Burning Dislike

Burning Dislike

Ethnic Violence in High Schools

Martín Sánchez-Jankowski

UNIVERSITY OF CALIFORNIA PRESS

University of California Press, one of the most
distinguished university presses in the United States,
enriches lives around the world by advancing scholarship
in the humanities, social sciences, and natural sciences.
Its activities are supported by the UC Press Foundation
and by philanthropic contributions from individuals
and institutions. For more information, visit
www.ucpress.edu.

University of California Press

Oakland, California

Library of Congress Cataloging-in-Publication Data

Names: Sánchez-Jankowski, Martín, author.
Title: Burning dislike : ethnic violence in high schools /
    Martín Sánchez-Jankowski.
Description: Oakland, California : University of
    California Press, [2016] | "2016 | Includes
    bibliographical references and index.
Identifiers: LCCN 2016005855 (print) | LCCN 2016007273
    (ebook) | ISBN 9780520289192 (cloth : alk. paper) |
    ISBN 9780520289215 (pbk. : alk. paper) |
    ISBN 9780520963870 (Epub)
Subjects: LCSH: School violence—United States. | Ethnic
    conflict—United States. | High schools—Social
    aspects—United States.
Classification: LCC LB3013.32 .S29 2016 (print) | LCC
    LB3013.32 (ebook) | DDC 371.7/820973—dc23
LC record available at http://lccn.loc.gov/2016005855

24 23 22 21 20 19 18 17 16

10 9 8 7 6 5 4 3 2 1

To my brother Mike and my sister-in-law Sharon

*and to my
brothers-in-law Frank and Luciano*

*and my
sisters-in-law Inga and Denise*

for their histories of support and affection

I think one can accept it as a general and constant rule that among civilized nations warlike passions become rarer and less active as social conditions get nearer to equality.

—Alexis de Tocqueville, *Democracy in America*, 1835–39

Contents

Figures and Tables

Preface

This book originates from a time when I was engaged in a study on educational inequalities within American urban high schools. While conducting that research I encountered a number of incidents of violence between students from different ethnic backgrounds. These incidents became more frequent, and one day they erupted into a full-scale riot that caused the school to be evacuated for purposes of restoring order. Not only did the violence cause injuries and extensive property damage, but instruction was suspended for a number of days to clean up the building and allow the students to collect themselves. As it turned out, this same violence occurred again two weeks later and required a further suspension of instruction. This violence between students from different ethnic backgrounds was so intense, destructive, and disruptive that I decided it had to be studied as part of a broader analysis of the obstacles encountered by urban school communities that were trying to improve the educational experience of all students.

Having decided on the need to study interethnic violence in high schools, I sought financial support to carry it out. I received generous support from the Robert Wood Johnson Foundation's Investigators in Health Policy Research Program. The Foundation's mission "to improve the health and health care of all Americans" involved the issue of violence in poor urban communities, which has consistently presented a greater public health threat to residents of these areas, particularly young people, than all other forms of disease. Thus they were willing to fund a research project intended to understand how interethnic violence in schools works so that this understanding might inform the broader effort to improve public health approaches directed at eradicating or reducing the impact of violence on those it touches.

I want to thank the Robert Wood Johnson Foundation for its financial support of the 2000–3 portion of this study. In particular I would like to thank Dr. David C. Colby, currently vice president of public policy for the foundation, for his support of the research project. I know he must have wondered about how the findings from this study have been applied; I can tell him that they have allowed me to consult with various school officials in California who have been experiencing the problems addressed in this book and to make suggestions that have prevented many potential injuries to students and eliminated or reduced building destruction and educational disruptions. Dr. Colby's support, and the Foundation's financial support, have accomplished a good deal of what he hoped. It is my wish that the publication of this book will assist a wider population of school officials who are facing this social problem.

Many people helped me in conducting the study or writing the book. As the reader will learn, the book is based on two studies of ethnic school violence conducted some twenty-six years apart. The first study was done while I was a research assistant for Professor Ithiel de Sola Pool of MIT's Political Science Department, who was asked by city government officials to evaluate the newly initiated court-ordered school busing program to desegregate Boston's public schools. Though he has passed away, I need to thank him for having sent me to the two Boston schools to conduct the research that constitutes a part of the analysis found in this book. I was not happy about doing the participant-observation research at the time, but it was essential for me to gain a fuller understanding of the social dynamics of interethnic violence in schools. I also need to thank his late wife, Jean MacKenzie Pool, who was able to locate all my notes from the Pool archives for me.

Obviously, many school authorities (school administrators, teachers, police, security guards) aided the research, as well countless students. I would like to publicly thank all of them for this help even though I will not be able to use their names because of the commitment I gave them, which was also required by the University of California at Berkeley's Institutional Review Board, to protect their identity.

I am grateful to several local residents in Los Angeles and Oakland who allowed me to use parts of their property to observe students walking to and from school. They all were concerned about the violence and wanted to do what they could to stop it from occurring.

In the writing of the book, I could not have wished for more help than I received from Claude Fischer, Corey Abramson, and Christine Trost, who read the manuscript and provided detailed comments. These comments were important in helping me rethink parts of my analysis and in making the book better. I would also like to thank two anonymous reviewers of the manuscript for UC Press, whose comments and suggestions greatly aided me in clarifying important points in the text, as well as the assistance of UC Press executive editor Naomi Schneider, whom I have had the pleasure of working with on a number of books.

I would also like to acknowledge my brother-in-law Frank's graciousness in allowing me to share his apartment while conducting the field research for the Los Angeles portion of this study.

Last, but certainly not least, I thank my wife, Carmen, for keeping our home in wonderful working order while I was out of town. She endured my being gone five days a week, five months a year, for three years. During this time she was the single parent to our three boys, who were ages fourteen, ten, and eight when the research first started, while she also worked full time as a social worker in a kidney dialysis clinic. She is special to me, and to all those who know her.

This book highlights the importance of the impact of a changing social ecology on the social dynamics of ethnic violence. As the reader proceeds through the text it will become increasingly clear that the ethnic violence dynamics I observed in the high school context directly relate to much of the sociological and political science literatures on ethnic conflict. Thus many findings of this book will contribute to understanding and, ideally, addressing the more general phenomenon of ethnic violence.

Introduction

All violence, all that is dreary and repels, is not power,
but the absence of power.

—Ralph Waldo Emerson, "Character" Lecture, 1864–65

Leanora Benitez screams, "What do you mean my son was in a fight and is on the way to the hospital? How can this happen in school? How did you let this happen? I get him up and off to school to learn, and you're supposed to keep him safe!" As Mrs. Benitez begins to cry, Mr. Talbot, the principal at Los Angeles's Chumash High School, responds, "Yes, I understand, Mrs. Benitez, I'm so sorry about this. I can assure you that we all take that responsibility seriously, but at the moment we have a lot of students who do not want to cooperate with each other."[1]

There is probably no civil society throughout the world that does not respect both the mission to educate its citizens and that mission's academic setting. Whether school is held outdoors, in a makeshift one-room structure, or on a multibuilding campus, it is imagined and treated as a special place. In many ways schools are idealized in our society as safe, peaceful places in which to learn. Yet people have entered schools and violated this ideal, even inflicting physical harm on participants in their routine activities.[2] In some places in the United States, especially schools in middle-class areas, these violent events are rare, though costly in terms of human suffering. In other places, such as many lower-class inner-city schools, they occur with such regularity that they have become a part of a school's everyday routines, albeit disruptive and disturbing ones. Whatever the number of violent events taking place in any particular school, it is fair to say that these events are universally thought to be unacceptable.[3]

School shootings are occasionally prominent in the news, particularly when they exact a considerable toll in human life.[4] However, a close look at these stories of violence reveals a decidedly social-class division in both the types of violence that occur and the public attention they receive. In the incidents at Columbine (Aurora, Colorado), Heath (Heath, Kentucky), and Westside High Schools (Westside, Arkansas), suburban or small-town settings where students' families' represented a wide spectrum of socioeconomic backgrounds, the violence was considered shockingly unusual and received considerable national attention. However, violence in inner-city schools where the majority of students come from low-income families has not received the same media attention, for two reasons. First, it generally does not involve large numbers of kids being shot in one event. Second, there exists a common perception that violence is so routine in inner-city neighborhoods as to be simply an aspect of lower-class life and, thus, while regrettable, not terribly shocking or unexpected.[5]

Despite this general trend in perceptions and coverage, one type of violence in low-income schools does receive attention when it occurs, and that is violence between students from different ethnic groups.[6] There would seem to be two primary reasons for the attention. First, this type of violence does not, even in low-income neighborhoods, occur routinely. Second, because the United States is ethnically diverse, ethnic violence in schools is a public indication that the school is failing to socialize its students into the American creed of tolerance for ethnic differences and to foster the "E Pluribus Unum" process of acquiring a shared American identity.[7] Obviously, any reported violence between ethnic groups in schools stimulates unease and gains the attention of school officials, the media, and the general public precisely because it has implications for the vitality of everyday interactions in the general society.

This type of school violence, based on ethnicity, is the central topic of this book. I will investigate it using systematic direct observations of behaviors leading up to violent incidents, as well as behaviors occurring during and after the confrontations. In doing so, I will use a set of sequential data that is not generally found in the existing scholarship.

HIGH SCHOOL VIOLENCE

Conscious violence between ethnic groups occurs in both middle and high school, but it is particularly destructive when it happens in high schools. To more fully understand the phenomenon of ethnic violence in high schools, it will be helpful to compare it to schools where ethnic change is occurring but violence is not.

What motivates young people to engage in violence while they are attending school? The research on high school violence has been growing, but not to the degree that the more general topic of violence has. The literature on school violence can be roughly divided into four categories. The first category comprises studies that try to understand the very violent and deviant acts that are rather rare events. Examples include the shootings at Columbine High School in Colorado, Westside Middle School in Arkansas, and Heath High School in Kentucky, whose destructiveness and apparent meaninglessness shocked and alarmed many Americans. Research on these events seemed to be required for the general public to understand their cause, if for no other reason than to calm fears that if it could happen to children in bucolic community schools designed for safety and learning, it could happen anywhere.[8]

The second category of studies on school violence has to do with bullying and fights. The vast majority of these studies focus on attacks that inflict some type of physical damage to the victim, such as rape, interpersonal fights, and assaults associated with robbery, or on surveillance to gauge and avert the threat of such attacks.[9] Research on bullying has been particularly prevalent because it is at present (2015) a more general phenomenon involving students from various socioeconomic backgrounds attending both public and private elementary, middle, and high schools.[10]

Some research has found that bullying is associated with perpetrators acting as gatekeepers in a sort of "rite of passage" to a higher-status group, or as punishers of those who deviate from the existing norms. Other research finds that individuals who bully have personal issues related to self-esteem and frustration that they project onto a chosen target. The victims of bullying also have self-esteem and efficacy issues that make them attractive targets.[11] Further, there is evidence that a great deal, perhaps most, of bullying is associated with social settings where status categories have been established and there is ambiguity involving the status hierarchy's middle categories. Consequently, bullying is quite prevalent in social environments divided into a hierarchy of status groups that find their status predicated on the subjective judgments of students in the other status categories. Thus, in an effort to maintain their position or move up the status hierarchy, students try to lower the status position of competitors by using bullying tactics such as spreading rumors about them, insulting them, turning friends against them, and ostracizing them. When these tactics are used aggressively without the worry of reprisal, the probability of violence increases.[12] Interestingly, some studies find an association between the antecedent behaviors of the perpetrators and the victims. The perpetrators attempt to establish dominance because they feel inferior to individuals of a higher status and want to be accepted, and the victims attempt to withdraw from being socially recognized because they too feel inferior and want to avoid being made to feel worse. So in some cases there is an odd symbiotic relationship where the victims share in the dynamic of bullying even while they want to avoid the injuries they receive, while the bullies will blame them for their own aggression.[13]

The evidence within this category suggests that violence is caused by emotionally challenged or disturbed youth who are trying to build a particular sense of selfhood using aggression as part of a developmental process that involves becoming and remaining popular among a large number of people within their social world.[14] The identified factors leading to this situation are the behavioral difficulties associated with disrupted or dysfunctional family life, including child abuse and competition for limited emotional and material resources.[15] Although the research is not specifically focused on ethnic violence (in fact, most of it does not mention ethnicity as a primary cause), aspects of bullying can exist in ethnic school violence. The present study will investigate this further.

A third category of school violence research does not involve acts that are substantively different from those mentioned in the previous two categories but occurs in particular schools, namely inner-city schools where violence has been an issue for some time.[16] At least three factors have been identified as particularly relevant to the violence in these schools. First, the schools are in low-income communities that are socially disorganized to such an extent that they cannot control violence anywhere that it occurs, including in the school.[17] Second, there are a greater number of inner-city youth from broken homes who feel abandoned, unloved, frustrated, and angry; and single parents are incapable of preventing their children's use of violence.[18] Third, these inner-city schools produce a climate that promotes the escalation of aggressive behavior into violence.[19] Much of this research describes what keeps individuals in these schools from controlling their own or their community members' drives toward violent behavior. Little attempt has been made to explain why individuals in specific contexts engage in violence in these schools but do not in other contexts, or how conditions promoting violence relate specifically to ethnic violence in the schools.

Finally, a fourth category of research on school violence has focused on the influence of ethnic identity as a precipitating cause. This topic has received more media coverage than other topics related to school violence, but it is rarely found in academic research, partly because it occurs less often than violence between individuals of the same group, and partly because in much of the violence between individuals from different groups ethnicity has not been an issue.[20] The studies that have concentrated on interethnic violence have often utilized versions of the "relative deprivation" and "defended neighborhood" theories to explain it.[21] However, a recent study of ethnic violence in Israeli schools has developed a theory that incorporates the impact of neighborhood dynamics in explaining ethnic student violence.[22] This framework is more inclusive than the individual-focused ones and its contribution quite promising, though there remain questions about how and why the particular conditions of the neighborhood are carried into the school. Clearly there is a relationship, but its exact nature and its contribution to initiating and maintaining the violence are not addressed in any detailed way by the existing research.

In sum, there are three main competing explanations about the origins of school violence: (1) biologically based explanations that focus on how the nature and functioning of the brain can drive an individual to violent behavior;[23] (2) structural explanations emphasizing the arrangements in the larger society that influence individuals to fight over scarce resources;[24] and (3) social-interactional explanations emphasizing factors like emotions, concerns over status, or defense against attacks on an individual's character.[25] Yet with regard to ethnically driven violence in schools, which occurs far less frequently than violence between individuals where ethnicity is not a factor, far less is known. No form of violence has more potential to involve large numbers of students, produce large numbers of physical injuries, disrupt instructional time, and cause significant physical damage to school structures than violence over ethnic issues. Once ethnic violence begins, no other form of violence is more destructive to the school environment. What exactly is it about ethnicity that leads to fights between youth in a school setting? In what situations do fights occur? Why do some youth fight while others of similar social backgrounds do not? Why are some fights more aggressive and destructive than others? What factors keep fights going, and how do they do this? What factors inhibit, slow, or stop ethnic violence once it has started? All of these questions have something in common. They point to the idea that there is an episodic content to ethnic violence, and consequently answers to them, even if only partial answers, should improve our understanding of what Randall Collins has theoretically described as the total process of violent episodes.[26]

One reason for our general lack of a clear empirical understanding of how school violence proceeds, regardless of whether it is ethnically motivated, has been that very few researchers have directly observed the violence itself, let alone the full context in which it occurs. This is not surprising; violence obviously does not occur at predictable times, making it difficult for a researcher to be on site when it does. In the case of school violence, the fact that most researchers are usually adults, and thus not a normal part of the students' social world, deters youth from engaging in violence for fear of being identified and turned into the authorities for punishment. Finally, some researchers feel that studying rather than policing violence is condoning or enabling it, either of which is inappropriate for social research.[27]

To overcome these problems the present analysis uses evidence obtained from directly observing interethnic violence in high schools. My goal is to concentrate on the processes involved in interethnic violence by specifically observing how it works in the everyday lives of students at various schools in three different cities during different time periods. Within this framework I will (1) identify and specify how structural conditions facilitate the possibility for ethnic violence in school; (2) describe how various structural, emotional, and interactional factors work to start an ethnic violent incident, continue it, and end it; and (3) determine how the factors associated with one phase of ethnic school violence keep that phase going while others work to begin a new phase.

Previous approaches focusing on biology, structure, and social interactions have been necessary to provide direction for any investigation of violence occurring in high schools, but none alone have been sufficient for understanding why students from different ethnic backgrounds engage in violence against each other in some schools but not in others, how fighting between ethnic groups develops, what keeps fights going, and why fighting between groups ends. For that we need to empirically identify what it is about the ethnic identity of individual students that works with biology, structure, and social interaction to produce physical violence. The empirical chapters that follow the ensuing theoretical chapter are an effort to contribute toward that end.

STUDY DESIGN AND METHODOLOGY

Ethnic violence occurs in both middle and high schools but is particularly problematic in high schools. Thus the present study was designed to clarify how the dynamics associated with interethnic violence play out in the everyday routines of high schools where interethnic violence occurs. To catalog these processes it was necessary to observe these dynamics firsthand, so a strategy was developed to gather such data. A brief description of the study's design follows (for more detail, see the Methodological Appendix).

The first task was to create a list of high schools throughout the United States that were experiencing interethnic violence. The list was obtained from an extensive review of newspapers throughout the United States that reported ethnic violence within the high schools of their geographic area. The data indicated that the vast majority of the violence was between African American and Latino students (with the latter being primarily of Central American and Mexican origins). There were schools that reported violence between other groups, but in each of these cases at least one of the conflicting groups was either Latino or African American: For example, one school reported violence between Albanian students and Latino and African American students; another reported violence between Armenian and Latino students. However, the number of cases involving groups other than Latinos and African Americans was very small.[28] Given that a large number of California high schools (eighty-four) were experiencing interethnic violence, that they included the same ethnic groups involved in this type of conflict throughout the country, and that their proximity enabled me to visit them more quickly and more often, I chose to study California high schools. Further, I decided to draw up a separate list of schools to study where ethnic change was occurring in the neighborhoods from which they drew their students but where there was no reporting of violence. This would allow for an analysis of what was different about the two sets of schools.[29]

A list of seventy-three schools from the five largest metropolitan areas in California reporting ethnic change in their student bodies was gathered and placed in a computer file. It was divided into two groups: schools reporting some level of ethnic violence (thirty-one) and schools reporting no ethnic violence (forty-two). Because a reasonable hypothesis exists that violence is more likely in lower-income neighborhoods, schools were then identified as low income/working class (a majority of students coming from low-income and working-class families) or middle class (a majority of students coming from middle-class families). Of the thirty-one schools reporting ethnic violence, all had a student body that was primarily low income and working class. Of the forty-two schools reporting no ethnic violence, twenty-nine had a student body that was primarily low income or working class, while thirteen had a student body that was primarily middle class.

From the group of schools that had reported ethnic change and violence, all of which were lower class, I randomly generated two schools from the computer file: one came from the Los Angeles area and one from the Oakland area. I then randomly generated from the computer file two lower-class and two middle-class schools that had reported ethnic change but no ethnic violence. This produced a total of six schools, two from low-income schools reporting violence, two from low-income schools reporting no violence, and two from middle-income schools reporting no violence (see table I.1). As it turned out, all the schools selected by the random computer-assisted process were from the greater Los Angeles and Oakland, California, areas.

This sample permitted me to study the full range of interethnic violence, from schools where conflict had already begun to schools where there was a potential for conflict but as yet it had not occurred. As it would turn out, the random sample of schools chosen was perfect for answering nearly all of the questions I was interested in. This was because two of the four schools that did not have any violence occurring in them when the study began developed intense interethnic violence and I was present for the entire process. The other two schools that did not have any violence when they were chosen remained without any violence both during the time of the fieldwork and five years after the research was completed. In brief, the sample chosen turned out to provide me with an excellent opportunity to observe the full range of interethnic violence from its inception to its end because I could study it on three levels: the school, the individual actors, and the incidents of violence and nonviolence.

My general observational approach was to systematically note what was said and done, how it was said and done, the behaviors and context in which it occurred; and how subjects' words and actions worked to produce various social outcomes. This approach had the advantage of reporting not just the subjects' words and actions but the larger patterns in which those words and actions played a role .

Fieldwork for the study commenced in September 2000 and ended in June 2003. The study started two weeks before classes began for the academic year and ended two weeks after the academic year finished.

TABLE I.1   SCHOOLS IN THE STUDY

Location and School	Dominant Social Class*	Status of Violence
Los Angeles		
Tongva High School	Lower class	Active violence at start of 2000
Chumash High School	Lower class	Violence begins after study begins
De Neve High School	Middle class	No violence
Oakland		
Miwok High School	Lower class	Active violence at start of 2000
Kaiser High School	Lower class	Violence begins after study begins
Ohlone High School	Middle class	No violence
Boston		
Shawmut High School	Lower class	Active violence at start of 1974
Paul Revere High School	Lower class	Active violence at start of 1974

*Middle- and lower-class schools were so designated using three criteria: (1) 2000–2003 Current Population Survey statistics regarding the median income for the geographic area that the school drew its students from; (2) the median housing price for the geographic area that the school drew its students from; and (3) the percentage of the students in the school that were eligible for the Federal School Nutrition Program. Finally, adjustments were made for the cost of living in Los Angeles and Oakland, California.

That meant starting at the end of August and ending at the end of June each year. I began the study in Los Angeles and after the first semester switched to Oakland. The following year I began in Oakland and switched to Los Angeles. For the third year I switched between the locations every thirty-five days. I spent a portion of each week at each school depending on what general activities were occurring within them. This allowed me the flexibility to be at schools that were "hot" (i.e., very active) with violence in order to observe the various conditions and dynamics associated with it. It also allowed me to follow tips about the presence of underlying disaffection that could evolve into violence and see when, where, and how violence would emerge. As it turned out, this strategy proved to be particularly effective in allowing me to observe both the full range of violent activities in the schools and the process they followed. In addition, I compared my observations with accounts of the violence that I missed in an effort to maximize accuracy.

Data gathering for my 2000–2003 fieldwork started before school began as students were going from home to school, then during school hours, and then after school as the students were returning home or were attending a school sporting event. More detail concerning the data-gathering process is in the Methodological Appendix, but briefly the data consist of both verbal and physical behavioral observations. Verbal behavior included the statements that subjects made as well as the symbolic mechanisms they used in making them. Physical behavior included the various movements individuals made that I carefully defined as aggressive. Some of these were movements in which no physical contact was made but intimidation was intended or occurred; other movements were overt acts of striking a person with a part of the body like the head, hand, fingers, elbow, knee, or foot or of using an object as a weapon. The other behaviors observed and recorded had to do with responses to these acts on the part of the students directly involved, witnesses, and others who were told of the acts later.

Since emotions play such an important role in both instigating and maintaining violent acts, it was important to observe their role in interethnic violence within the schools studied. Emotions have often been described as elements that are internal to the psyche of the individual and thus invisible to the naked eye. However, emotional dispositions are not merely invisible entities within the body; nor do they lie silent in the brain.[30] They can be considered (1) physically present in the brain as electronic impulses messaging a particular sensation that is often described in common sense language as a "feeling"; (2) present in the body as reflex expressions of their existence; (3) behavioral in what action is taken to accommodate or alleviate them; and (4) observable.

A full range of accommodations are at the individual's disposal to deal with emotions, such as enduring the feeling, repressing it, or aggressing toward the identified object causing it. Each will have an effect on the person's disposition (mood), bodily reaction (feeling, twitching, sweating, etc.), and social behavior (actions taken). In most cases there will be observable verbal expressions and physical signs. For example, in conjunction with social context, which was vital in assessing their presence, the emotional disposition of (1) *fear* was identified with facial expressions, eye widening, twitching, and sweating; that of (2) *hatred* with facial squinting, clenching of fists, pressing or biting of the lip, forceful breathing, and verbal expressions of extreme dislike; and that of (3) *resentment* with physical avoidance of members of the other group, expressed by walking away in nonhostile encounters or by refusal to cooperate with members of the other group in nonhostile circumstances, angry verbal outbursts about, or directed to, members of the other group that erupted suddenly in a previously nonhostile conversation, and verbal denigration of the ideas and behaviors of members of the other group whenever the opportunity presented itself.

Thus all of these emotions had physical, verbal, and behavioral elements that could be observed. What is more, emotions were assigned to a particular event only when more than one of the verbal and physical indicators listed above were observed in a specific incident. For example, if there was an interaction in which one of the participants threatened another with injury if the other did not give him all his money and the threatened person began to request that he be left alone (i.e., requested the removal of the threat), and this was accompanied by sweating, eye widening, twitching, a tightening of facial muscles, and/or verbal expressions of fear that were followed by physically aggressive action toward the threatener, then it would be categorized as aggression emanating from fear. In addition to the physical expressions observed, the context in which they took place and how others interpreted their meaning were used to identify what emotion(s) were operative, being expressed both verbally and in action, and responded to by others. The point here is that I did not label the presence of an emotion in initiating and/or maintaining a violent encounter without physical and verbal evidence from that particular situation to support it.

Finally, my field notes consisted of both the physical behaviors and the verbal statements of the subjects that I interacted with or observed. I recorded the observations using a formal shorthand technique that I had learned, and this allowed me both to record the various subjects' statements nearly verbatim and to capture the interactive behavior more fully. The data were then transferred every evening to a computer-assisted qualitative data program called Folio Views.[31] A coding scheme to organize the data had been devised before the study began. This scheme was elaborated as the study progressed and as new codes were required to organize additional new kinds of data and new topics to be considered for the analysis stage.

After leaving the field in 2004, I recalled that I had yet another entire set of observations on the very same topic that I had collected twenty-six years earlier when I was a graduate student at MIT. At that time, an agency within the city government of Boston had asked my adviser, Professor Ithiel de Sola Pool, to conduct research on the school busing program that US district court judge W. Arthur Garrity had ordered to eliminate de facto segregation in the Boston public schools. The research was to be based on aggregate data associated with issues like school attendance, acts of violence, and academic achievement, and on the behaviors of students, faculty, administrators, parents, and nonstudent members of the local school community. Since I was my adviser's assigned research assistant, he asked me to go to the schools and be the observer of everyday behavior. He indicated that access had already been arranged with both school officials and the various police departments that were assigned to keep the peace. Thus I did go to the schools and was granted access to the facilities at the school as well as the grounds surrounding it. In addition, I had access to the places where the African American students in Roxbury were being bused as well as to the buses they were riding. In addition to the schools, I attended the various neighborhood community centers that many youth from both the white and the African American communities used for socializing. I took very detailed notes using three-by-five–inch note cards and organized them into cardboard boxes under different substantive topics. I would hand in my notes to my adviser biweekly. It was my understanding that he was to use them to produce a report on various issues arising from the court-ordered deseg-regation program to address the implementation of quality education at the schools involved. After I had completed two years of research, the project officially ended. I forgot about the notes I had taken during this period until I was about to begin my research on interethnic school vio-lence in California. I then thought that the evidence from the Boston project twenty-six years earlier would be interesting to review for the present research project. I retrieved my original notes by contacting the widow of my adviser, who located them in his old office. I traveled to Cambridge, Massachusetts, picked up the four large boxes of my notes, and had them sent to my office in California. After the completion of the research in Los Angeles and Oakland I read and coded each note from the Boston project to match the codes used for the Los Angeles and Oak-land study and then added them to the Los Angeles and Oakland Folio Views data set. This integrated data set proved to be extremely valuable because I could analyze ethnic violence in schools some twenty-six years apart to see which patterns remained consistent over this long period and which had changed. Further, the fact that African Americans were being victimized by Irish Americans as they attended school in Boston in 1974, yet were the very group victimizing Mexicans as they attended school in Los Angeles and Oakland in 2000, requires readers to shed any preju-dices they may harbor that certain groups are more likely to be victimizers or victims. It forces one to focus on *the conditions* that influence members of one ethnic group to victimize members of another or become victims of another.

Readers may ask whether my being Mexican, male, and fifty-five years old at the time of the research in Los Angeles and Oakland had an impact on what I was able to see and hear. The answer turns out to be that it did not. It should be remembered that the Oakland and L.A. communities from which the schools were drawing their students contained both Mexican and African Americans of both genders and various ages, so I did not stand out as an "outsider." In the case of Boston, I was twenty-nine when the research began, but I was not a member of either of the antagonistic groups (Irish and African American), and I did not physically look like either group. Further, as my presence became common and there were no negative repercussions for those who had displayed aggressive speech or behavior in front of me, no apparent inhibitions were exhibited.

I analyzed the data collected to answer the following questions: What precipitates ethnic violence? What forms does it assume? What keeps it going? How do people react to it when they are directly involved as well as after they have been involved? How do those who are not directly involved in violence react? In what ways is ethnic violence different from violence having nothing to do with ethnicity? I sought to connect the answers to these empirical questions with theories of ethnic violence.

Every study that deals directly with living subjects raises some ethical issues, but a study of violence among adolescents is obviously permeated with them. I presented the study for approval to the Institutional Review Board at Berkeley, which has a history of being very protective of subjects. Following IRB protocol, I informed the staffs in each school about the study, had teachers introduce me and the study to their homerooms, and made a presentation about the study to the local PTA. I obtained advanced written consent from the administrators, faculty, and the parents of all students who were formally interviewed, though the formal interview data are not used in the present book.

The present research project was the same as a participant observation study of a local community; it is just that each of the communities I investigated consisted of fifteen hundred to three thousand youth attending a school. Although I was a part of the students' environment, and in that sense participated in it, I did as much as I could to avoid interfering with it. In that regard, for those interested, appended to each quote used in the text is a backnote describing how the conversation was recorded, the context of the conversation, and where I was when I recorded it. In addition, I told the Los Angeles School District Police, the Los Angeles City Police, and the Oakland Police that as part of my research I would be present in the school and among the students as they traveled to and from school. The anonymity and confidentiality of every individual who was a part of the study were rigorously maintained, and their identities remain anonymous in the text of this book. Thus all of the names of schools and individuals that appear in this book are fictitious.

From the start to the finish of this research project, which also includes the Boston research project of some twenty-six years earlier, I observed a lot of violence. Some may wonder how I could view more violence than the security guards that were employed by the school to deter it, and the answer is straightforward. The security guards were reluctant to intervene either because they were from the neighborhood and identified with one of the conflict groups or because they were afraid of getting injured in the process. Thus they regularly occupied physical-social spaces where they knew there was little chance that violence would occur, whereas I was intent on placing myself precisely in those spaces where violence was most likely to occur.

I watched students who might have been hurt and many who were. It was disturbing. Luckily no students whom I observed were mortally wounded during the research, although some were taken to medical facilities for treatment. Any research that deals with crime, whether or not that crime involves violence, is faced with moral, ethical, and legal dilemmas, and the choices made will never measure up to the satisfaction of everyone, including the researcher. For example, if the researcher who sees something illegal calls the police and they arrive to stop and arrest people, the researcher ceases to be a researcher and becomes an extension of law enforcement as a quasi-vigilante agent. If the researcher does not tell the police, the police make an arrest, and the researcher is subpoenaed to testify, then not only will the study be completely compromised, but more importantly the researcher will have violated the pledge not to cause harm to any subject of the study. That pledge is mandated by federal government regulations concerning research on human subjects. Finally, there is the problem of personally intervening to stop violence without any official authority to do so, and the added risk of causing physical harm to the subject or oneself in the attempt. This situation makes for less than optimal choices. It could be argued that, for all the reasons just mentioned, direct observation research should not be conducted. However, violence in schools, regardless of whether it has anything to do with ethnicity, remains a serious problem. Reliance solely on law enforcement or on research using survey and in-depth interviewing techniques of victims and victimizers will not provide us with information about the dynamic processes associated with where, when, and how violence operates. Without this information, effective interventions will remain incomplete and individuals will continue to experience unnecessary physical harm while attending school and some reduction in learning due to interruptions in the school's social order. I chose to complete this research with the intent of taking what I learned and providing it to all interested parties that wanted to develop policies to reduce school violence. I can report that the research did produce rich data on ethnic violence and that I have been able to consult with various school districts in their efforts to develop programs to stop the violence. Therefore, while I was uneasy about observing individuals getting injured, the recommendations that emerged from the study have prevented other students from being hurt by ethnic violence. I hope this book may be of aid to other schools' students as well.

Before moving to the next section, I offer a brief word on the presentation of data in the book. My analysis is based on patterned thoughts and behaviors among various individuals as they dealt with ethnic violence in their daily lives in these high schools. Thus the examples I present are to be understood to represent *patterns* of observed expressions of thought and physical behaviors, not singular events. A pattern was identified when some verbal or behavioral event occurred twenty or more times, or, if fewer than twenty times, that it occurred when the circumstances were the same. If an expression or behavior was idiosyncratic to a particular person, place, or time it will be reported as such.

The quotes I present did not come from formal interviews because I believe that statements made by individuals while they are interacting within their natural environment are much less inhibited than tape-recorded responses to formal questions and over time are a more accurate representation of their thought processes on substantive issues. As the reader will see, I use the respondent's exact language, recorded using a formal shorthand technique that I learned; this is important for accuracy and identification of meaning even if the reader (as well as the author) considers what is said as distasteful or troubling to read, as in the case of epithets like *nigger, wetback,* and *white trash.*

Finally, I previously mentioned that I did collect data from formal interviews with administrators, teachers, parents, and students but that these data are not included in present manuscript. I mentioned this to highlight that the quotes offered in the text are from individuals' "normal" conversations. Nonetheless, I also need to clarify that the data I gathered from the in-depth interviews were designed to obtain information on an issue related to but substantively different from the one dealt with in this book. I will use those data in a subsequent project.

CONSIDERATIONS OF ETHNICITY, RACE, CLASS, AND GENDER

A few more points should be raised before the plan of the book is outlined. The first has to do with the concept of ethnicity. In this book, I consider ethnicity to be composed of a number of factors that individuals are socialized to understand as being a part of the group they belong to: these factors include language, values, religion, customs, a common history, names, and sometimes phenotype (i.e., "race"). Phenotype usually becomes salient when members of a group come into direct contact with another group or are provided information as an introduction to the existence of another group. In either case, the role of phenotype becomes salient when it is required as a marker for group inclusion and made a justification for exclusion, as well as for evaluation of superiority or inferiority within a hierarchy of ethnic groups and the establishment of group-defined norms for behaving with members of other groups. Some ethnic groups, such as Filipinos, Mexicans, and Puerto Ricans, will not emphasize phenotype because the evolution of their group and its accompanying cultural characteristics resulted from the blending of two or more groups with divergent physical features. However, phenotypes for these groups often become useful for establishing status hierarchies within the group as well as functional for intergroup relations by creating markers to identify in-group/out-group members and the subsequent social boundaries that will affect both everyday, neutral and hostile interactions. As we will see in this study, African, Irish, and Mexican American high school students used "race" markers to indicate who belonged to what group and in the process established a status group hierarchy that favored their group over others and was used to justify the legitimacy of their group's interest demands. In the present study, the distinction of race entered Irish and African American relations primarily as a way for the two groups to indicate their strikingly different phenotypes, but even the Irish students were aware that the concept of race as phenotype was fluid because American citizens of British origins had historically considered them "racially" different and that part of their own group's evolution had involved a change in their racial classification.[32]

Violence in high schools is too often attributed to gang members or to other individuals with psychological problems who adhere to a general culture of violence. In cases of ethnic violence in the schools, gang members will become involved but will do so late in the process. What is most important to highlight, and will be shown throughout this book, is that structural circumstances related to social change together with the economic constraints facing those involved will draw the general population of students into participating.

Finally, a few words on the impact of social class and gender as they relate to the violence discussed here. Male students participated more frequently in violent actions than female students. Yet although female students engaged less in direct violence, they did play both a functional, and at times significant, role in its process. Thus I will describe their actions only at those times when their role in the violence was noteworthy.

Social class is a vital part of the argument advanced in this book. Two of the schools in this study (one in L.A. and one in Oakland) were experiencing ethnic change and were composed of students from African American and Mexican ethnic backgrounds but experienced no incidents of violence related to ethnic issues. The difference was that these schools were composed of students from middle-class families where conflicts that did exist (including various forms of bullying) were in general effectively mediated by school authorities and parents. Thus, as with gender, where female students are discussed in relation to certain occasions when they were active in and/or contributed to the violence, middle-class schools will be discussed in those sections where comparison between them and lower-class schools helps clarify what is being described.

PLAN OF THIS BOOK

The book begins with a theoretical chapter that outlines the entire dynamic of ethnic violence in schools and provides a road map for the empirical chapters that follow. The empirical chapters describe the reasons for how and why ethnic violence happens and works the way it does, information that to date has been difficult to obtain. They demonstrate that it has a natural history of phases and component stages, a beginning and end. Part I of the book, "Tinder," contains two chapters that identify the macro and meso social conditions that set the stage for ethnic conflict and how they promote its onset. Part 2, "Flames," contains two chapters on the factors that cause a specific violent incident to occur, the structural content of the incident, and the dynamics of the interactions that keep it going. The second of these two chapters describes the types of violent incidents involved in the ethnic conflicts of these schools and their progressive phases. Part 3, "Embers," presents two chapters on the factors that lead to a cessation of hostilities and the mechanisms by which the peace is maintained. The Conclusion draws on what has been learned from the study about the dynamics of ethnic conflict when it occurs in high schools and offers concrete policy suggestions for school officials to effectively combat this problem. A methodological appendix completes the text.

CHAPTER I

Toward an Understanding of Ethnic Violence in Schools

The thornbush is the old obstacle in the road. It must catch fire if you want to go further.

—Franz Kafka, *The Third Octavo Notebook*, November 21, 1917

Violence in this study has been defined as an act of aggression aimed at causing some degree of pain or physical injury to the targeted individual(s). What distinguishes its various forms has more to do with the motive and target of the aggression than it does with either the type of aggressive movement involved or the tools used. In this regard, the motive for ethnic violence in schools is to injure someone because of his or her observed or assumed ethnic identity. Ethnic violence has some behavioral characteristics similar to other forms of violence, but the dynamic through which it completes its life course assumes a particular pattern. This chapter will outline the life course characteristics of ethnic violence in schools, by which I mean the course that it takes from start to finish.[1] Many of the tenets advanced in the present theory can also be ascribed to ethnic violence that takes place in contexts other than a school, as well as various forms of nonethnic violence. However, the sequencing of these other phenomena could very well be different.

A number of theories offer explanations for why ethnic violence occurs in schools, but they address ethnic violence in general wherever it may occur. As we will see, some aspects of these theories are relevant to ethnic violence in school, but because the school occupies a unique physical, social, and cultural location in American society they do not fully explain the school phenomenon. Randall Collins and Donald L. Horowitz propose two of the theories most pertinent to school violence.[2] While they deal directly with violence in great depth, including the issue of ethnicity associated with it, they still do not cover the full dynamics of ethnic violence.

Collins's theory has enormous breadth in that it attempts to theorize the micro processes of violence across social environments and targets. It focuses on the individual and what gets him or her to engage in violence; and although a number of interactional factors (e.g., competition or an argument) may provide the impetus for violence, the engine that drives all violence is what he calls a "forward panic." This forward panic is "a pattern developing in time, the buildup of tension/fear and the shift to sudden weakness of the victim . . . [that] opens the dark tunnel down into which people collectively fall."[3] Obviously, in part this concept suggests that individuals have a dark side that enables them to do evil things in the right situation. Thus it would seem that there is nothing unique about any particular situation, including one that involves ethnic violence, since once the processes begin they have a life of their own. The argument assumes that all violence is more or less phenomenologically the same; the only thing that differs is the situational content that triggers a sequence.

Although there is much to be learned from this perspective, it eliminates, or at minimum blurs, factors that work together to create variance in the types of violence. Factors at the macro level, like the history of social interaction between individuals and groups, economic pressures within and between groups, and current social structural arrangements, as well as factors at the micro level, like the motives, timing, type of involvement chosen, and structure of engagement (length, intensity, targets), all play a part in the character of the violence engaged in as well as its interactional path. Thus if one accepts Randall Collins's approach, all violence is phenomenologically similar. Yet earlier I proposed a definition of violence as the use of physical force to damage or injure another person. Further, I suggested that the common denominator for all that is generally referred to as violence begins with some aspect of "aggression," or the act of initiating hostile action toward other persons. However, where, when, with whom, how, and why that aggression takes place are significant in producing phenomenologically different forms such as sexual violence, domestic violence, and war, to name a few. All can involve aggression in the form of physical force and bodily injuries, but the sociological character and interpretation of each are different.

Ethnic violence is one such form. It is differentiated from other forms of violence in that it takes place when two or more people from different ethnic groups attack one another and when the reason for the attack has specifically to do with both ethnic identity and the identification of an ethnic other. While some of the reasons for this type of attack will be similar to those found in other forms of violence, there are some important differences in the micro dynamics related to where, when, with whom, how, and so on, as well as significant differences in the macro (i.e., structural) and meso (i.e., situational) conditions that both bring about this type of violence and shape the trajectory it assumes.[4]

Whereas Collins's theoretical approach is focused on the micro processes involved in general violence that would include ethnic-oriented violence, Donald Horowitz's conceptual framework is directed toward the macro and meso conditions that encompass ethnic conflict generally and ethnic riots more specifically.[5] Within this framework, there is a buildup of tension between members of each group, as Collins also theorizes, and the victimizers employ some form of instrumental calculus to choose targets that will produce the desired objective, such as revenge, deterrence, or an expression of protest. Horowitz then argues that a social provocation occurs in which the dynamics of group action take control, creating a frenzy that results in numerous injuries and deaths. One of the most important parts of his work for the issues that the present book confronts is his argument that the "deadly ethnic riot" has a rhythmic process that plays out in a particular way.[6] Nonetheless, despite the important implications of his study for our understanding of ethnic violence in schools, Horowitz's primary concern with explaining violence that leads to deaths, such as the deadly ethnic riot and war, establishes some limits to his conceptual framework's ability to explain other forms of ethnic violence involving simply a few individuals, informal groups engaged in a brawl, or ethnic riots where there is no premeditated attempt to cause fatalities and where no fatalities occur. Thus for ethnic violence among students attending high schools there is a need to identify which processional facets are the same as those described by Horowitz and which are different.

The theory I present below focuses on a variety of forms of aggression in high school that produce physical and psychological trauma, although not necessarily fatalities. High school is a particularly fruitful place to examine interethnic violence precisely because society considers it completely off limits for that kind of behavior. Obviously, some of the formal propositions I advance will be applicable to the more general phenomenon of violence (as well as ethnic violence more broadly), but my main concern is to offer a theory of ethnic violence among students attending public schools in the United States. In drafting this theory, which is derived from the present study's data in dialogue with existing models and presented as a road map of what will follow in the substantive chapters, I shall rely heavily on the metaphor of fires, particular forest fires, to explain the phenomenon of ethnic violence in schools.

KINDLING: THE HISTORY OF ETHNIC CONFLICT

Although on occasions fire can be used strategically as a productive mechanism, it is generally dangerous because it can damage and destroy the physical, social, and psychological objects it touches. Aggression associated with ethnicity in high schools has the same power, and, interestingly, its "life course" assumes characteristics most often observed in fires. The origins of an encounter involving interethnic violence are usually associated with the acts that immediately precede it, but the broader social origins of ethnic violence lie in the historical experience of the ethnic groups before they enter the host country.[7] The first encounter with members from other groups, as well as the group's historical record of socioeconomic mobility, plays a significant role in group relations. Each group has a history through which it will interpret present events and develop what it understands to be appropriate modes of interaction with other groups. How the other group responds to these modes of interaction is, in turn, predicated on its interpretation of these behaviors in light of its own historical experience. Thus the origins of ethnic violence are imbedded in the social interactive histories of all the participating groups. This evolutionary process of an ethnic group in its relationships with other groups provides the social ecology for future interactions.

To return to the fire analogy, the story of forest fires begins with the type of vegetation in a particular locale. That vegetation is the result of what developed, either naturally or with human intervention, a number of years before. Thus both natural evolution and deliberate human intervention determine the kind of vegetation that will exist in a particular place and time. The case of California provides just such an example because most of the state has a dry climate and this has forced native plants to develop the capability of existing for very long dry periods. This process has created plants that are durable but structurally brittle and vulnerable to fire.

In addition, arborists in California made decisions to intervene and plant the eucalyptus tree for shade. Native to the dry climate of Australia, the eucalyptus could grow to extraordinary heights with shade foliage in conditions of very little moisture. As it turned out, California had a perfect climate for eucalyptus and they proliferated there. The tree's structural composition was dry and brittle just like that of the natural flora. Thus not only was it vulnerable to fire, but it burned quickly with extreme heat and broke into small hot embers that the winds spewed a considerable distance, igniting new fires. In the social environment, an ethnic group's historical development and the state's attempt to improve life for some groups and not for others can also create the conditions and situations that provoke volatile and violent episodes between ethnic groups.

CLIMATE AND WEATHER: SOCIAL CONDITIONS AND STRUCTURAL CHANGE

The content of social situations is greatly determined by the structural conditions in which they occur. These social conditions that affect the relations between groups and individuals of a particular locale in part reflect the macro structural conditions affecting the nation, state, or city. Many of these conditions are related to the economy and the problems associated with managing to make a comfortable life within it. Some arise from general problems such as a national recession or a business's outsourcing of production to take advantage of less expensive labor.[8] Other conditions can simply be the change in business preferences for certain ethnic groups to do particular labor, creating a situation where one ethnic group gets job opportunities at the expense of another group or is viewed that way by a group not being hired at the same rate.[9] In addition, employers sometimes recruit particular ethnic workers to replace incumbent employees so they can increase their economic advantages (avoid unionization, reduce wages and benefits, and increase productivity with longer hours). These practices create conflict between the groups, and where there is a long history of such situations, as in the United States, the structural circumstances present at the time and any history between currently interacting groups related to past conflicts over economic spoils create ripe conditions for group violence.[10]

In addition to problems within the structure of the labor market, the housing market can create conditions for ethnic tension and conflict. For example, newly arriving ethnic groups seeking housing find that the housing market is unable to provide them with options, constraining them to live in a specific area. Often this means high concentrations of diverse peoples living in limited space, forcing members of their populations to have unrelenting contact with each other. This is a recipe for increasing conflict between the groups.[11]

Social circumstances can also create a climate predisposing to ethnic violence. The first of these concerns the cultural orientations of the various groups interacting in a particular locale. The greater the degree of difference in cultural orientation between the groups, the greater their alienation, dislike, resentment, and prejudice toward each other. Religion plays a large role, mainly because religious beliefs usually encompass morals, values, and worldviews that can be a source of significant difference in what is considered "right," "just," and "sacred." In addition to religion, specific customs associated with different cultures can play a role in organizing interactions between ethnic groups, particularly the case of the clothing, food, and behavior thought to be appropriate for in-group and out-group members. The tensions between Jews, Moslems, Christians, Hindus, and Sikhs, all of whom have issues with some elements of the customs (religion, dress, food, and behavior) associated with the rival groups, are examples, and who fights with whom against whom varies by country and region as insults to these customs occur or as competition for limited resources (material, natural, informational, cultural, etc.) increases.

Last, the primary language spoken by a group establishes communicative boundaries between themselves and other groups and influences interactions. Much of what will be used to establish legitimate membership in an ethnic group is determined by language preference, ability, and usage. Likewise, much that will be used to misinterpret the motives of others from a different ethnic group will be drawn from conversations in which languages vary among those directly involved, or those listening to them.

Ultimately these preconditions—greater material competition, wide cultural differences, and frequent close encounters—create a climate that makes ethnic conflict possible, but it is the immediate socioeconomic conditions (i.e., the "weather") in a particular locale that make ethnic violence probable.[12] Essentially, the immediate social pressures create a "current condition" that escalates the possibility of conflict just as the presence of extremely hot weather with high winds increases the risk of a fire occurring and decreases the fire authority's ability to combat it. Some examples of these social pressures are the existence of a segmented labor market with a large supply of unskilled or semiskilled laborers who are forced to compete for a small number of jobs;[13] a recession or the exodus of businesses that formerly employed significant numbers of people in low-skilled jobs;[14] ethnic or racial discrimination in the occupational and housing markets that reduces the options of those who have been the targets of this bias;[15] and a reduction in governmental benefits for those who are having difficulty in securing a job, housing, and health care.[16] States within the United States and cities within states differ in demographic composition, economy, and history of social relations, which creates variation in the types of situations faced in different locales even when the same ethnic groups exist in significant numbers.[17] The conditions present at any one time can simply follow the general climatic pattern and create a hazardous situation for some limited period of time, or they can deviate from the general trend by being more intense or being present for a longer-than-normal period (e.g., in the natural realm, drought or extra-rainy and wet conditions). Crises such as tornadoes, hurricanes, and floods can create strains on those who confront them;[18] riots can produce environments where ethnic tensions and hostilities grow.[19] These specific conditions are responsible for establishing an incendiary situation among ethnic groups, and I conceptualize them as "social weather." I do this because these conditions occur during a specific time and space and represent a sharp accentuation of a general "social climate." Therefore, despite the general societal belief that schools should be exempt from any type of violence, the fact that ethnic violence occurs in a public high school underscores the point that it is a part of, and cannot be separated from, the local social environment.

FLINTS AND SPARKS: FRICTION AND AGGRESSION IN ETHNIC GROUP INTERACTIONS

Having identified the preconditions for ethnic violence, let me now identify the factors that are likely to initiate it. Like fires, ethnic violence requires an energy source to start it. Usually we refer to these energy sources as sparks, but sparks themselves must be started by something. The sparks initiating ethnic violence emerge from the frictions associated with the interactions of individuals from each group. These interactions are often awkward because people have different criteria of what is appropriate behavior in public places. What is appropriate for some groups is not for others, and friction arises when behaviors are thought to be offensive to various members of a group.[20] The acts considered by members of a group to be offensive to their tastes precipitate a psychological reaction in which the offended group considers members of the other group crude and inferior. Social tensions arise when these acts continue on a regular basis and begin to be publicly acknowledged with signs of disapproval. These signs generally send a message, intended or not, that the offended party finds the act beneath him or her and vulgar, and once this signal has been made there is a counter-reaction from the opposing group indicating that they have been insulted by people who are pretentious or in no social position to make this accusation. Over time these interactions constitute social friction, which, as the number of irritating interactions increase, sparks an aggressive verbal exchange. In this instance, cultural differences in everyday encounters create incidents of misunderstanding that lead to insults threatening individuals' status and pride, which in turn stimulate an aggressive reaction (i.e., sparks).

Sparks can also emerge from interactions that are contaminated from the beginning. These interactions occur when members of one group try to take advantage of members of the other group through trickery, persuasion, or coercion. This pattern can remain peaceful until one of the parties violates the existing relationship by overzealously using an increased level of aggression to deceive and compel, or to resist such behaviors. This produces the intensity required to initiate (i.e., spark) an escalation to violence.[21]

SMOKE AND FIRE: PASSIONS AND VIOLENT ETHNIC CLASHES

Sparks by themselves do not automatically cause a fire. Many sparks simply burn out in the air. Often in the early stages of interethnic relations this is exactly what happens. People let go of the emotions that led to an aggressive verbal exchange and possibly physical gestures. Sometimes, even when exchanges create enough animosity so that assault seems imminent, the passions required to move it to the next stage of physical violence are not yet fully realized. In these situations individuals verbally express themselves but then walk away. Thus we have smoke but no fire.

On other occasions, however, interpersonal conflicts creating intense passions (smoke) do explode into a full-grown violent ethnic clash (fire). For this to occur it is necessary that one or more individuals involved in a tense encounter be motivated to not step away in an effort to avoid a violent clash. This motivation emanates from two key elements related to the human desire to satisfy emergent needs. One set of needs is associated directly with the body, while the other is associated with the social world in which the individuals interact. Within the first set, the key ingredient is the desire to satisfy needs related directly to the person's body, such as hunger, thirst, sleep, pain, temperature discomfort (too cold or hot), fear, anxiety, or rage. Some of these needs may be real and others delusional, but when they play a role in a social encounter they can lead to aggression in an effort to satisfy them.[22] Therefore, in some encounters that include individuals from different ethnic groups, the ensuing violence arises from an internal desire to relieve physical and psychological discomfort, irritation, or discontent that has nothing to do with ethnicity.[23]

Within the second set of emergent needs, the key factor is the desire to gain and maintain a high social status in the hierarchy of that aspect of society that the individual favors and respects. These needs originate in the socialization process associated with parents, authorities, and the individual's ethnic group and in the ever-changing priorities of their peer group or the larger society. Thus this desire is intimately involved with efforts to fulfill the social obligations associated with perceived ethnic and peer group expectations and is directly related to establishing a sense of personal identity through some form of solidarity. Most often this will be expressed as a desire for group approval and will be articulated as performing one's "duty" in contributing to the community's existence in a way that honors the group's assumptions and procedures.[24] The merging of the personal "I desire" with the identified group's "we are" provides the driving force in moving individuals toward active violence and is associated with wanting peers to approve, admire, and venerate their behavior. Of course, this presupposes that, for status to be gained or maintained, the group for which the individual seeks approval must find the use of violence acceptable or appropriate, at least within certain contexts.

To this point I have been concerned with the factors that create conflicts between individuals from different ethnic groups. As the saying goes, "Where there's smoke there's fire," and this can be true for the development of ethnic violence as well. The process by which ethnic conflict evolves into ethnic violence begins when members of a particular ethnicity acting as a quasi-organized group use physical aggression to satisfy their needs and desires, and in so doing indicate by declaration or insinuation that they have picked their targets because of their ethnicity. In brief, members of the various ethnicities see the conflict in the school as based, not on disagreements between individuals, but on the fact that they belong to different ethnic groups; and this realization allows the movement from individual-oriented violence to group violence.

For group violence to escalate there must be additional stimulants. The first of these stimulants is associated with emotions, and several emotions play a significant role. Especially potent are the fear, hatred, and resentment that individuals experience when they feel that their body, material possessions, physical space, religious beliefs, or sense of identity at their most private core have been violated because of their ethnic background.

A second stimulant of group violence has to do with passions. Although the term *passions* is often used interchangeably with *emotions,* to better understand the progression of intergroup violence we must treat passions and emotions as linked but not synonymous. I am using *passion* to indicate the existence in a person, or group, of an *intense* and *overpowering* emotion like vengeance, revenge, or the resolve to rectify what is believed to be an act(s) of injustice toward them and/or members of their ethnic group.[25] Thus passions become the high-octane stimulant to complete the tasks that proceeded from desires, needs, and emotions. Together, desires, needs, emotions, and passions form a chain reaction necessary for the intensification of ethnic group violence.[26]

FROM FLAMES TO FIRESTORM: RIOTS AND STAMPEDES

We know that fires, left unattended, can grow into firestorms. The same progression can occur with ethnic violence.[27] The movement from a fire to a firestorm begins with the use of available resources to increase the intensity of the conflict. Intensity involves the capability to keep all the potential actors enthusiastically engaged. If we were talking about a fire we would refer to the availability of combustible material and the oxygen necessary to build the fire's intensity. In the case of ethnic violence the combustible material is the number of individuals that can be recruited for combat by persuasion or coercion. The "oxygen" is provided by the onlookers who encourage the violence, the media that either accurately report events or irresponsibly embellish the events for purposes of self-promotion, and community political leaders whose approval, or lack of disapproval, is driven by the need to support constituent concerns and issues.[28] Each provides the additional ingredients to increase the quantity and intensity of violent incidents.

Clearly, a fire and a firestorm differ in scope as well as intensity. In the case of ethnic school violence the firestorm usually is associated with "frenzied behavior" like riots and stampedes. Wind is the necessary natural resource for fires, and group dynamics, like crowd behavior, is the natural resource for ethnic violence.[29] First, when individuals from a particular ethnic group learn that coethnics are fighting with others from a different ethnic group in their immediate social vicinity, they will quickly look to start a fight with individuals they identify as their current antagonists from a different ethnic group. The impetus for the aggression is fear that if they do not attack first they will be vulnerable to being attacked and hurt. They are also impelled by a code of solidarity. When their coethnics are immediately engaged in conflict, their group expects them to demonstrate solidarity by joining the fight against members of the rival ethnic group. They are afraid that coethnics will call them cowards who did not come to the aid of their coethnics. This label is particularly powerful during the period of adolescence, when youth are seeking and avoiding labels in the pursuit of establishing a desired and acceptable identity.[30]

The second way crowd aggression among high school youth is generated is within the context of an organized group action. A small number of individuals decide and organize to attack members of a rival ethnic group. Once the fighting begins, new participants are drawn into the fighting, not out of fear, but because the fighting would be exciting and fun.[31]

Thus, to return to the fire metaphor, if we consider the dynamics when individuals from respective ethnicities continue to join the fighting, they resemble the traditional firestorm that builds as it relentlessly consumes increasing amounts of resources in proceeding to adjacent areas. When a fight between rival ethnic groups breaks out in one area and individuals in a different part of the school hear of this and also begin to fight each other, the situation more closely resembles a fire that spreads as the wind blows hot embers to new spots, thereby creating a storm as it engulfs additional areas.

DYING EMBERS: THE CESSATION OF VIOLENCE

Like fires, ethnic violence does end at a definite point. This happens by one of two processes. The first is that there are no compelling reasons or emotions to continue the fighting. In essence, it has run its course and there is nothing to fight about, either because the conditions that precipitated the fighting have significantly changed or because the emotions that kept it going are no longer present or as intense. The second process is that law enforcement (i.e., official state agents) has laid down such a blanket of control that violence is no longer possible. This second process is like the extinguishing of a fire by members of the fire department.

However, relief is tempered by the awareness that violence could again arise at any time. Consequently, both school personnel and law enforcement are increasingly vigilant, actively looking for signs that individuals or groups are planning to engage in physical violence. The larger strategy is to isolate individuals and remove them from the general population before they recruit enough students to "the cause." Of course, in many cases "the cause" has lost its relevance and simply faded into the background of those moral justifications associated with macro community issues, replaced by more immediate concerns with self-defined individual justice and the accompanying emotions of avenging perceived past transgressions against the self. This new condition is like that discussed in theories of revolutions where after the cessation of a considerable amount of violence some remnants that started the action (fire) and kept it going persist, despite widespread expectations that the storm is over.[32] This period is one of change. The exact nature of the change depends on how a number of contingent factors develop: the continued presence of issues that initiated the conflict; the continued presence of individuals who participated in the violence and did not totally renounce it; and the group dynamic in which individual/ethnic group identities interact with social pressures of acceptance and rejection that attracted individuals to intergroup violence, just as a sinkhole consumes objects unfortunate enough to be stuck in it.

Once this transition period has passed and there has been no group conflict for months, a period of peace is established. Given that history for youth passes "at the speed of light," most of the students will consider the days of conflict as ancient history, but school authorities will see the current situation as an opportunity to establish new policies to confront and monitor violence more generally and ethnic violence in particular. This requires that school officials think of ways to persuade the local authorities to improve the community conditions that precipitated the conflict and to remediate the conditions that made the school a fertile place for conflict to flourish. In essence, in this period school officials will do what they can to create new material and social resources that will at minimum provide a retardant and at maximum a resilient environment to ethnic violence.[33] In social terms this means school authorities will change what they can and wait until the demographics of the neighborhood change.[34] As the ethnic demographics of the neighborhood change, with more newcomers arriving and more members of the incumbent group exiting, violence in the schools will pass from being "ethnic group oriented" to being individual and "nonethnic." Thus, in the new demographic condition, violence is likely in schools whose students come from low-income families, but it will no longer be based on ethnicity or on the symbols that are part of a larger strain in ethnic group relations and will instead assume the characteristics of antagonism between individuals as individuals.

In summary, what society often understands in terms of individual pathology—the use of violence in everyday life—cannot be properly understood without examining social groups. Psychologists, economists, political scientists, even Max Weber, want to reduce social behavior to the actions of individuals. There is a sui generis aspect of "the group," which is why we require sociological analyses and why the existing models are inadequate.[35] In this regard, ethnic violence is more likely in schools where the students come from low-income families; where an increasing number of new students come from ethnic backgrounds different from those of the current student body; where there is general tension between the ethnic groups over a variety of issues that include maintenance of an ethnic identity associated with a physical place; where there is competition for limited resources to aid the socioeconomic well-being of each group's members; and where there is a struggle between members of these ethnic groups to attain enough political power to control the allocation of resources to groups. These underlying tensions solicit a reaction that often involves some level of violence in order for the remediation process to occur. Finally, once ethnic violence starts in a school there is a natural history to it that will be described in the empirical chapters that follow.

PART ONE

Tinder

CHAPTER 2

Kindling

The History of Ethnic Conflict

People are trapped in history and history is trapped in them.
—James Baldwin, *Notes of a Native Son,* 1955

Most researchers of violence, regardless of their conceptual framework, agree that the overwhelming majority of violent incidents are catalyzed by prior conditions involving one or more individuals. The question has always been to empirically identify these prior conditions and how they work to produce the violence. I begin with Randall Collins because his book has been the most exhaustive treatment of violence, offering a large array of hypotheses. In discussing the role of ethnicity in the phenomenology of violence, Collins acknowledges that racial prejudice and "structural conditions in the background, more long-term in nature, affect whether ethnic groups have an antagonistic relationship." Because he believes that ethnic antagonisms do not often lead to violence like riots, he focuses on what is necessary for collective ethnic violence like riots to occur. He argues that four sequences, or "acts," lead to the violent ethnic riot. They include long-standing trouble (presumably, though this is never explicit, between the groups), followed by "act one," when there is a perceived provocation, then "act two," when there is a lull, and finally "act three," when there is an outburst of violence that is one-sided and can be repeated. Since he asserts that violence is not easy for anyone to engage in, the process by which individuals act violently involves what he calls the "forward panic," a series of events that include the "buildup of tension/fear with the shift to the sudden weakness of the victim that opens the dark tunnel down into which people collectively [like a crowd] fall."[1] Of course, much of this is a statement about the relationship between ethnicity and riot violence, which we will have more to say about later in the empirical chapters on such events, rather than about other forms of violence where ethnicity plays a primary role.

There are of course other theories concerning ethnic violence centered on individual and group roles in racism and reactions to it, as well as struggles over the control of valued resources and political representation.[2] However, most of the theoretical propositions concerning ethnic violence, including Collins's, tend to look at the factors that are relatively immediate to the time violence is enacted, such as an ethnic/racial slight, a threat, or a physically aggressive move, and this misses some of the details that lead up to a violent action. Even Collins uses the phrase *confrontational tension* to conceptualize the situation immediately before violence occurs, and no doubt there are times when a "confrontational tension" exists. Nonetheless, in the case of ethnic violence, generally conditions have occurred in the past that influence individuals' use of violence against members of a different ethnic group. Here we are faced with a number of questions: When individuals engage in violence against members of other ethnic groups, what prior conditions have influenced these events, how far back do they go in group and personal history, and how and why do they work to cause the violence? The answer I found is that three factors set the stage for ethnic violence to begin and continue to intensify, each of which has been developing for some time. They include a personal identity linked to a particular ethnicity, a sense of history related to the ethnic group that one identifies with, and the use of prejudice to navigate relations with both members of one's group and members of other groups. I shall consider each of these in order, and we will see that they produce different outcomes in lower- and middle-class schools.

THE ROLE OF GROUP HISTORY IN THE PROCESS OF ETHNIC SORTING

All youth, especially those in adolescent development, are engaged in identity formation, but some elements of this process provide the conditions for interethnic violence to become a serious problem. One of these elements has to do with the role that ethnicity assumes in a person's individual identity. Part of deciding "Who am I?" typically has to do with a person's ethnic origins. When this is the case, the individual must separate him- or herself from others on the basis of ethnic origins. This process is more intense when one must separate oneself from many individuals with differing ethnic origins. It may be facilitated through family socialization, or non-family members' identification of the individual with a particular ethnic group, or both. One's ethnic identity includes the attributes shared by members of the group: physical features, name, language, religion, and a group's history.[3] Although the process just described is common to most individuals, in this study it was especially crucial in establishing an environment where ethnic violence in schools became likely.

There is no automatic connection between the historical legacy of an ethnic group and its members' involvement in violence. However, there is evidence that a group's historical legacy makes it more likely to be victimized. The present research found that how the youth in the study's schools understood their group's history was more important in fueling ethnic violence than previous theories would suggest. Youth can use their group's history to emphasize both its proud accomplishments and its victimization. Victimization in the United States amplifies a group's sense of worth by emphasizing the obstacles it has overcome and justifying claims for special attention.

The students in the present study used group history to discriminate group members from non-group members, foster solidarity, prejudge others, and rationalize actions that would create antagonistic relations between students from different ethnicities as well as to maintain the ethnic violence once it started. Students turned to group history to emphasize the accomplishments of their group and establish a sense of common destiny. Ethnic youth from middle-class families attending a high school with a predominantly middle-class student body used group history to demonstrate how their ethnic group had advanced since its arrival in the United States and the contributions their members had made to the nation. In the middle-class-dominated schools, a sense of group history contributed to reducing antagonism between groups, and celebration of ethnic differences and the benefits they provided to everyone established a basis for preventing ethnic antagonism. Teachers in both middle-class and lower-class schools extolled ethnic diversity, but student reactions differed sharply. In lower-class schools students displayed dissatisfaction, antipathy, and resistance,[4] whereas in the middle-class schools students responded to ethnic diversity with interest, enjoyment, and acceptance. The comments of Denise, an African American attending Los Angeles's lower-class Chumash High School, and Enrique, a Mexican American attending Los Angeles's middle-class De Neve High School, are representative of this pattern.[5]

Denise: This is a dumb week in history class. Mr. Smith [pseudonym] keeps telling us about Mexican cultural stuff, but I don't care about that shit, do you? This is America, we don't need to know about Mexico and what they do there, and I don't care if it's supposed to make the Mexicans in class feel better. If they need that, why don't they just go back there?[6]

Enrique: I really liked yesterday when we were learning about the African and African American culture, and they brought in all their food. It'll be interesting to see all the different kinds of African stuff that's still in America. Tomorrow's when they'll show the different things that are African in Latin America, including food, and that'll be real interesting too. [Everyone makes a verbal gesture in agreement.][7]

As was mentioned in the Introduction, the evolution of ethnic antagonisms into violence generally occurs in schools that draw their student population from low-income families. More will be said about why this is the case in the next chapter, but in evaluating the influence that a sense of group history has in setting the stage for ethnic violence one must keep in mind what kinds of schools are most affected. Among the lower-class students group history served to explain the differences between the groups they were forced to interact with, but the emphasis was primarily on the hardships endured by their group and the unjust nature of that hardship. There is no doubt that lower-class students were very sensitive to their socioeconomic position and felt that they needed to explain their present position through group history. Thus their use of group history incorporated three themes: the unjustified hardship imposed on members of their group, and by extension their families; the severity of the hardship suffered by members of their group; and the length of time their group had endured hardship.[8]

The general pattern among students who mentioned group history in both free conversation and formal classroom discussions was to focus on the suffering and hardship that their forebears had endured and thereby to establish that their group was morally wronged and that their predecessors were entitled to be regarded as heroes and not villains or pathetic failures.[9] The lower-class students who discussed ethnic histories generally engaged in a competition over whose group had suffered or was suffering the most. These students attempted to establish a rank order of suffering for the various ethnic groups: contending, for example, that slavery was worse than indentured servitude, agricultural work was worse than industrial work, or piecework was worse than hourly wage labor. The comments of JaRod, Peter, and Antonia are representative. JaRod was an African American attending Oakland's Miwok High School:

> We had to live through the slavery shit and then fucking Jim Crow and they're complaining about being migrant workers. They ain't anywhere near what we went through, and they ain't got no right to be ask'n for special help or anything, and especially if the help is the same as us.[10]

Peter was an Irish American attending Boston's Paul Revere High School:

> The fucking niggers talking about they had to deal with slavery and this and that, hell slavery is been dead for a hundred years. They try to make people think they got it bad, but that's just a bunch of shit. They ain't had to deal with as much prejudice and discrimination as us [Irish] in this town. They ain't been here as long as us and had to deal with them Protestant upper-class fuckers like we had to. So, they ain't got no right talking about being so discriminated against all the time so they'd have to come to our school. [He is talking about court-ordered busing to achieve numerical equality in schools.][11]

Antonia was a Mexican American attending Los Angeles's Chumash High School:

> They [African Americans] are always talking about slavery did this to them and that to them and that is why they deserve to live where they want to now and not have people like us [Mexican Americans] around them if they don't want, but we were here before they were in the US and we got all our land stolen from us, then they kicked us out of the US and try to keep us from coming back to our own land. Plus, when they do let us in they make us take the shitty jobs that nobody wants, even African Americans won't take them! So, I don't care what the bastards say, we had it worse than them for longer and they can go to hell if they don't like us![12]

Along with the kind of oppression a group suffered, the length of time it was treated poorly was important in establishing the group's legitimacy as a heroic example of fortitude in the face of struggle. It was used to support a positive image for all members of the group and oneself in particular.[13] The comments of Marco, Candace, and Logan are representative. Marco was a Mexican American attending Oakland's Miwok High School:

> Us Mexicans have been on the bottom in California forever. Nobody but the Indians has had to put up with as much discrimination as us. The Anglos don't like us 'cause we look and talk different from them, and the *mayates* [literally means "bug" and is used as a derogatory word for African Americans] don't like us 'cause we talk different than them and work harder and better than them. In fact, we're better than the Anglos too, because we work at jobs they won't do.[14]

Candace was an Irish American attending Boston's Shawmut High School:

> Nobody's been kept down like us Irish. Nobody gave us anything, we worked shitty jobs and still work shitty jobs here [Boston] cause Protestants don't like us. So, I don't know what the blacks are talking about when they talk that discrimination stuff, 'cause we had it worse than them for a hell of a lot longer and done better. We're [Irish] better than other groups in the US because we got ahead even though everybody's [other groups in the US] against us.[15]

Logan was an African American attending Los Angeles's Chumash High School:

> Yeah, the shit we've put up with for hundreds of years is nothing like any of them other motherfucking groups! We been held back from slavery to even now, but we just keep coming on and showing everybody who's better. Look at all the black people that's invented stuff, entertainers, and sports stars and shit. Ain't no other group can show that and faced the shit we have. The whites think they're superior, but it should be pretty clear they ain't nothing compared to us.[16]

In the formation of a group history to build a positive personal identity, the final element that contributed to the evolution of ethnic violence in the schools was the blaming of other groups for one's own group's experience with hardship. These regularly included the groups that each group was currently forced to interact with. For the Irish, it was African Americans who took jobs that they, or other European American group members, were trying to unionize, making their group's life more difficult; and it was African Americans that challenged their privileged position of employment in city jobs such as police and firefighting, constraining their group's opportunities.[17] The comments of Sidney and Jody are representative. Sidney was an Irish American attending Boston's Shawmut High School:

> Them fucking niggers! They always complaining racism, so they can take the jobs away from us on the police force and fire department. Ain't nobody discriminated against them, they just too fuckin' stupid to pass the test to get in; but them pointy-head liberals [academics] and the courts will feel sorry for 'em and take jobs away from us [Irish Americans] who worked hard to get 'em.[18]

Jody was an Irish American student attending Boston's Paul Revere High School:

> No, it's upsetting that my cousin might not get a city job because the blacks want to say they been discriminated against. They want stuff just given to

them even though they don't work for it. So why should we be put in a bad way just because they're black and can say anything?[19]

For African Americans, Mexicans were making their life worse by taking jobs that were attractive and would have been theirs if the Mexicans had not been around and willing to work for less money. The comments of Edward and Mona are representative. Edward was an African American attending Chumash High School in Los Angeles:

> Hey, who can like Mexicans? Everybody knows that they take jobs. They gonna work for nothin' so the jobs is only good for them. We ain't gonna take jobs that can't pay the bills, so then all the jobs are theirs and we get nothing.[20]

Mona was an African American student at Oakland's Kaiser High School:

> I know my mom's been having a lot of trouble gettin' a job. So is her friends, and I think it's 'cause of all the Mexicans who is working for hardly no money. . . . Nothin's going to get better until they start to do things like deport them.[21]

For the Mexicans it was African Americans that had made their life more difficult because they always sided with Anglos on immigration issues and tried to delegitimize attempts by other ethnic groups to receive societal aid. The comments of Diego and Laura represent this line of thinking. Diego was a Mexican American student attending Oakland's Kaiser High School:

> The blacks want you to feel sorry for them because of racism, but they are racist toward us. They always think Mexicans shouldn't live here just like the Anglos. So both of them is on the same side against us getting a better life.[22]

Laura was a Mexican American attending Los Angeles's Tongva High School:

> The Anglos and blacks is trying to say we [Mexicans] need to be stopped from coming to America and send the rest of us back. They're trying to make life worse for us, not better![23]

I frequently encountered statements like this by African American and Mexican students in the low-income schools of Oakland and Los Angeles, but rarely in the more middle-class schools in both cities.[24]

Group history can be effective in building personal identity and a positive self-image. It is also effective in building a worldview that divides people into "we" and "they" (i.e., the act of discriminating) and forming prejudice that is essential in initiating and sustaining social conflict between groups. The comments made by the students comparing ethnic experiences and expressing hostilities were not made as "after-the-fact" rationalizations. They were expressed in each of the schools before episodes of violence started.[25] Thus the students' understanding of ethnic history was critical in setting the conditions for violence to occur.[26]

GROUP HISTORY AND DISCRIMINATION

One of the obvious points about ethnic conflict is that some form of group sorting has previously taken place. Individuals choose group alliances as a result of both family socialization and their "normal" everyday interactions with what constitute the constituent elements of their and other "social groups." As part of the socialization process, individuals learn "clues" that will be useful to assign an individual to one or another group. Certainly a key aspect of this sorting, or group identity formation, involves physical and cultural factors, usually considered to have been endowed at birth, that correspond to the characteristics that family, friends, or acquaintances attribute to a specific ethnic group. These include features of the body, names, language, religion, and group history.[27] Part of the act of discriminating, which is essentially deciding who is in one's group and who is not, involves making generalizations about the characteristics of one's own group as well as others'.[28] The students I studied in these schools used this formula, but in different ethnic groups the content of the formula varied in kind or degree. There was an evaluative component: individuals believed that the content associated with their group was unique or generally better than that found in other groups.[29] The result of this tendency was the development and use of stereotypes. The generalizations that constitute stereotypes usually have some accuracy or at least are not totally false. However, *stereotyping* is biased in that it leaves the holder in jeopardy of making errors in assessing a single individual. Volumes of research have shown that stereotyping does not allow for nuanced perceptions of variation within populations.[30] Nonetheless, stereotypes are used in everyday life by most people, and the students in this study relied on them to define groups and to assess the intentions of other students toward themselves. By using stereotypes, students could produce discrete social categories that removed a very significant amount of social ambiguity from their world.[31] The comments of Andrea and Lane are representative. Andrea was a Mexican American student at Los Angeles's Chumash High School:

> My brother tells me the blacks think they're better than us in everything and just try to move us out of the way and take over everything. They'll just push you any time they want something, and that goes for the girls too. They just don't have any good manners, so I know that when they come around I got to be careful about not doing anything they don't like, 'cause they'll just get physical with you. I really don't like them 'cause that's the way they all are.[32]

Lane was an African American student at Oakland's Kaiser High School:

> Fucking Mexicans! They just stick to themselves and walk around like they're afraid of us or don't like anybody that ain't Mexican or shit. They are so fucking irritating to be around, and I don't trust them 'cause if you be kidding with them they either say nothing and keep walking and stuff. I just want to hit the fuckers and say, "Wake up! There's more students here that ain't Mexican than there is Mexican!" [Everyone laughs and nods in agreement.][33]

For the teenagers in this study, and most likely adolescents generally, stereotyping not only provided a road map for interacting with other individuals but, as I will discuss in the subsequent section, helped them develop a personal identity as well. Stereotyping also established the conditions that made aggression between social groups, particularly ethnic groups, more likely because it provided a basis for rationalizing future and past aggressive behaviors.[34] The comments of Keysha, Susan, Ted, and Ronald are representative of stereotyping. Keysha was an African American student at Oakland's Kaiser High School:

> Them Mexes [Mexicans] is really stupid. They'll haul shit if somebody tells 'em to, and that's why Whitey likes them. They got no self-respect when it comes to work, they're just really stupid. I can't think of slower-thinking group than them fuckers. [There is laughter from others she is talking with.] It just shows you, you got to be who you are, and I'm thankful of who I am and not one of them Mexican fools that just work and fuck like rats! [Everyone in the group laughs and agrees.][35]

Susana was a Mexican American student at Los Angeles's Chumash High School:

> I'm getting tired of the way the teachers always try to tell us about blacks and how bad they got it. We [Mexicans] have had it bad too, and I'm glad I work hard for what I get and am from a culture that's always worked hard

and not been lazy and loud like they are. They always want to say things about us, but nobody wants to hire them 'cause they're rude and never work hard on the job. My dad always complains about how they work and how they're always missing work and stuff. Other people at the hair shop also say the same thing. Plus, they just like to steal things from other people, and this is always on the news. [Both of her friends nod in agreement.][36]

Ted was an Irish American student attending Boston's Shawmut High School:

Well, you got to be proud of who you are and not like the niggers who hate what they are. I am so glad to be Irish 'cause we were treated like dirt by the Protestants, but we kept working and didn't complain all the time, and now we got Irish millionaires, politicians, and sports greats. What they got? Just laziness and stupidity. They [African Americans] just had too much inbreeding during slavery, you know? [Everyone laughs and agrees.][37]

Ronald was an African American student attending Boston's Paul Revere High School:

I fuck'n don't want to go to that cracker school! ["Cracker" is a name often used by African Americans to describe "racial whites."] Why would I want to do that? The fuck'n Irish run this city, and any of them that gots brains is not livin' in that part of town, so I got to go to school with a bunch of white trash that's stupid and uncouth. So why should we go there? Those people [the Irish] is drunks and degenerates, and everybody knows that; and that's exactly why any of them that's smart got the hell out of there! This is fucked up! [All five members of the group he is talking with verbally agree with him.][38]

Like these four students, most of the students attending the schools in this study held stereotypical views of the other group they had to interact with well before violence between the groups occurred. There is, of course, the issue of whether all the individuals think this way or whether they just say this in a group situation because they know what the prevailing view is of the other group. It is always difficult to determine in a natural setting that is nonexperimental what a person "really thinks." It is probable that there was variation in what was "really thought" among each of the groups, but the prevailing "in-group" stereotypical views of the "out-group" were socially so influential that they appeared to be generally internalized to provide members with a cognitive map to the "socially appropriate" view of individuals in the other group.

A caveat to this finding must be mentioned. My findings on stereotyping are not an attempt to generalize to all cognitive processes, though some elements of general cognitive processes are involved in determining "in-group" and "out-group" identification. I am simply drawing attention to the fact that stereotyping is a critical element leading to ethnic conflicts.

PERSONAL IDENTITY AND PREJUDICE

Individuals establish their identity during adolescence within a particular social environment,[39] and in most cases the social environment is similar to their parents' and thus provides generational continuity.[40] However, in some cases adolescents form their identities in the midst of social change. In this study social change involved the shift from an ethnically homogeneous to an ethnically heterogeneous neighborhood. Transitions are often difficult no matter what their content may be, and how this social change is understood by those experiencing it says a good deal about how people will react to it. Individuals within a particular ethnic group have generally viewed the arrival of new people from a different ethnic group as a threat to their way of life.[41] Although such change can certainly alter life as incumbent residents experience it, they can live next to people of a different ethnic group and still maintain their traditional way of life: that is, they can live separately together. This was the case in the middle-class areas and schools that I studied. However, it was not the case in the poor and working-class areas and schools. The reasons for this will be discussed later in this chapter. The point here is that in mixed ethnic environments personal identity, which includes some element of ethnic identity, often involves prejudice and discrimination in the cognitive process.[42]

FORMULATING HISTORICAL PREJUDICE

Prejudging is something that everyone does every day. It is simply the use of a shortcut logic to guide individuals on how to act in the presence of or with other individuals at a given time. I define it as a shortcut in that it uses information gathered in the past to establish social categories, place individuals in these categories (through discrimination), and prescribe appropriate and functional behavior as an alternative to allowing oneself to be guided by the interpretive content of the interaction itself.[43] Thus people will prejudge individuals and contexts in order to navigate basic everyday interactions.[44] The problem is that prejudice is often, though not always, based on faulty assumptions because it relies on information that is incomplete, inaccurate, or obsolete. This can contaminate the interaction, making it brief, cursory, and unpleasant. In essence, it can, as Samuel Roundfield Lucas has argued, establish a field of "damaged social relations."[45] The fact that it is very common to all individuals makes it particularly insidious in accounting for its total impact on individual and group relations. Only when the articulation of the prejudice is blatant or profane is it clearly identified and more easily explained. So where does that leave us in the analysis of preconditions of ethnic group violence? In brief, once people have developed the criteria to distinguish their group from all others, using the available information to formulate generalizations about other groups (i.e., stereotypes), prejudice carries these endeavors forward into interaction.[46] Thus prejudice was one of the preconditions for violent behavior between the different ethnic students attending the schools of the present study.

The prejudice that resulted from the mental activities of group members to distinguish themselves from others involved stories about the trials, tribulations, and triumphs of the group to create solidarity, carve out an existence, and form an identity. In most groups the "worth of their celebrated triumphs" is predicated on the obstacles overcome to achieve them, and if a group does not overcome obstacles, both the private and public aspects of the group's identity have less status. Thus, for the students in this study, achieving group worth by overcoming difficulties made both significant and modest gains worthy of inclusion in the group's history and identity.[47] The comments of Tom, an Irish American from Boston's Shawmut High School, are representative:

> Fucking niggers is always complaining about this and that, but when we first got here we didn't have a pot to piss in. We were just "Mick" scum to everybody [the word *Mick* being a derogatory term used by the English and American Protestants to refer to Irish Catholics], but we fuckin' worked shit jobs and elected our people to government that could help us, and that helped cities to get better too. . . . Yeah, us Irish know how to work hard and overcome things and make things better.[48]

Clearly, the students in this study perceived that their ethnic group made gains through historical conflict with others. This dynamic carried with it a set of beliefs, true or false, about the other group (stereotypes and prejudices) and affected motives and behaviors toward members of the other group(s). The primary source of these beliefs was stories told by family, friends, and community members, but some used selected material from ethnic history books and courses to bolster them. However, what kept the prejudice dynamic active among the students was the conviction that the perceived motives of members of the other groups were well established and that those who did not heed the wisdom of this information and act accordingly risked being physically hurt. Moreover, they deserved what they would get for having ignored that wisdom. The comments of Erica and John are representative of this. Erica was a Mexican American attending Los Angeles's Chumash High School:

> You just have to know that the blacks is going to beat the shit out you if they get a chance. They done that to my cousin and my older brother when they first went to their school in another section of town. My mom said that happened when she went to school too. . . . Look, we know what they're like, so you got to protect yourself around them and if you don't and get hurt, everybody will say, "We told you."[49]

John was an African American attending Shawmut High School in Boston:

> Them motherfuckin' Irish trash has been trying to fuck us up forever. So not knowing that is to be brain dead! So if you get fucked up by them you deserving it, you know?! That's just the way they are and always been, so you got to do what you have to to protect yourself. [Everyone nods in agreement.][50]

The prejudicial thinking at this stage related to past history and not to how the individuals themselves were currently being treated. Nonetheless, the youth took the historical accounts, whether true or false, seriously. Thus historical grievance provided the "kindling" without which violence would not have otherwise occurred. Some of the individuals making these comments would engage in physical violence with members of the other ethnic group in the coming months, but when these comments were recorded they had not themselves experienced it. Further, this prejudicial thinking establishes not only that other groups have been guilty of past transgression against members of one's own group but also that they have the ability to inflict harm on one's own group in the present. Take the representative comments of Sheila and Hector. Sheila was an African American student attending Shawmut High School in Boston:

> I hate the Irish in this town. You know how many times one of us has been beat up by them for no reason? They always want to attack us when there is a lot of them together. So, hell, you know they want to do it to us [now] for coming to their school, and there sure is enough of them to do it too![51]

Hector was a Mexican American attending Kaiser High School in Oakland:

Them *mayates* is mean as hell. They have really beat up a number of us when we've been anywhere near their neighborhoods. A number of people have said they were beat so bad they almost died, in fact one guy said that if the police hadn't come by he would have been dead. Now, there's a lot of them going to this school, so you know that they will be able to do this here too. [The three girls he is talking to nod in agreement.][52]

The prejudice among the adolescents in this study was generally expressed in clear, strong, and often deliberately uncouth terms. However, because it was based on beliefs that their group had been violated by the other(s), it provided a moral shield to resist adult arguments that it was both inappropriate and distasteful. Thus each of the groups felt that their preconceived stereotype of other groups was justified given the group's history and the history of their group's relationship to them. The comments of Caitlin, Carlos, and Ida are representative. Caitlin was an Irish American student at Boston's Paul Revere High School:

People in the suburbs are all in a huff and call us racist and things because we say we don't want to have anything to do with them [African Americans], but they never have to be around them. They [African Americans] are crude and violent and they always have tried to take over everything. So them liberal whites is just ignorant, because if they'd know them the way that we do they wouldn't say a damn thing! [All four people nod in the affirmative.][53]

Carlos was a Mexican American attending Chumash High School:

Fuck, them *blacks* are always trying to take your money, your girl, and your music [electronic devices]. They say we're racist, but we ain't! If they wouldn't act that way then we wouldn't say they do, so I don't listen to their shit. [A group of six other students all verbally agree with him.][54]

Ida was an African American at Boston's Shawmut High School:

Them is all white trash, them Irish is. They racist to the core and so prejudiced they won't give no one a chance, but they live like little rats. . . . Yeah, they are like that because the other whites don't think they are any good and then they just try to take it out on us. They probably go to church and take communion too, but God knows they is dead wrong![55]

The prejudices found among the students of this study who were experiencing ethnic change in their neighborhood and school were intensified by personal needs associated with adolescent development. First, since most of the students in these situations had already sorted themselves and other students into discrete categories, they coveted acceptance by their ethnic peer group. What they wanted to avoid at all costs was to be shunned by their ethnic peers, and this led to group conformity in ethnic relations.[56] The comments of Patricia and Richard are representative. Patricia was an African American student at Oakland's Kaiser High School and was talking to another female student:

> Yeah, you say that Mexicans haven't done nothing to you, but just keep saying that and see all the shit you take from the others here [peer group]! They goin' to call you a sellout of the race [African Americans], so I'd shut the fuck up about that shit if I were you.[57]

Richard was an Irish American student at Boston's Shawmut High School:

> Hey, I better keep my fucking mouth shut, but that talk about killing niggers is fucking crazy! But everybody here [in the school] is so pissed off that even the girls will hate anybody who doesn't hate the niggers. I don't want that [having girls hate him], who would?![58]

As previous research has shown, adolescence is a time when individuals search for a sense of self based on criteria different from those of the adult world.[59] Thus the desire to establish an identity is centered on what the coveted peer group understands as necessary for assimilation into it, for acceptance by the group, for a personal identity, and for temporary group solidarity in intergroup relations. Prejudging others' worth is part of an attempt, by comparison, to develop one's own sense of self, and prejudgments will include ethnic difference when ethnicity is a part of the adolescent's immediate environment. Thus in those environments one observes ethnic prejudice with a moral justification. The comments of Jenna and Yale are representative of this. Jenna was a Mexican American student at Los Angeles's Tongva High School:

> Denise is not somebody I want to hang around with or be like, she acts just like the blacks and thinks she is going take every boy she wants and have sex with them. She doesn't care about being decent, she just wants to take whatever she wants. She is so greedy, and there is no way I want to hang around with her and do what she thinks is fun. She's definitely going to end up just like the black girls who do the same thing and get pregnant and have to raise a baby with no one who will marry her![60]

Yale was an African American at Oakland's Kaiser High School:

> Mexicans are so "kiss-ass" and act like they're just sheep. You know they're like mice, all scared of everything. They got no sense of how somebody should act. All they do is take shit, and who can have dignity like that? You like to be like that? Well, hell no, nobody whose got any pride wants to be like them. I don't, you don't, ain't nobody we know who wants to be a man be acting like the shit they do. They just a fucking pathetic group![61]

Further, as was mentioned earlier, the moral element in the prejudice found among the adolescents in the present study enabled them to resist adult arguments that it was inappropriate and distasteful. The comments of Gabriella and Mark are representative. Gabriella was a Mexican American student at Los Angeles's Chumash High School:

> Them blacks is so sick. They got no sense of right and wrong, they'll just as soon rob, kill, or want to fuck you any time they can. There is no time that I ain't watching them, 'cause if you don't they'll mess you up. . . . Yeah, my mom and dad, but mostly my mom, says, "Don't say things bad about the blacks 'cause they ain't all like that," but she's at home and don't get around much. So she don't hear all the things that have gone on with other Mexicans having to deal with the blacks.[62]

Mark was an African American student at Oakland's Kaiser High School:

> Yeah, who can't hate the fucking Mexicans in this school, and I was telling my brother why, but my dad told me not to be so prejudiced. I say, "Okay, Dad, you say that, but they taking all our jobs and they ain't even legal." . . . Yeah, well, my dad can say that shit because he got a job with the city and ain't got to worry like the rest of us. So there ain't no fuckin' way that I'd ever hire or help any one of them fuckers [Mexicans], 'cause they only care about themselves and we [African Americans] got to do the same.[63]

In sum, these beliefs increased the chances for violence because they led students to see others' actions as threatening. After each episode of violence students engaged in or heard about they felt these beliefs to be justified, and this in turn reduced their threshold of resistance to engaging in violence later. Further, once a violent act started, participants used these beliefs to demonize their opponents and increase the intensity of the fight, as well as to rationalize their involvement and their plans for future involvement.[64]

MIDDLE-CLASS SCHOOLS

Much of the information in this chapter related directly to lower-class schools, because that is where most ethnic violence occurs. This raises an obvious question: If acts of discriminating, stereotyping, and prejudging are a "normal" part of adolescent youth's creation of an identity, why are middle-class schools not also vulnerable to ethnic violence? The answer is that while adolescents in middle-class schools do employ discrimination, stereotyping, and prejudice in forming a personal identity, the influence of middle-class norms within each area from which the schools drew their student bodies created a difference in how and why they were used. In brief, it established an environment where violence between ethnic groups was considered unnecessary. For example, the parents of students that attended the middle-class schools in this study had acquired the capital to purchase homes in the area because the housing stock was structurally and aesthetically desirable. The schools were reputed to prepare their students to be accepted by a university of their choice. The adolescents were overwhelmingly second generation, were assimilated to American cultural norms, spoke only English or preferred to use it in everyday interactions, and were culturally assimilated to the prevailing American middle-class values, goals, and preferences. Thus these schools, like the lower-class schools, were homogeneous in social class, but because the neighborhoods from which the students came were not identified with a particular ethnic group the students did not experience a sense that their ethnic background was relevant to whom they associated with or how their peers would evaluate them. Their ethnic background gave them a family history to be proud of but was not directly linked to who they were, wanted to be, or were accepted as.[65] The comments of Neal and Tina provide two examples of this. Neal was an African American attending Los Angeles's De Neve High School. Here he was talking to three other students (two African Americans and one Mexican) who were new to the school that year:

> I mean, there are people here from all kinds of backgrounds, but that doesn't mean anything big in this school. Everybody gets to celebrate their ethnic heritage here, and people are cool with it because it's just a celebration. Hey, look, it don't take a genius to see that no matter what your family background is everybody in this school is pretty much American, you know? I mean, even with somebody like me, I got nothing in common with Africans and I can tell you the Mexicans in this school don't have any connection to Mexicans in Mexico. Look, we like the same stuff, do the same things, and want to go to college. So there's really no difference, we're just like the other Americans.[66]

Tina was a Mexican American student attending Ohlone High School in Oakland; here she was in a conversation with two other Mexican American students:

> Yeah, just the other day this guy at the [amusement park] is asking me about what gangs my brother hangs with at school, and I am like, this is too weird because look at this school, it is like middle class with the only gang being the sports teams or social clubs! That shit this guy was talking about gangs

was just barrio shit, that's all. [The other three students laugh.] Aren't we the most American school there could be?! The Mexican students here, or most of them, can't speak Spanish and don't know Mexican culture. I think everybody, I know I am, is proud of being Mexican, but most of us have lived all our lives here and are really just American like everybody else in this school.[67]

Thus discriminating, stereotyping, and prejudging are based on nonethnic criteria, allowing the ethnic heritage of the students to be something to celebrate and not stigmatize. The comments of Julon and Claudia are representative of these beliefs. Julon was an African American student attending Los Angeles's De Neve High School:

I know what you're saying, so don't talk to her. That girl [she is African American] is messed up, she thinks she knows everything and she's ugly too! [The others in the conversation laugh.] Couple of the Mexican girls in that group are real good looking, but they all think they are hot shit, so none of us are having anything to do with them. A couple of days ago two of the guys in their group asked if we'd help them with a school event and Sharri and Amari said "no" 'cause anything they're going to do is really going to be boring.[68]

Claudia was a Mexican American student attending Oakland area's Ohlone High School:

I really like this school and am glad my dad got transferred to this job here. It is so different from the one that I came from where everybody decided if you were black or Mexican, or if you were an immigrant or Mexican American. It was crazy because they just decided what you were like even though they didn't even know you. It was just crazy. Here nobody cares what you are, just whether they think you're worth hanging out with. I mean I don't like that they decide if you're pretty or smart or can hook them up with drugs, but it's really better than the racial stuff that people would actually fight about in the last school I went to.[69]

SOME CONCLUDING COMMENTS

This chapter described key elements forming the preconditions for physical violence between ethnic groups in high schools. These elements are all part of a psychological development that takes place within most youths and the groups they will ultimately be identified with. The four significant elements were (1) determining who was in their ethnic group and who was not, (2) stereotyping those who were excluded from their group on the basis of their interpretation of historical accounts of past relationships, (3) building personal identity during this developmental stage in a mixed ethnic environment undergoing social change, and

(4) using prejudice to reduced perceived risks in navigating social relations with members of the out-group. While a good deal of the research on ethnic violence identifies each of these as a perverted element that produces antagonistic or "broken" social relations, I have found them to be aspects of the general processes faced by most individuals as they develop. Indeed, they are so much a part of normal development that there is no cost-free way to eliminate them.[70] If we were so concerned about social conflict, and were able to eliminate them, it would be like being worried about fires and eliminating all vegetation, or at least the vegetation that would be particularly combustible, like eucalyptus trees in California or the various deciduous trees in other parts of the country. If successful, our efforts might well create a landscape that few people would recognize, or even want to live in. In other words, the processes that I have found operative among the students of these schools are in no way deviant. They are quite ordinary. However, these natural sequences in personal development can become dangerous when the social conditions in which they take place become extreme. Thus, when the process of forming an identity takes place in a stressful social environment the danger of group conflicts arises, just as when natural vegetation is placed in drought conditions, the danger of fires arises.

In discussing these elements that form the foundation for violence in schools, I do not intend to posit a causal sequence that runs from the natural act of discriminating to stereotyping, from identity formation to prejudice, and finally from prejudice to violence. What I did find was that all these elements were present among the students in this study. We will have the opportunity to see the important role they played in initiating aggression toward individuals in the various identified out-groups when we follow the same individuals identified in this chapter and observe them (as well as a host of others) engaged in violence when ethnic conflict became a regular occurrence. Each of these elements alone could be socially benign. Yet when they are all present in certain harsh socioeconomic conditions they become kindling for the conflagration of ethnic violence in lower-class high schools.

CHAPTER 3

Climate and Weather

Social Conditions and Structural Change

Dogs bark at a person they do not know.
—Heraclitus, *Fragments*, 500 CE

The previous chapter was concerned with identifying and analyzing the factors that provided the historical and social psychological basis for ethnic violence to occur—in terms of the fire metaphor, the kindling. In the case of fires, while certain kinds of vegetation are particularly likely to produce intense fires, certain environmental conditions must be present that make them especially combustible. This chapter will analyze the circumstances that transform certain long-standing social conditions into potentially volatile situations. However, before beginning to analyze the transformation referred to above, I wish to make clear that while this book has some important implications for understanding the sociology of ethnic conflict more generally, its primary focus is not the general category of ethnic conflict. Rather, it is concerned with one expression of it—physical violence among ethnic groups in schools in the United States. Obviously conflict between ethnic groups can take place without physical violence, and we see this in such areas as market behaviors, politics, and sports.

There are two main kinds of research on ethnic violence. The first uses survey techniques to look at attitudes related to violent intent or self-reported violent behavior and thus is concerned with the formation of bigoted and hostile attitudes toward social groups that over time lead to aggressive and violent behavior. Within this research, negative attitudes toward certain groups of people—disliking them, seeing them as a threat, or feeling socioeconomically deprived by them—and positive attitudes toward the use of violence are enough to explain why people engage in violence.[1] The second type of research focuses on the immediate events that precipitate a physically violent encounter—the micro interactions that set the stage for violence between individuals and initiate physical aggression.[2] It is concerned with the content of an immediate encounter: that is, the meaning that the actors apply to the symbols that elicit an emotion leading to an aggressive behavioral response.[3]

Although both of these perspectives can explain some aspects of violence that will be empirically investigated in later chapters, they miss a particularly important phase in the development of the conditions leading to violence. On a time line, this period is located between the earlier conditions that form attitudes and beliefs leading to prejudice, bigotry, and disdain toward members of a particular ethnic group and the immediate interaction between individuals that turns into a violent encounter. This period fuses the beliefs and prejudices that have been historically developed and passed on to succeeding generations by family, friends, and institutional leaders with the interactions that individuals experience with members of the various out-groups in the neighborhoods and schools in which they associate. Thus this chapter will describe how ethnic change converts the social condition of historic interethnic conflict into a dangerous possibility for the eruption of interethnic violence.

NEIGHBORHOOD EXPERIENCE

Although a public high school's geographic district comprises many neighborhoods, they are usually (except in the case of magnet or charter schools) spatially connected in such a way that the residents generally share a similar socio-geographic experience. So what experiences are especially important in establishing ripe conditions for interethnic violence? In this study, a set of economic and social concerns within the school's enrolling neighborhoods proved to be the most salient in creating a volatile environment.

Economic Apprehensions

The first of these had to do with economics, particularly the economics of housing. Every realtor will tell prospective buyers of a house that "the value of a house" and its price will depend on three factors: "location, location, location." What they mean is that any house's exchange value will depend on a combination of objective and subjective factors that residents and prospective buyers place on a particular location. Thus people attempt to buy houses that combine what they need (i.e., use value) with the probability of increasing their wealth as the property increases in equity (i.e., exchange value). Here lies the economic basis for the creation of an environment of heightened ethnic tensions.[4]

Those already living in the area, especially those who have been living there for some time, have a financial commitment to homes they actually live in as well as to the neighborhood where the housing is located. Like other homeowners, people of modest means will look to buy housing that is affordable, adequate to meet their living needs, and more prestigious than their former housing because it is structurally more sound, has more space within the unit and between houses, and is more accessible to public services like transportation to retail stores with greater variety of inventory, to their work, and to schools thought to provide better educational opportunities for their families. They consider this improvement to be a calculated investment that will build equity for their future. Thus, when members of a different ethnic group begin to buy houses in that area, incumbent residents are vigilant and concerned with how the new residents will influence the current value of their homes. When there is information, regardless of its accuracy, that the new residents' presence may negatively affect the value of their homes, incumbent residents are not only concerned about their current investment but outright afraid that devaluation of their housing property will reduce their net wealth, lower their current economic status, and destroy their hopes for their and their children's future. Therefore, the first condition affecting interethnic conflict is evidence of a decline, or a potential decline, in the area's housing prices with the influx of a new ethnic group.[5]

Let us examine the sociological backdrop. In the Los Angeles and Oakland neighborhoods of the present study, African Americans had been the primary residents for more than twenty years. Mexican Americans were the new ethnic group purchasing homes in those neighborhoods. It is well documented that both groups faced discrimination in the housing market from real estate brokers and lending agencies that limited their opportunities for purchasing a house in certain metropolitan locations.[6] It is also well documented that members of these groups were aware of the value of houses in particular areas and wanted to purchase houses that would provide equity.[7] Finally, the fact that their opportunities were more limited made them even more anxious about protecting their investment. Given that segregation is not random but engineered by financial institutions, minority communities are artificially composed of families having a specific range of occupations and incomes.[8] Consequently, in this study incumbents' concerns about whether ethnic changes in the community could affect their housing investment were more likely, though not exclusively, to be expressed by members of the minority working and middle class who had bought their homes and had a mortgage to pay. The comments of Royce, Claudia, and Cindy are representative. Royce was an African American student at Los Angeles's Chumash High School:

> Yeah, there is all the Mexicans coming and changing the neighborhood, and so you know it's goin' to make a big difference. Our home is definitely going to be worth less than when my dad and mom bought it, and they're really worried about that; and I can't blame them 'cause the house and the two cars is all we got really.[9]

Claudia was a Mexican American student attending Oakland's Miwok High School:

> My dad's worried that he shouldn't have bought our home in a black neighborhood 'cause he may lose money, but said we needed a bigger house and this was the only place we could afford. So he said, "I don't care how tough it is in the school with the blacks, we can't financially move."[10]

Cindy was an Irish American student at Boston's Paul Revere High School:

> You got all them blacks coming to school here and you know what that means. There's goin' to be more crime, and all our houses are going to be worth nothing, 'cause look what happened in Dorchester and Roxbury. My mom said to our neighbor when they were talking two nights ago that we got all our money in the house and don't want it to dry up [lose money] because the niggers are coming to school over here.[11]

Educational Apprehensions

In addition to worries about maintaining housing values, incumbent residents in these changing neighborhoods expressed concern about whether newcomers would lower the quality of education in the local schools and make it more difficult for the incumbents' children to get into college.[12] Not all the students were focused on going to college, but of those that were the comments of Jenny and Damien exemplify this concern. Jenny was an Irish American attending Boston's Shawmut High School:

I just hope that the school can still give me a good education 'cause I really want to go to college. Remember, the blacks are bad students, but they get affirmative action and we get nothing. I got to earn my way into college, and I know that the teachers will be forced to make the classes easier because of them, and that's not going to help me get into college.[13]

Damien was an African American attending Oakland's Kaiser High School:

I got to believe that if there is a whole lot of Mexican students in this school the teachers are going to have to make everything simple for them 'cause hardly any of them can speak English, or they don't speak it too good, and so we will have a harder time getting to college because of them. So that's fucked up and I don't want them here![14]

Dashed Expectations

Of course, newly arrived students saw a different reality. Whether they had come because their parents sought better housing or better education, many had hoped that the new school would be better than their old ones. The comments of Aldo and Germina are representative. Aldo was an African American attending Boston's Revere High School:

I thought I would get a better education by going to this school because there was all the nonsense at [previous high school] with people skipping class and making noise in class so we couldn't learn. But them whites really hate us, and so there ain't going to be a better education there. It could have been a good place to go to school, but the way they carry on about us coming, it won't be.[15]

Germina was a Mexican American attending Oakland's Miwok High School:

The blacks don't like us and don't want us to live and go to school here, and that's really disappointing to me. I came here from a school in Mexico and thought I would get a better education, but it really is not what I thought I'd get, and the blacks make it really no good at all. I really don't want to be in this neighborhood 'cause they don't want us and I don't really know why.[16]

In addition to being disillusioned with the quality of education at their new school, newcomer youth were surprised, disappointed, anxious, and resentful about the community's negative reactions to their arrival. Most of them had never thought there would be a problem with living in the new neighborhood and attending the new school. Two representative comments come from Shawna and Felix. Shawna was an African American attending Boston's Shawmut High School:

Well, I did know that the folks in [this neighborhood] were against us [African American students] coming to their school, but I had no idea they hated us this much. They really hate us with everything they got. It's just really mind blowing that somebody could hate you this much and not even know you. That's really messed up![17]

Felix was a Mexican American attending Los Angeles's Chumash High School:

After we moved to the neighborhood, they [African Americans] were really saying some real shit to me. I thought they were just kidding, but they really did pour on the hate. I mean I think they really hate us, and that kind of surprises me; I mean it just seems kind of weird that they'd hate us more than the whites, but that's the way it is.[18]

The students from families that had purchased their house in the new area now believed that the hostility they were experiencing from the incumbent students posed a risk to their parents' investments and ability to improve their family's future. The comments of Alina and Cristiano are representative of these feelings. Alina was a Mexican American attending Oakland's Kaiser High School:

My dad was telling my uncle that he move here [the present neighborhood] so that the family would have more room in the house and that he could use it [the house] to borrow money for us to go to college and that now he was worried that someone might set the house on fire to get rid of us [Mexicans]. I'm really upset about this, and I never even thought of it [the financial risk] when we just arrived and started to think of the school we was going to. But they [blacks] don't like us at their school. I really can say that I don't like them for this, and even if things change I'll still not like them [African Americans] for what they're doing now.[19]

Cristiano was a Mexican American attending Los Angeles's Tongva High School:

Danny [one of the group's friends] got beat up yesterday as he went home from getting something at the *tienda* [small store] a few streets over. They took all his money and broke the little finger on his left hand. I told my mom that I was not really wanting to live here, she said that they bought the house to have the chance to live a better life. . . . So, yeah, I don't like the blacks for putting all this up in the air and making my dad and mom worry all the time.[20]

Social Apprehensions

Apprehensions associated with social interactions created another experience that worked to build an environment of antagonism between the groups. When two groups live in the same area there is a tendency for individuals to associate with their own group.[21] This sorting process establishes ethnic segregation, whether individuals are motivated by their own inner promptings to affiliate or by normative pressures. However, in the present study individuals expressed four considerations that influenced them toward group identification, association, and solidarity.

First, some students entered high school with prior antagonistic personal experiences, either their own or their relatives', with members of the other ethnic group they had been forced to interact with; examples were being robbed, insulted with ethnic slurs, or shunned. They brought with them a reluctance to meet members of the "other" group. Wilson and Amelia's accounts are typical of the boys' and girls' comments respectively. Wilson was an African American attending Boston's Shawmut High School:

> Hey, let me tell you when I was twelve, me and my two sisters were going to the Red Sox game and we were sitting in the bleachers. Well, at about the third inning a bunch of Irish guys start using racist comments about one of the players and I mean really bad ones. My older sister turns around and looks at them and right after that they poured beer on her head and when she turned to push them, one of them hit her in the face, and then we all got into it. I just don't want to deal with them animals in any way, so when I see them I just go the other way.[22]

Amelia was a Mexican American student attending Los Angeles's Chumash High School:

> I kind of don't say much to African Americans 'cause they really used to say all kinds of bad things when I would walk by them on my way to work, and I just don't like being around them now. . . . I would be just walking by and saying nothing and they would start with trying to pick me up and when I didn't say anything they would start with me being a whore and stuff. It was awful all the things they'd say, and even the black girls who were there laughed. So I'm going to just not say anything to them and keep to myself 'cause I don't want to be around them.[23]

The second source of social apprehension was how individuals compared their economic experience in the United States to that of other groups. This is usually referred to as a sense of "relative deprivation." It played a significant role in group relations in the schools of this study.[24] For African Americans, the dominant theme was that their experience was particularly harsh; no other group's experience could compare, and it remained so to the present. Thus no other group had the right to make their situation more difficult or to take away the positive elements of life they had struggled to create.[25] The recent Mexican inhabitants in the neighborhood were seen as having taken jobs that African Americans were entitled to. These jobs, along with loans from the financial institutions that African Americans were being denied, allowed them to buy homes in their neighborhood.[26] The comments of DeShaun and Courtney were typical of those expressing this position. DeShaun was an African American attending Oakland's Miwok High School:

> You see them fucking Mexicans coming here [the neighborhood], and you know they got their money from jobs they take away from us. They know what they're doing so I don't like the fuckers much. I mean they take our jobs and then they get the white bankers to give them money to live in our neighborhood too![27]

Courtney was an African American attending Los Angeles's Chumash High School:

> I really don't like seeing Mexicans living around here 'cause my brothers can't get any construction work anymore and it just reminds me of that. They [the Mexicans] will work for almost nothing, and the whites will just hire them 'cause of it . . . and my father says that on top of that the white banks will loan them money but they won't give us any 'cause they don't want us to move next to them [whites].[28]

The Mexican population believed that despite being subjected to societal prejudice and economic hardship they were constantly being neglected in favor of African Americans. They felt invisible to the general Anglo (i.e., white) community. What is more, they believed that African Americans had a number of opportunities withheld from the Mexican population and were frustrated because they thought the African American community did not take advantage of them. The comments of Facundo, a Mexican American student attending Oakland's Kaiser High School, and Renata, a Mexican American attending Los Angeles's Tongva High School, are representative.

> *Facundo:* The blacks are always complaining that they're discriminated against, but it's us [Mexicans] that is discriminated against. They [US government] try to keep us out and then pay us very low wages compared to Anglos and blacks. Then even though we have all this prejudice against us they help blacks get into college and not us. . . . They [African Americans] just get all the help and they don't do anything with it and then complain about us.[29]

> *Renata:* I am so tired of the blacks complaining that we take their jobs. My dad and mom work really hard at jobs that don't pay shit, and every time they try to get a good job in government [city government] they give it to

blacks 'cause they say they been discriminated against. They get breaks we don't and still complain.[30]

In Boston, I regularly heard Irish students and adults in the community complain that they had to hear African Americans "whine" about their living situation. In fact, they believed the African Americans were better off than the Irish. They most vigorously protested that their economic situation was quite difficult and that they could use some help from the government but that help was always given to African Americans, who did little with it to improve their lives. Take the comments of Connor and Deirdre, both of whom were typical of those feeling this way. Connor was an Irish American attending Boston's Shawmut High School:

> We Irish get nothing from anybody, and a lot of us are just as poor as the niggers, but the government only helps them 'cause they always talk about slavery and shit like that. They been without slavery for hundred fucking years and they still don't get any better. It's them that's fucked up, not anybody doing stuff to them, and so the government should give more help to people like us who need a little instead of wasting it on them.[31]

Deirdre was an Irish American attending Boston's Paul Revere High School:

> I really think what the government gives blacks is not right. There are a whole bunch of other people that need help and work hard, like us here. We need a little help to make things better for our families, but all the governments just help blacks because they complain and whine the most that they are discriminated against. If they would actually work harder they wouldn't get discriminated against, but they won't, so why do they keep giving everything to them?[32]

In sum, these grievances in and of themselves do not cause violence to occur; they simply intensify underlying feelings of insecurity (both personal and group) that the changes to the community and school have created. However, as we will see in subsequent chapters, once violence between individuals from both groups occurs, these feelings cause emotions to intensify and events to escalate.

Cultural Apprehensions

The third issue that concerned the host group was that the local subculture they had helped to build and maintain in the neighborhood was in danger of being significantly changed by the new ethnic group.[33] This anxiety was reaffirmed as they interacted with members of the new group. Information about jobs and services, food, entertainment, and, most important, the criteria establishing status in the community were changing because of the increased presence of new residents from a different ethnic group. Not only did this create a period of confusion, but it heightened the yearning among the incumbent residents for the return of the "good old days."[34] This can be seen in the comments of Shawana and Brandon, both of whom were young but still products of the social order developed when the local community had been occupied by the previously homogeneous, or at least dominant, ethnic group. Shawana was an African American attending Los Angeles's Tongva High School:

> The neighborhood was fine before the Mexicans came, and now that they're here things is changing in bad ways. They're just different in everything, language, clothes, religion, and how they behave, just everything. I really don't like their stuff [language spoken, clothes, religion, etc.], but I now got to deal with them and it ain't as much fun. I liked things the way we had it before they came, and the rest of us do too because it was better. [A number of the people she is talking with indicate verbally that they agree with her.][35]

Brandon was an Irish American attending Boston's Shawmut High School:

> Before Judge Garrity ordered the busing this was a nice school, but once he made the blacks come here it's been the pits. It's not just that they want to fight us all the time, it's just that they act so fucking odd and none of us [Irish Americans] like it. . . . Plus, if we were to let them live in our neighborhood too, they'd really fuck everything up that we like. You know, they'd just do things the way they like instead of the way we like and everything would be different and bad if you ask me. I like the way we do things, and I want to keep it that way and not go toward the ways niggers like to do things. [Others in the group verbally indicate that they agree with him.][36]

The host community also worried about how an influx of newcomers threatened their neighborhood's historical identification with a specific ethnic group. Many areas may be named after an ethnic group, as in the case of Little Italy, Little Armenia, Korean Town, Chinatown, Greek Town, Japan Town, Spanish Harlem; and even if they are not, the area's name may be famously associated with an ethnic group, as in the case of Harlem (African American) in New York, Pilsen (originally Czech, later Mexican) in Chicago, North Beach in San Francisco (Italian), South Boston (Irish), or Hamtramck in Detroit (Polish). Often the identity of the inhabitants is integrally linked to the area, so when another ethnic group begins to move in they are viewed as invaders and threats to the collective and individual identities of current residents.[37] The comments of Bartin and Clare are typical of those holding this view. Bartin was an African American attending Los Angeles's Chumash High School:

> Naw, I ain't about to leave here [this neighborhood] just because them wet-backs [Mexicans] keep coming in. This is always been our neighborhood and this is who I am. You dig? I'm proud to being part of it, so I'll die before I let them force me out of here. Or better yet, some of them can die trying to take it from us. [The others that are part of the conversation all laugh, nod, or say something that indicates their agreement.][38]

Clare was an Irish American attending Boston's Shawmut High School:

> We are all from [the area of Boston the school is located in] and this is who we are. Everybody's proud of being from here, and there ain't no way that they'll make us go from here. We're [she names area as part of personal identity], not some black ghetto, and ain't no way they're making us change that![39]

SCHOOL EXPERIENCE

There is some evidence that how factors directly related to schools themselves and to how they operate on a daily basis play a role in stimulating violence among the students.[40] These factors include school codes, culture, and social organization. David Eitle and Tamara Eitle found that school codes and culture, along with the percentage of African American students, were strong predictors of school violence, whereas a school's organizational structure had no impact.[41] However, I found in the present study that schools' social organization had a very important impact on establishing conditions for violence. Like most schools, those in the present study tried to group students in ways that would maximize their opportunities to learn. Sometimes they did this by "tracking," or grouping students by levels of educational competence and giving them a common curriculum intended to meet their interests and aptitudes. Tracking is associated not only with several educational problems but also with the creation of an environment susceptible to intense interethnic violence.[42]

In schools that use "tracking," the theoretical basis for the practice is that students' shared curriculum and shared level of educational competence allow more classroom activities to take on a group character, so that students socially interact more with each other and the instructor on specific educational issues, as in the case of group discussions and projects. However, because "tracking" groups of students by achievement criteria (test scores, grades) and not social criteria such as ethnicity, means that in lower-class schools undergoing ethnically oriented demographic change classroom activities will give individuals having emotional dislikes, resentments, hatreds, anxieties, and tensions no way to avoid each other.[43]

Here is a representative incident from the present study. It happened in a general (i.e., nonadvanced) placement class composed of both Mexican and African American students. As the teacher was looking over his notes to start the class, a group of African American students were talking loudly and laughing. When the teacher began the class and the African Americans were still talking, one of the Mexican Americans said loudly, "Can you stop talking so we can hear Mr. K?" One of the African Americans was offended at being told this and said, "Who are you to mouth off? You shouldn't even be in this country because you can't even understand English." The other African Americans started to laugh. Then, another Mexican American student said, "Well, you been in this country for two hundred years and you still can't speak English right." The other Mexican American students didn't laugh, but some grinned. Two of the African Americans then said, "You just a bunch of dumbasses, and we'll see you after class and knock some sense into you all." Thereupon one threw a pencil at the Mexican American who had said that African Americans did not speak English well. At this point the teacher aggressively intervened and said that any more talk by any student would get a pass to the office for disciplinary action. Although the students stopped talking to each other, tensions remained high for the entire class, and before the teacher dismissed the class he called the office to report the possibility of violence after class. Two security guards were posted outside the room as the bell rang to signal the end of class, but in a later class that day the same students engaged in a ferocious fight.[44] In brief, the tracking system did not allow students to easily avoid during the school day classmates of the ethnic group that they had problems with and thus provided the conditions where frictions would inevitably be violently acted out.

Of course, some schools have no formal tracking system, but in most there is a system that for all practical purposes closely resembles tracking. The provision of courses labeled "honors classes" or "advanced placement" courses that include more complex college-level material separates students who are more educationally skilled from those who are considered "average" or below and thus is a form of tracking, albeit related to specific courses rather than a full curriculum.[45] The social consequence of this particular organizational scheme in each of the schools of the present study was the same as those found in the schools having formal tracking. It placed students from differing ethnic backgrounds in the non–advanced placement courses together. It forced social contact and created an environment perfect for interethnic friction and intense conflict.[46] The comments of Miranda and Caleb are representative of students' feelings about being in classes with the opposing ethnic group. Miranda was a Mexican American attending Oakland's Kaiser High School:

> I really don't like being in this class because there are a lot of blacks in the class and they don't like us, and that just makes me feel really nervous to be around them. Then when I get out and seen how they acted toward us in class, you know they laugh whenever we make comments like we are really dumb about what we are saying, I just really detest them stupid asses and want to hit them.[47]

Caleb was an African American attending Los Angeles's Tongva High School:

> It's so irritating to be in that class with them [Mexicans] 'cause they just are so slow in getting the instructions of the teacher and then they ask stupid questions 'cause the teacher just told us the answer. Most of them should be in grade school because they really are not smart enough, but the school just puts them there so it looks like they're educating immigrants. It's just too fucking frustrating and I really can't stand that I got to be with them and feel like hitting them 'cause they're just dumbing down everything.[48]

Although tracking does contribute to a fertile environment for conflict, its effects regarding violence are not uniform across tracks. In the present study, students who were assigned to the upper tracks were less likely to express antagonistic views about students from other ethnic groups. While they may have held negative views about members of other ethnic groups, they were reluctant to articulate them. It was found that their reluctance was based on the belief that they had more to lose than to gain by saying negative things about people from another group. Generally, these students thought that if they did and their remark initiated a fight for which they were suspended, they would have a harder time getting into college, and nearly all the students in the upper tracks had college as a common goal. Representative attitudes can be seen in the words of Delfina and Justin. Delfina was a Mexican American attending Los Angeles's Chumash High School:

> I don't want to get into any arguments with other students, and especially the African American students, because they will just keep it up and then it

could turn ugly and then I got a lot more problems—like getting into trouble with my teachers or even worse, having to go to the principal's office. I just want to get out of this school and into a good college, and I've worked too hard to mess that up with a screaming session. [Both of the people she is talking to say they completely agree with her.][49]

Justin was an African American student at Oakland's Miwok High School:

There ain't no way that I'm getting into an argument with the Mexes, 'cause it will just end in a fistfight with them and that definitely ain't worth it—they're not worth it! All that stuff is bad, and only bad things can happen to me if I'd do it, so don't count me in on anything like getting into it with them. The most important thing to me is staying clean and getting into a good college, man. . . . Well, if I can't get out a situation 'cause I got dragged into it, I'll fight, but I'm going to stay away from this shit [interethnic fighting] because it will just mess me up and that's not worth it.[50]

Although the ethnic conflict and violence in the schools of the present study indicate that ethnic desegregation can raise violence, the above finding suggests that segregating individuals by academic criteria does decrease the probability of violence for students in the higher academic tracks.[51] However, for students in the lower tracks, or what may be described as the general school population (i.e., nonelite), desegregation of ethnic groups dominated by low-income families provided the social conditions for antagonisms, conflict, and violence.[52] Ethnic students from middle-income or higher-income families did not have the same experience, and more will be said about them later.

THE IMPACT OF SCHOOL CURRICULUM

All of the schools in the present study attempted to foster positive attitudes about cross-cultural understanding and cooperation by designing and implementing curricular and extracurricular activities to maximize exposure between groups. When these communities were not experiencing rapid demographic changes this policy may have been benign, but when they were, as they were during the present study, the more administrators, councilors, and teachers encouraged understanding, tolerance, and cooperation in school activities, the more their efforts galvanized the very attitudes that would encourage violent confrontations. For the teachers it was frustrating. Take the comments of Jerry and Belinda. Jerry was a social science teacher at Boston's Shawmut High School:

The idea of promoting tolerance is good, but doing it while we are trying to teach is just a lose-lose situation. The students don't listen to you, or just let it bounce off them, and you spend time doing that and not getting to the material they will need to pass the general exams to get into college. Plus, the students listen to us telling them to be tolerant and they just look at you as though you're crazy. It is totally frustrating, because when you can get students from both sides to talk after class they bluntly tell you that they hate those on the other side. But the administration keeps telling us to do it, and we do it.[53]

Belinda is an English teacher at Los Angeles's Tongva High School:

I really am frustrated with this new effort to promote tolerance in the school. The administration wants all the teachers, especially in the social sciences and humanities to integrate it into their courses, and I now spend a good deal of time putting this into my unit plans, but it is a waste of time. These students don't want to hear this and they will tell you that to your face if you bother to ask them. Basically, they've already made up their minds and they are not interested in tolerance. The tolerance train left the station a number of months ago.[54]

The students felt that while what the teachers were saying was good in theory, they did not fully understand the situation and the treachery of the group that students were in conflict with. The comments of Fiona, Rudy, Damario, and Alyssa are typical for the students attending all the schools experiencing violence in this study. Fiona was an Irish American student at Boston's Shawmut High School:

The principal and teachers want us to get along with the niggers and understand where they're coming from, but they don't have to deal with them. When you do that, there ain't nothing to understand 'cause they'll just knife you and not think nothing about it. My brother got beat up and knifed real bad by them at a Bruins [local Boston Professional Hockey team] game.[55]

Rudy was an African American student at Boston's Paul Revere High School:

You listen to the shit that the teachers and school officials say we should do. You know, like trying to show some compassion for others different from yourself, but that's just bull. The whites in this school is just animals, and like animals they'll rip you apart when they got you alone. So, maybe what the teachers say is okay with some other groups, but not with what I got to deal with it ain't. Them Irish motherfuckers jumped me and two friends walking around the Commons [Boston Commons is a public park in the middle of the city], and so there ain't nothin' to be compassionate about.[56]

Damario is a Mexican American student attending Oakland's Miwok High School:

> No way am I going to think African Americans can be lived with here in this school. They jumped me at a music event down around the park while me and some friends were having a picnic. I was sore for a week or more. There just fucking pigs. Them teachers don't know what's it like to have to deal with them, so this "Let's be understanding to one another" won't work here.[57]

Alyssa was an African American student at Los Angeles's Chumash High School:

> My teachers been promoting understanding and tolerance between us and the Mexicans, and that's good, but they don't know how it is with the Mexicans. They're sneaky and if they don't like what you say they'll try to cut you. They tried that shit with me about a year ago, and two of my "homes" [other African American students] stepped in to save me from getting stabbed by these Mexican girls that had razor blades. . . . No, I ain't into forgetting and forgiving any of them at this time, so the teachers are just talking shit![58]

What is particularly instructive about these comments is that students from each side of the conflict had had negative experiences with members of the other group, or people close to them had. Thus the school staff's efforts to promote understanding and cooperation were negated by the students' experiential understandings of current interethnic relations.

In sum, the factors identified in this chapter helped promote interethnic aggression and violence in schools. Clearly compulsory schooling forces teenagers together in one location several hours a day every week for nine to ten months a year. Such an arrangement, even without ethnic competition, envy, antagonism, and hostility, provides a fertile environment for frustration and aggression. Add to that those students who feel structurally trapped within a school and we find a perfect environmental condition for violent eruptions between students.[59]

THE LACK OF AN ESCAPE OPTION

Ethnic succession in neighborhoods has been a consistent feature of the American urban experience.[60] In the neighborhoods of the present study, the influx of Mexicans into traditional African American neighborhoods in Los Angeles and Oakland and the influx of African American students into the traditionally Irish American schools of Boston caused residents to consider moving. Some of the African American residents of Los

Angeles and Oakland were able to move to new neighborhoods that were in the process of changing from predominantly "white" areas to mixed African American, and some of the Irish Americans were able to move to other "white" areas in the greater Boston region.[61] However, many students who found themselves with discomfiting new neighbors had no financial resources to move to another area. This was true for both the new residents, like Mexicans in Los Angeles and Oakland who because of limited capital and prejudice in the real estate market could purchase or rent homes in only such areas, and for the existing African and Irish American residents who because of limited capital and prejudice in the real estate market could not sell their homes and move to another area. Consequently individuals from two ethnic groups felt trapped and embattled. With no options and no illusions of receiving any aid to get them out of this fix, they felt their only option was to protect their economic property and social life at all costs. They were not classically what Suttles calls "defended neighborhoods" but "defended subneighborhoods" (i.e., parts of neighborhoods), and, like any group of people who think that they are "cornered," they readied themselves to resist with determination.[62] The comments of Delores, Logan, and Dalia are all representative of this resolve. I have chosen to use quotes from both male and female students (more than usual) to highlight that, regardless of gender, students who feel that everything they have is invested in a particular area will resolve to fight when they conclude that fighting is their only option to protect what they have. Delores was an Irish American attending Boston's Shawmut High School:

> Yeah, my dad tried to find out if he could get a loan so we could move to Lynn, but the bank wouldn't give him one. I don't really know why, but maybe 'cause he don't make that much money being a street cleaner for the city. All I know is we're going to have to stay here, and so my mom told me that we're all going to have to fight real hard to keep the blacks from coming here to school. I agree with my mom 'cause we don't have any choice.[63]

Logan was an African American attending Los Angeles's Tongva High School:

> You hear that Micah and his family are going to Pomona to live 'cause they don't like that the Mexicans are living here now. I'll bet my mom wishes she could do that, 'cause she told me that if she could she'd move to the Valley. My aunt thinks that the prices for housing is going to go down now that the Mexicans are here, so she's been trying to see if she can get a loan for my mom, but my mom says it's not possible and we going to have to stay. I really don't want to live next to them, but what's the choice? I feel like making it hard on

them so they stop coming and we can keep what we got here, 'cause if we don't they'll just keep coming and we won't have anything left to the 'hood.[64]

Dalia was a Mexican American attending Oakland's Kaiser High School:

> I told my dad about all the trouble here, but he said that there's nothing he can do about it because he put all his money into our new house. So he just told me to stand up for my rights and don't back down, and that's what I'm going to do. I don't care if it's one of them African American bitches or a guy, if they try to force me to do something or hurt one my friends, I'm going to fight them, and I don't care how many times I got to do it 'cause there ain't no other choice.[65]

FRAGILE ELEMENTS OF COOPERATION

Most of this chapter has been concerned with describing the social conditions that make ethnic violence between groups possible and probable and reporting the negative attitudes that members of each group have toward the other. However, not all the students in each group had these attitudes. Some students were quite comfortable with members of the other group and even provided mutual assistance in academic class work and participated with them in extracurricular activities like sports and various social clubs. They were also close enough to share feelings of insecurity, stress, happiness, and sadness and to give and accept advice. In brief, not all the students had negative experiences with members of the opposing ethnic group. To be sure this was a small minority of students from each group, and despite their positive experiences with members of the other group these students would come to be overwhelmed by the events in which they would be expected to support coethnics and would be taken by their ethnic adversaries as potential targets. As the violent events unfolded in each of their schools, all of the students who had had positive feelings (I recorded thirty-seven, though there were undoubtedly more) before the violence erupted assumed a belligerent and actively negative position toward the other group once the violence began. In sum, the students with friends in the opposing group were swept up into their respective groups and supported them.[66]

SOME CONCLUDING COMMENTS

The sentiments expressed by students in this chapter and chapter 2 have been harsh and explicitly bigoted. They were present not just among students but among large numbers of residents throughout transition neighborhoods where ethnic "difference" had to be confronted daily. None of the factors described in this chapter cause violence; rather, they establish the conditions for violence to start and continue at an intense level. Thus, when material conditions and the sense of comfortable social relations are disrupted or challenged, language and cultural differences become salient and any identifications associated with phenotype (i.e., racial identifiers) become useful in promoting hostilities between the groups. The actual factors that initiate violence, which are not the same as those described in this and the preceding chapter, will be dealt with in the following two chapters.

We have now seen the underlying conditions that make ethnic violence in school likely: an increase in ethnic diversity in the schools as a new group moves into the neighborhood (or, in the Boston case, is bused into the school); conditions of scarcity in the school and the wider neighborhood that set the new group and the incumbent group in competition; no options for moving out of the area to avoid conflict and a decrease in family wealth; a set of deep, hostile attitudes that youth in each group have about the motives and behavior of youth from other groups; and a regular, forced interaction that is part of the school day. Using the fire metaphor, this chapter compared these social conditions to the climate and weather conditions that make a fire more likely. Nonetheless, just as the presence of kindling and fire-promoting climatic and weather conditions do not in and of themselves make for fire, so these conditions alone do not make for violence. For that to occur, a *spark* is required, and that is the subject of the next chapter.

PART TWO

Flames

CHAPTER 4

Sparks and Smoke

The Start of Ethnic Violence

It is easier to exclude harmful passions than to rule them.
—Seneca, *Dialogue on Anger*, (50 CE [?])

The last two chapters described the conditions that increase the chances of violence: group and individual identity formation; neighborhood change and the personal and group insecurities associated with it; individuals' experiences (some good, but mostly bad) dealing generally with members of different ethnic groups as well as the specific groups currently moving to their area; the larger structural conditions that shape those experiences, making incumbent groups view newcomers' incursion as a threat to the value of their housing, the quality of their schools, and the traditions of their neighborhood, and the difficulty that incumbents and newcomers have in moving elsewhere. This chapter describes when, how, and why ethnic violence in high schools actually breaks out, but it is important to remember that the acts of discriminating and prejudging presented in the previous two chapters are brought to the interactional process and are an integral part of when, how, and why the violence begins. There were six phases to this violence; this chapter traces the first two. With each new phase, increasing numbers of individuals became involved in the violence.

BEGINNINGS

Sociologist Randall Collins argues that engaging in violence is not easy for individuals and consequently does not occur all the time. Collins postulates that certain social-psychological factors create a generalized tension among individuals that builds to a point where these individuals simply shed their inhibitions (primarily fear of being hurt) and react violently. They are then drawn into a panic mode, in which they continue in a trancelike state.[1] This is an interesting hypothesis for empirical investigation, as are a number of other hypotheses such as frustration-aggression, innate drives for dominance and submission, struggles over group status, and struggles over material possessions.[2] What all these hypotheses have in common is an attempt to identify the tension present within individuals that causes them to engage in violent behavior, but none specify the exact character of the initiating agent that caused them to act this way at a particular time. For example, not every individual who has felt frustration wants to dominate a situation, nor does every person who seeks status and material possessions engage in violence. When it came to ethnic violence in the schools I studied, two emotions linked to specific actions that the students engaged in were critical to starting the process of violence: *resentment* toward members of the other group that evolved into *loathing*.

Three actions involving these emotions slowly began to take place. The first was the act of shunning, which both groups participated in as they interacted outside the classroom. For members of the new group within the school, shunning was based on resentments about being made to feel socially unaccepted. Two typical responses were those of Alphonso, a Mexican American attending Oakland's Kaiser High School, and Rosalyn, an African American attending Boston's Paul Revere High School.

> *Alphonso:* My adviser asked me if I do anything with the African Americans here at school, and I told her I really never talk or do anything with any black 'cause they don't like us and they'll just ignore you anyway. She said I should try, and I said okay, but I'm definitely not going to because I really don't like them for the way they're acting.[3]

> *Rosalyn:* My history teacher asked me the other day if I was interacting with any of the white students and I told her I didn't 'cause they hate us and don't want us here so what would be the point. She said that not all the white students felt that way and I should try, but she don't seem to get it that none of them is going to want to talk to us 'cause their whole community don't want us.[4]

In each of these statements we can see that although the students are told they should try to interact with members of the other ethnic group, both say they will not. Further, when I observed these two students, and others like them, they did not shyly try to avoid members of the other group but actively shunned them even when it seemed that friendly inter-action could occur.[5] A typical example involved Alejandro, a Mexican American attending Oakland's Kaiser High School. Alejandro was in line waiting to buy candy at the school's dispensary during one of the recess periods. Two African American students, one male, one female, turned to see who was behind them in line. They started a conversation with Alejandro about the fact that the school football team had lost their second playoff game and were out of the tournament, and as they were talking they offered some of their popcorn to Alejandro. He declined the offer, turned, and walked away. Approximately three minutes later he joined up with four Mexican American students. Everyone seemed to understand what was happening, because immediately after Alejandro left, the African American male student shrugged his shoulders and said, "Fuck them!"[6]

For the incumbent group, shunning was based on a variety of resent-ments toward the new group in the neighborhood. The first of these was resenting that the new group had moved into the neighborhood that the incumbent group considered theirs by virtue of their tenure. The com-ments of Jordan, an African American student attending L.A.'s Chu-mash High School, were representative:

> I fucking can't get over them Mexicans coming here and messing up every-thing that we built here! So many folks [black people] worked so hard get-ting things the way we want—you know the way *we* want and not what whites want—and now the Mexicans are coming to fuck everything up![7]

Second, the incumbent group resented that Mexicans, or any other group, could move into their area, whereas they could not move to another area. The comments of Kioka, an African American attending Oakland's Miwok High School, exemplify this:

> It just ain't fair that now Mexicans be coming to our school and all. I mean they get money and they can move wherever they want, but we get money and the whites are so racist that they won't let us go to anything but another black area . . . so yeah, we got to stay here with them cause we ain't got nowhere to go. My dad just resents the Mexicans for this, and you know I can see what he means.[8]

The third resentment sprang from incumbents' fear that the social system they knew could change in a way that they disliked or liked less than what they currently had. The comments of Caitlin, an Irish Amer-ican at Paul Revere High School in Boston, are representative:

> I feel exactly like you do about this. I liked it [the neighborhood] the way things are, and now with the blacks coming to school here it's just different.

Things are like different, don't you think? . . . Even though we don't associate with them [African Americans], they're just here, and they're going to change things 'cause they like different stuff than us. They don't fucking need to come here and make things worse for us.[9]

For the incumbents and the newcomers, the act of shunning not only emanated from feelings of resentment but in itself reinforced the resentment of the shunners and intensified the resentment of those being shunned. As we will see later, at the end of the violence process shunning would cease and the groups would become more integrated, but in the first phase shunning played a critical role in paving the way for violence to emerge.

The second action that helped set the stage for violence evolved from shunning and involved the formation of small social groups—cliques— that were intended to establish bonds and create psychological support, not only as part of normal adolescence, but as an adaptation to this time of social change and the personal insecurity it had caused. When a multitude of new students from another ethnicity come into a school, the criteria for establishing and maintaining group social status and hierarchies are uncertain. This creates a period of flux for all the students, and during it I observed a multiplicity of ethnically separated social groups all trying to create a social system that felt comfortable to them.[10] While the vast majority of these groups were not organized for anything but benign social interaction (i.e., were nonviolent), the fact that they existed would eventually facilitate the second stage of ethnic violence in the schools, which will be discussed below.

The third action was that students from the incumbent ethnic group formed ad hoc bands for the express purpose of physically and/or financially injuring students from the other ethnic group. These new bands were composed of individuals who displayed a particularly agitated state of mind. The group action that they had decided to engage in was an attempt to cope with general feelings of resentment that the newcomers were living in the neighborhood, that the school was not as it used to be, and that there was no satisfying solution to the unwanted changes. These resentments formed a kernel of emotions that were not resolved and festered into the more intense feeling of *loathing*. Nearly all the members that participated in these bands expressed loathing toward students from the other ethnic group that was used to justify engaging in malicious actions. Loathing was a stronger sentiment than resentment in that it incorporated hatred toward members of the new group. I observed that students who loathed the new group wanted to inflict physical pain on its members.[11] However, although loathing was a necessary condition for ultimately engaging in violent behavior it was insufficient for making violence routine. For that to occur, individuals harboring loathing needed to form a social group.

During adolescence, needs for group affiliation and approval are particularly intense, and this provides an environment conducive to developing group aggression.[12] The first phases of ethnic violence (see figure 4.1) began with these ad hoc bands of students composed of friends and friends of friends beginning to express resentment toward the newly arriving ethnic students. Their discussions were openly public, in that the expressions of resentment were not concealed so that only those in close proximity could hear them. Even though very crass statements were often made about students who were ethnically different, the conversations about how to react were more private. Most of the talk was simply about resenting the new students for coming to their school, but as soon as the talk turned to loathing these students, some talked about "making them pay for coming." A representative example involved Damien, an African American at Los Angeles's Chumash High School:

> Check it out, you been seeing all those Mexes coming to school? I fucking hate the motherfuckers being here! We need to make them pay, and so if they want to come here they should give up some money or something. I say we tax them on the way to school, what do you think? [Three members of the group say they'll participate.][13]

Once loathing toward the newcomers had spread among the incumbents in the lower-class schools, the resulting incidents of ad hoc violence (see table 4.1 for definitions of types of violence) followed two patterns. In the first pattern, violence was started by male students, with female students sometimes, although less often, joining in. Within this pattern one would generally observe three or more young male students from the incumbent ethnicity (Irish in Boston's schools and African Americans in Los Angeles and Oakland schools) waiting until one of the newcomers (African Americans in Boston, Mexican Americans in Los Angeles and Oakland) walked past them, then making some disparaging remark about the newcomer's ethnicity, and using any response by the newcomer as an excuse to attack that person. In the second pattern, sometime during the day one or more members of the incumbent group identified a newcomer as a potential target for violence. At some later point in the day, three or more incumbent group members, most often male, who had coordinated when they could all attack that person, walked up to the newcomer and made inflammatory statements

LOS ANGELES/OAKLAND

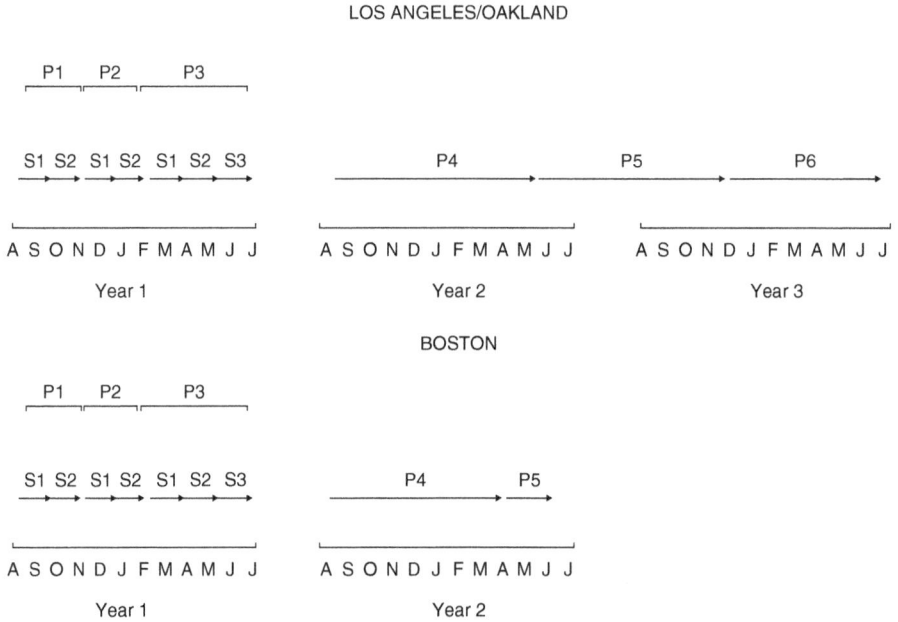

FIGURE 4.1. Phases and stages of ethnic violence within schools. The data for this figure come from the author's field notes. The lines provide representations of general durations of different phases in ethnic violence among the Boston, L.A., and Oakland schools of this study. The symbols "P1" through "P6" are for phases in the violence that are discussed in the text. Above P1 through P6 are data for L.A. and Oakland and below are for Boston data. The stages (S1, S2, etc.), also discussed in the text, are numbered in sequence within the phases.

about his or her ethnic background and then almost immediately began hitting and kicking the newcomer, adding verbal statements like "You should have stayed in your own area." The amount of force, as measured in both the number of blows and the power used with each blow, varied depending on the victim's response and an assessment of whether the victim had suffered enough pain. These incidents lasted between three and seven minutes, with an average of four minutes (see figure 4.2, "ad hoc at school").[14] A typical example involved Wilson, an African American attending Oakland's Kaiser High School. Seeing a Mexican American student walking past the group of male students he regularly associated with, he said to the Mexican, "Go back to Mexico or wherever your fucking home is." The Mexican did not respond and kept walking. Wilson and three other African American students walked up to him and started to deliver punches and kicks. The Mexican American

TABLE 4.1   FORMS OF ETHNIC VIOLENCE IN THE SCHOOLS

Form of Violence	Definition
Individual violence	Physical combat between two individuals based on their being members of different ethnic groups.
Ad hoc group violence	Physical combat in which three or more individuals spontaneously form a group based on the ascriptive criteria related to their ethnicity to defend one or more individuals considered coethnics or to harass/ punish members of the rival ethnic group, though there is no further identification with the spontaneous group past the present event
Brawl	Physical combat between groups of individuals (both formal and informal) acting without any organizing element of planning, strategy, tactics, or coordination.
Riot type 1 (protest oriented)	An unrestrained public disturbance that involves large numbers of individual students, usually more than fifty, engaged in concerted aggressive acts of protest toward targeted individuals in authority and objects related to that authority, such as office equipment (desks, chairs, computers, windows, doors, signs, etc.) and personal possessions of authority figures, whether related to school activities (documents, lesson plans, cameras, computers) or not (automobiles, purses, wallets, keys, glasses).
Riot type 2 (entertainment oriented)	An unrestrained public disturbance that involves large numbers of individual students, usually more than fifty, who have overcome personal inhibitions to engage in concerted acts of aggression toward random physical property on the school campus for amusement and entertainment.
Riot type 3 (animosity oriented)	An unrestrained public disturbance that involves large numbers of individual students, usually more than fifty, engaging in aggression toward targeted ethnic students whom they consider to be their ethnic group's enemy.
Stampede	An unrestrained public disturbance involving large numbers of individual students, usually more than fifty, frenziedly moving toward a physical space considered safe from the perceived reason to leave their original location.

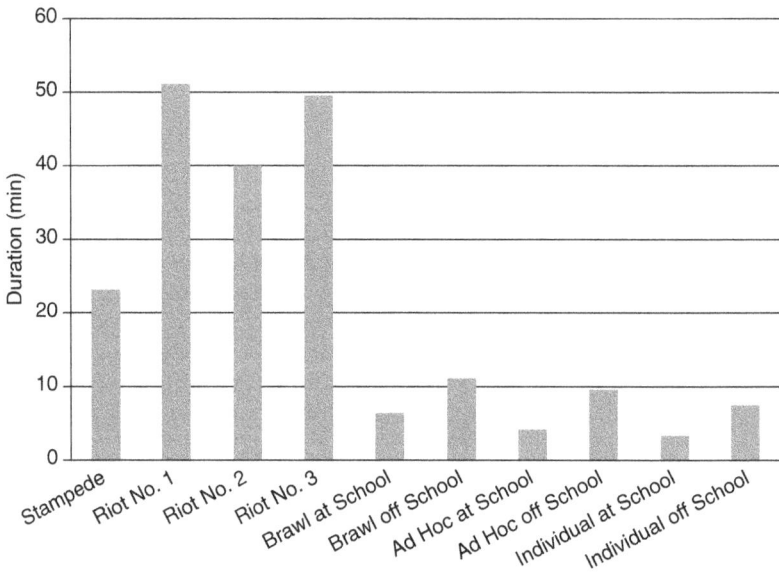

FIGURE 4.2. Average duration of violent acts. Data for this figure are derived from my field notes. Because I could not be at every school at the same time, or on every part of each school's campus during a school day, the data cannot reflect the total numbers of each type of violent event that occurred but only the events I directly observed and recorded with a stopwatch. See the Methodological Appendix for the totals of each form of violence.

student still said nothing, but he did defend himself by trying to block the blows. Wilson and the others continued to rapidly hit the Mexican with full force. Then, after about a minute Wilson said, "That's enough for this motherfucker," and added to the Mexican before kicking him a final time in the leg, "Do you get it? You should keep to your area, not ours!"[15] Wilson and the others then ran off when one of their group informed them that a security guard was coming.[16] The victim had large welts on his face and was helped by the security staff to the school nurse for attention.[17]

During this first phase in the violence these small bands of male students would continue to confront the new ethnic students by approaching them on the way to and from school, demanding that they give them all their money. There were two typical interactions. In one the victim handed over the money without protest. In the other, the victims might mildly protest, saying something like "You're taking all the money I'm getting for the week to eat." Neither response deterred the perpetrators from taking the money that the victims had. However, the type of aggression used by these predatory bands differed depending on the victim's reaction. When there was compliance with no form of protest, the predatory group would push the victim quite hard during the first interaction to indicate they were serious about causing bodily injury. This was verbally reinforced immediately after the push. However, if the predatory group encountered any resistance by the victim, either a verbal protest or a refusal to relinquish the money, they would rapidly, repeatedly, and with considerable force, punch and kick the victim for about two minutes. Afterwards they made comments indicating that these attacks relieved feelings of resentment, loathing, and frustration and satisfied greedy desires. It was quite common to hear participants from the predatory group say, "That felt good," "Now I'm relaxed," "They'll know they shouldn't have come to our school," "I'll put better use to this money than they would have," "I always wanted to get the new iPod, so now I'll be able to get it," and so on.

Generally the assaulting bands (each band did not include the same students each time) would pick out particular members of the other group for attack, usually students who were physically smaller or traveling in smaller groups. The attackers regularly hit and injured the victims in the process of robbing them, although the injuries were not as bad as in subsequent stages of the violence when all those involved felt greater threat.

For the victims of these predatory bands, the situation was dire, but they did try to manage. For example, the Mexican students who were the victims of this first wave of violence in both Los Angeles and Oakland tried to avoid being forced to give up their lunch money two to three times a week by either taking an alternative route to and from school or having a family member drive them to and from school. Generally, these efforts were only successful for a short time before they were confronted and asked to pay while they were in school.

Why did the victims not tell the authorities? The answer was that when these bands began to extort money and strike their victims the number of new ethnic students was relatively small. They felt more isolated and vulnerable to physical harm than if they simply gave the assaulting students the money. Further, they believed that if they told the authorities they would be more harshly punished the next time they were robbed because the authorities were not capable of protecting them. Fear was powerful, as this representative comment by Huberto, a Mexican American student at L.A.'s Chumash High School, indicates:

> I'm just going to give them what they want 'cause if I don't they're just going to trap me somewhere and beat the shit out of me. . . . What do you mean,

tell the police? The police ain't going to be around to help me all the time, so I got to give them the money they want. I hate them [African Americans] for this shit, but I've just got to give it to 'em.[18]

To emphasize this point, during the three-year research period in Los Angeles and Oakland, only three students told school authorities about being robbed, and in only one of the cases did the victims identify the perpetrators. In that case, students were arrested for the robbery. Two weeks later, three Mexican students were beaten severely by a group of four individuals wearing hoods over their heads. After this incident the robbing of Mexican students continued and no one notified the authorities. In fact, in six cases that I could document, fear of reprisal was so great that when the students told their parents about being forced to give up their lunch money to African American students, the parents decided to give their kids a packed lunch. Then if they were forced to give up their money they would have something to eat. Thus the threat of making things worse was particularly influential in determining how Mexicans managed this type of hostile interaction during this first phase of violence in their school.[19]

As time went on, even though the new students continued to give in to the incumbent students' aggression, feelings of loathing intensified.[20] This counterintuitive development was directly related to growing frustration among members of the incumbent group. The first source of this frustration was associated with the ever-increasing numbers of ethnic students (Mexicans in California and African Americans in Boston) coming to the school and the feelings of impotence to stop it.[21] The second source was less obvious but also related to psychological feelings of impotence. In this second case, it was the newcomers' continued acquiescence during those occasions when they were outnumbered and trapped that stimulated feelings among some incumbents (Irish in Boston and African Americans in California) that a lack of resistance to their aggression cheated them from attaining a power over the newcomers.

It was during this first phase in the violence, a phase in which violence began to occur on a regular basis, that students from the incumbent ethnicity would attack the newcomers. Often other students witnessed these events. Some witnessing students supported the attacks with words of encouragement or passively watched without objecting to the attacks. The victims and their coethnics who were watching but felt outnumbered and helpless to intervene were so upset that networks within the newcomer group began to talk about taking revenge. Ultimately, what was most important in expanding the violence was not the initial attacks but the newcomers' perception that these attacks were not the intentions of a few deviant individuals but the sentiments of the entire incumbent group. The newcomers saw all members of the opposing group as their tormentors and potential targets for retaliation. The comments of Bartolo, a Mexican American attending L.A.'s Chumash High School, typify this thinking:

> Jerry and Nico got jumped by a number of blacks in the courtyard right after lunch before their next class. I heard from Sheila that something was going down, and I ran over there, and all the blacks watching it were just hollering for them to keep on hitting Jerry and Nico. It was fucked up. We ain't taking that shit from them, not any more shit. So whatever black is available is going to get it, 'cause all them think it's great to hurt us. [The other six Mexican students all nod in agreement.][22]

I heard twenty-one other statements like this one made by different Mexican American students at Chumash High School within ten days of this incident.

In each low-income school, it was members of the incumbent group who initiated acts of violence toward the other ethnic group. They acted not as individuals but as members of a group. These acts of aggression were intended to inflict pain, anxiety and gain material possessions. Two representative examples follow. The first incident involved a group of Irish American students attending Paul Revere High School. When the first wave of African American students was being bused from Roxbury to Revere High to comply with the court order to integrate Boston's Unified School District, local citizens directed their resentment and loathing to the courts and the intellectuals who they believed provided the ideological support for the busing. This was expressed by parents and community leaders at public events, on talk radio, and in the news media.[23] As for the students, most of whom were from Irish American backgrounds, the mixture of resentment, fear, and loathing was directed at the African American students that were being bused. One representative example involved Jason, an Irish American at Revere High:

> Fucking niggers are coming here, I hate those black fools! They're just fucking dirty and ugly, and I sure as hell don't want to have to share anything with them. After they start coming to this school, this whole place is going to get destroyed. Everything we got is just fucking going to die. I really do fucking hate them! So any time me my friends get a chance kick the shit out them we'll do it just like we been doing. [All of the other four agree with him

and at different times say, "I agree with you," "Yes, I know," and "You're right about that."][24]

A second example involved an Irish American named Tim. In a previous conversation where I was present he had said that he was worried that there was no way to stop the change in the school now that African Americans were attending. Tim, with four of his friends, watched an African American leaving a sporting event at school and said, "Just go back to where you belong, nigger!" then attacked him by hitting and kicking from all sides. When he fell and was unable to defend himself, one of the attackers took his watch and said, "You don't need this, you're too dumb to tell time." A custodian who had witnessed the fighting went to get the police. They arrived just after Tim and his group had split up and gone in different directions into larger crowds at the sporting event.[25] Tim and his four coethnics were never apprehended for the attack during the two years of the research.[26]

The final example involved Devon, an African American attending Oakland's Kaiser High School. Devon and three other friends said to a Mexican American male student on his way to school, "Give me your money, motherfucker!" After the Mexican American gave him the money Devon hit him in the face. The Mexican American was holding his face but did not say anything, whereupon one of Devon's friends hit the Mexican American five very strong blows, saying, "These fucking Mexicans is so fucking weak they won't even defend themselves, it makes me sick to be around the gutless fuckers!" He then hit him again and they all left.[27]

These acts by members of the incumbent ethnicities involved slightly different meanings. For the Irish Americans, taking the victims' money was more of a symbolic afterthought to the primary goal of inflicting pain and injury, a final "insult to injury" type of action, whereas for African Americans taking the money from the Mexicans was the primary goal of imposing anguish, and the infliction of physical injury was added as a type of insult. The reason for adding insult to injury was to symbolically establish, among one's own group and its adversaries, who had the power to dominate. Thereby status and "positive" solidarity (association from pride) were established for the dominating group and consternation and "negative" solidarity (association from trepidation) among the dominated group.

However, the differences in what constituted injury and insult were based more on the causes of social change in the two situations. In

Boston it was the courts that initiated the change, forcing the combatants on both sides into this conflict. The only way to resist the presence of the other group was to fight them physically and in the process add insult by taking their money. In L.A. and Oakland the social change was caused by new residents buying or renting housing units in the area, so resisting initially took the form of physically and financially hurting and intimidating the kids (and by extension their parents) in an effort to pressure them and their parents to seek a transfer to a different school, move to another area, or deter others from wanting to live in their area. The added insult was a symbol of the incumbent African American students' disgust with the new students' presence in what they considered "their school."

In sum, the first phase of violence was associated with loosely connected groups of students fighting each other, and within this phase the first stage (figure 4.1, P1, S1) involved members of the incumbent ethnic group attacking newcomers. In Los Angeles and Oakland, but not in Boston, some incumbent groups of students that participated in the attacks on the newcomers were members of the local street gang, but during this period gangs were not involved as gangs. In other words, gang members were involved, and gang leaders did not discourage their members' involvement in robbing newcomers or in acting with other members of the incumbent group to simply attack newcomers, but members were acting as individuals and not as formal representatives of the organization. However, in subsequent stages of the violence, gang members on both sides of the conflict would in fact participate as formal agents of the gang's organization.

NEWCOMERS' SELF-DEFENSE RESPONSE

Within three to four weeks of the start of this intimidation, and after a climate of fear, resentment, and hatred had developed throughout the general school population, a second stage within this first phase of the violence emerged (figure 4.1, P1, S2). In this second stage of ethnic violence in the schools studied, members of the new group began to respond to being victimized by forming groups for protection. These groups were not in any way formal. They were associations of individuals based on ethnicity for the primary purpose of self-protection from the incumbent group while newcomers were at school or traveling between home and school. Four psychological sentiments fueled this effort to form groups: unease, fear, protectiveness, and the sense of a common predicament. When these self-defense associations began, most of the individuals expressed all four sentiments. Two examples involved Joaquin and Marcy. Joaquin was a Mexican American student attending Los Angeles's Chumash High School:

> Hey, we been being hit on the way home for a couple of months, so I think we need to stay together, otherwise I'm a little nervous about getting robbed again, or just knocked silly for no reason by them [the African American students]. . . . If we don't protect each other who's going to? It's only us who they pick on.[28]

Marcy was an African American student at Boston's Shawmut High School:

> We got to keep together after school or them white trash is going to try and jump [attack] us. My mom was asking me if I was scared when I go to school, and I was telling her that sometimes I am, but most of the time I just feel a little worried about what might happen and then I tell her that we [African Americans] all hang together to protect each other 'cause none of the other folks [school personnel] are going to [protect them]. She says she feels better knowing that, and I said, "You feel better? I feel a whole lot better that we got each other's butts too!" [The other five all agree with her.][29]

During this period these self-defense alliances included students who would not have naturally associated with each other were it not for the external threat they all faced. The students themselves often recognized this. Two representative examples involved Juana and Adrian. Juana was a Mexican American student at Oakland's Kaiser High School:

> Yeah, I'll meet you and the others right after my last class. Is Enrique going to be there? . . . Yeah, I was just thinking that Enrique's okay, but I wouldn't be caught dead with him if it weren't for the blacks jumping us all the time, he's just too out of it![30]

Adrian was an African American student attending Boston's Paul Revere High School:

> That Nate is one fucked-up dude! [He is responding to Nate's behavior during lunch where he was throwing food at another person.] He'd be judged certifiably insane for the way he acts. Did you see him do all that crazy shit in class? Him hangin' with us is got to be just temporary until we get these white motherfuckers to stop messing with us or we all will get into trouble![31]

With the advent of these new self-defense associations the incumbent students were generally unable to extract money or pressure compliance to any of their immediate demands. A representative example occurred in Los Angeles when a group of nine Mexican American students (five male and four female) were walking home and a group of four African Americans who had been robbing them approached and said, "What's up?" followed by "We're here to collect for today." One of the Mexican American male students responded, "We ain't got any money for you today." The leader of the African American group said, "You give it to us or you're going to get it," and the Mexicans said, "We don't care, we ain't giving you any more money." When the African American students started to swing at the Mexican American male students, the latter began to swing back. The Mexican American girls who were part of the group joined their male colleagues. As the police were running toward the melee, all the African American students ran away without having extorted any money from the Mexican Americans, who waited for the police.

The Mexican American students had serious welts on their faces and bruises on other parts of their body, and the African Americans received scratches and bruises as well, but no one was seriously injured. After the incident the new saying that circulated among the Mexican Americans at Chumash High School was "If you want a piece of any one of us, you got to take the whole enchilada." It is not clear exactly how this phrase proliferated; perhaps it was simply an obvious play on the familiar, but it was present among the Mexican American students in every school in both Los Angeles and Oakland. What was clear was that even though confrontations continued, this new defensive tactic (i.e., traveling in groups to resist being victimized) was effective in eliminating the robberies and reducing the number of reported attacks against the Mexican American students. Further, I observed that this tactic had been successful twenty-six years earlier in reducing attacks on African Americans during the early stages of school integration in Boston.

The second stage in school violence was generally spread out over a four- to five-week period. In terms of the microinteractions of aggression that took place during this stage, before a fight occurred I observed evidence, from speech and physical behavior, of strong fear and resentment among newcomers, and of astonishment and insult among incumbents. *Fear* could be observed in students' pensive expressions and in movements of rubbing hands and clenching fists and was explicitly verbalized in statements like "I'm afraid," or "I'm scared." *Astonishment* was evident in wide eyes, quick looks, and startled body movement, as well as sounds and words like "That's unbelievable," or "That's amazing."

Insult and *resentment* were discernible through expressive statements such as "What he said was offensive" or "That's disgusting."

A particular pattern of aggression was associated with each of these sentiments. For the newcomers, fear was associated with what I will call "defensive aggression" because the blows were delivered with a minimal amount of force and with some hesitation, so that if a counterblow was delivered it could be blocked. Further, although this type of aggression presented a minimal level of intensity as compared to others that will be discussed next, the duration was for as long as necessary to protect oneself (on average from five to thirteen minutes).[32] However, when aggression by the newcomers was related to resentment rather than to fear, it was more offensive, by which I mean its intent was to inflict bodily pain. This involved the use of extreme force with each strike, with the strikes coming in rapid succession, and lasting as long as necessary to achieve the intended goal (generally five to fifteen minutes). A representative example of this occurred at Los Angeles's Tongva High School when a group of five African American students came up to four Mexican Americans and said, "You need to give us your money or you all are going to get your asses kicked here to Mexico!" and one of the Mexicans responded, "Fuck you! You ain't taking no more of my money, asshole!" Immediately the African Americans moved toward the Mexicans and the Mexicans charged at the African Americans, punching and kicking with full force. The African Americans were taken aback but responded with full force. Neither side was able to declare victory because both hit and got hit by the other. There were injuries to both the upper and lower body of each group member, since kicking as well as punching was involved. The level of aggression by the Mexicans was very high, and after the fight they expressed resentment that had been clear from the time it had begun.[33] The comments of Símon, a Mexican American, were typical:

> I'm not being forced by them fucking blacks to give them any money. They got no fucking right to do that shit, and I'm not putting up with it no longer. Every time they try that shit, I'll fight the fuckers![34]

For the incumbents, surprise at the newcomers' resistance fostered a type of aggression that is best described as "uncommitted offensive" because these individuals were on the offensive against their adversaries but were not totally committed to using maximum force for as long as might be necessary to obtain physical dominance. Thus the blows were delivered with little to moderate force for a short time that generally did not exceed two minutes. However, when incumbents felt insulted by the fact that the newcomers were now actively resisting, they went on the offensive in their attacks with great intensity and were committed to inflicting as much bodily injury for as long as was necessary to achieve physical dominance. These types of attacks generally lasted from three to eleven minutes. An example of this occurred at Oakland's Miwok High School when a group of five African American male students approached four Mexican Americans (three boys and one girl) and made fun of what one of the Mexican American boys was wearing. The Mexican Americans retorted by saying, "You blacks are just the most stupid people," and this stimulated the African Americans to charge the Mexicans and begin to viciously deliver blows. Recognizing that two of the Mexican boys were in pain, one of the African Americans pointed at all of them and said, "You insult me and the brother like that again and you won't be able to walk home!" The Mexicans did not say a word, but a week later when a group of African Americans threatened them if they did not give them their money they engaged in another fight.

During this stage, resentment from an insult or injustice provoked vigorous aggression against its perceived perpetrators.[35] The comments of Jeremy, an African American at Oakland's Kaiser High School who was a member of the dominating group, and Nicolas, a Mexican American student attending Los Angeles's Tongva High School who was a member of the dominated group, are representative of this resentment.

> *Jeremy:* Every fucking time they disrespect me I going to fuck them up [beat them up]! I mean every time! They better fucking understand that and stop that shit![36]
>
> *Nicolas:* Fuck them black assholes! I fucking don't care how many times they hit me; we're going to fight them every time they insult us. Fuck them![37]

INCUMBENTS' REASSERTION OF DOMINANCE

At this point, a new, second phase of the violence began as the incumbent students realized that a new situation had arisen. No longer would the new students sit idly by and allow themselves to be "picked on." Yet the incumbents' anxiety, resentment, and loathing had not gone away. The only aspect of the situation that had changed was a new resistance among newcomers that many in the incumbent group found annoying or revolting. For a short period of two to three weeks there were no reported incidents between members of each group. However, during this period there were discussions among members of the incumbent group about how to deal with the new situation, and these discussions resulted in a new outbreak of violence, in which incumbents reacted aggressively to newcomers' resistance (figure 4.1, P2, S1). An example occurred in one of Boston's local restaurants on a Saturday involving five young Irish Americans that attended Shawmut High School:

> *Troy:* There was some trouble between Fred [a friend] and some of them nigger bastards the other day. What was that about?
>
> *Ned:* Fred and couple of friends were fucking with them, and they weren't having it anymore. So I guess they [Fred and the group he was with] tried to slap 'em in shape, but the niggers all fought back. It ain't like Fred lost or anything, it was just a standoff, that's all.
>
> *Troy:* That's fucking disgusting!
>
> *Ernie:* You know this is the way them fuckers [African Americans] been acting lately, and if we let them they'll keep act'n that way. I tell you I ain't for that.
>
> *Ronald:* Well, if we goin' to do something we got to do some more planning, 'cause the old way ain't working.
>
> *Ned:* Okay, so let's do it.
>
> *Troy:* We can get together at my house tonight at seven. [They all nod in agreement.][38]

Later in the evening, walking to catch the subway to my apartment, I saw Ned, Ernie, Ronald, and Troy talking on a house porch.[39] Three days later they engaged in a fight with three African American students whom they surprised as they left their gym class.

Another incident involved Horace and three friends who had been extorting money from four small groups of Mexicans as they walked to and from Los Angeles's Chumash High School. Recently these four small groups had joined with other Mexicans to protect themselves from African American harassment. Horace's group decided to continue to extort lunch money from the groups by employing a new technique that used cell phones and the Internet to threaten the targeted groups to give them the money rather than to do it in person. They would first contact various members by e-mail or their cell phones to demand money, give instructions as to where to leave it, and threaten physical harm if they did not. The first reaction of the Mexicans was to listen to their phone messages or read their text messages and refuse to cooperate because they now felt safe traveling in relatively large groups of students. However, Horace and his friends began to single out one or two members of the targeted group of Mexicans and attack them in school when they were alone in the bathroom or traveling between classes. Five attacks were reported in a three-day period. The two attacks I observed were quick, averaging about three minutes, with multiple blows to the targeted person's body and face that left one boy bleeding from a gash in the forehead and a girl with welts on her face and shoulder.[40] All of the victimized students reported the attacks, but the students whom they were able to identify as their attackers had alibis that authorities were unable to disprove. No further action was forthcoming.

The second response of the incumbent student groups (African Americans in L.A. and Oakland and Irish Americans in Boston) to the new students' defensive strategies was to roam by foot or in their cars with the expressed purpose of randomly attacking them.[41] They did this for three reasons. The first reason was a sense of disbelief and outrage at the new students' defiance. Representative comments are from Dante, an African American living in Los Angeles and attending Chumash High School, and Rory, an Irish American attending Paul Revere High School in Boston:

> *Dante:* They [Mexican students] fucking did what? They fucking said "no?" God damn it! Who the fuck do they think they be saying "no" to? We're really goin' to fuck them up now! Blast the livin' fuckin' shit out of 'em next time![42]

> *Rory:* Did you see them fuckin' niggers fight back? They must be on some drugs or something 'cause they must not know whose town they're in. So next time really make the fuckers suffer![43]

Eight days after making this statement, Dante and three other African American students were detained by police for fighting, along with six Mexican American students. Dante and the other African American students were in possession of four steel rods.[44] In the case of Rory, three days after he made the above statement, he and six other students were detained for fighting, along with four African American students. They also had chains and baseball bats.[45]

The second reason for roaming and randomly attacking a new student was simply to have fun and provide entertainment for both the attacker and observers. An example of this occurred in Los Angeles's

Chumash High School. Five Mexican American students walking home were confronted by six African Americans who pulled up in a car next them, got out quickly, and started to hit them. After receiving numerous blows, the Mexicans simply covered their bodies for protection. At that point one of the African Americans said, "Time to exit!" and all of them started to laugh. Another said, "This roundup stuff is a gas, man," and the others all made verbal gestures of agreement and left in the car. All through this period, various African American male students could be heard talking about the fun that they had had going on "roundups" of Mexican students.[46] Another representative example occurred among a group of six students attending Oakland's Miwok High School:

> *Frank:* Did you and Lester go on a hunting trip [i.e., a "roundup"] this week?
>
> *Lem:* You know it, and it was a good one too! We had some uppity Tacos [Mexican students] that had to be put in their place.
>
> *Dion:* Did they beat you and the others' butts? [Everyone laughs.]
>
> *Lem:* You got to know better than that! We punished the motherfuckers, man, we don't ever get punished! Hey, if we weren't having fun we wouldn't do it. [All six of the students smile and nod affirmatively.][47]

The third reason that some students became involved in roaming and attacking students of the other ethnicity had to do with personal issues. They were in some way attempting to test themselves and see whether they could successfully meet a challenge or avert being the object of peer ostracism. These students were reluctant to become involved in violence on their own because they felt physically inadequate (too small or weak) and feared severe injuries or because they had moral reservations. Therefore, they participated as members of the group attacking students of the other ethnic group because it provided them the opportunity to overcome their fears. It gave them a chance to become more competent in physical combat and to show others in their group that they were one of the group and not to be ridiculed as deviant or weak. The comments of Paul and Silas are representative of such students. Paul was an Irish American attending Shawmut High School:

> I can't believe that I went with Mike last night to jump niggers that came into our neighborhood after school was out. We saw one of them who must have been being picked up by a relative or something because the bus taking the rest of them had already gone. I recognized him from one of my classes, and we jumped out of the car and hit and kicked the guy bad. I was sort of scared we would be seen and then get into trouble, but we did it and nothing hap-

pened so I was relieved. I never done anything like that before 'cause my mom would think it was wrong and so I felt good or something, I don't know, I just felt good. I mean I felt I was able to take care of myself, you know?[48]

Silas was an African American student attending L.A.'s Chumash High School:

My family, especially my mom, would think that the devil had gotten into me for going along with all the other guys while they attacked the Mexican guys. We hurt a number of them we could find going home from the game last night. . . . Well, I just kicked them, but it felt good that I could really do this when I always used to be afraid of doing stuff like this, and everybody was like congratulating people and that was good 'cause most times people just think I'm just a good student and sort of weak.[49]

Students like Paul and Silas who were physically small rarely fought while the victims were standing. They would wait until the adversary was already in a compromised position and then join the others of their group in hitting and kicking them.[50]

During this stage of conflict when the incumbent students tried to reassert their physical dominance, the patterns of violent confrontations were predicated on two sets of emotions in each student camp. The incumbents were *angry* over having their power challenged and in many ways neutralized by the newcomers' resistance and were *determined* to reassert dominance. For the victims, fear and the humiliation of having been violated were the most significant in determining the pattern of future aggression.

When anger was present, the incumbents' aggression went on for a relatively moderate length of time, generally from one to five minutes per incident. However, when the motive was to reassert dominance, the aggression was highly intense, with the incumbents using a great deal of force to injure their target, and with the attacks lasting for a longer time, generally five to ten minutes. A typical example was a fight that took place when students were returning home from Oakland's Kaiser High School. Ten African American students were gathered at the corner of a major intersection. About five minutes after small groups of Mexican American students started walking home on the other side of the street, the ten African Americans charged across the street and began attacking the Mexican Americans using pipes, sticks, combs, and heavy rope. The Mexican boys and girls fought back with whatever objects they could use for protection and/or weapons (usually backpacks, heavy rope, combs, nail files, and razor blades), but the African Americans fought with particular intensity and more organization. As the African Americans continued their attack they would make statements that the Mexicans could expect this all the time until they understood that the school belonged to the African Americans.[51] As happened in all of these types of incidents, youth were injured. In the example mentioned above, which lasted just under nine minutes, some youth received cuts or bruises, and there was one report of a broken bone.

Violated and humiliated by the incumbents during "normal" school interactions, the newcomers no longer responded with defensive physical blows to keep African Americans from injuring them. They fought back and used blows of great force to make the perpetrators pay in pain.[52] When victimized newcomers felt violated and engaged their victimizers in an offensive attack (i.e., in an effort to inflict bodily harm or at least pain), it lasted between five and six minutes. However, when victimized newcomers were afraid of being injured, they responded in a defensive manner and the fight lasted around ten minutes. An example of an act of aggression emanating from feelings of humiliation occurred when Felix, a Mexican American student attending Los Angeles's Tongva High School, walked by a group of five African American students at school who started to make fun of the way he was dressed. One of the African Americans grabbed Felix's shirt as he walked by. Felix immediately began to hit, kick, and scratch the African American. The other African Americans then tried to grab and hit Felix, but because Felix and the African American student had their fists up and were moving quickly the others had difficulty hitting him. This fight also lasted just over six minutes before school authorities broke it up. Even after the authorities had separated the two, Felix continued to scream at the African American that if he did that again he would hurt him worse.[53]

NEWCOMERS' RETALIATORY RESPONSES

In the second stage of phase 2 (figure 4.1, P2, S2), the newcomers formed groups that stopped being defensive and became aggressive. The groups were designed to be vigilante and were formed first by students who were friends. However, as the groups became more capable of defending themselves, they expanded because more students wanted to associate with them for purposes of protection. Whenever attacks on unsuspecting newcomers increased, the leaders of these newly formed "vigilante-type groups" of newcomers began to advocate retaliating against their tormentors. At this stage, youth gangs did not provide an organizational resource for the "newcomers" mainly because the area they had moved to was in fact "new" and the number of eligible gang members was still small. A new gang had not yet developed and local gangs associated with the previous neighborhoods where the newcomers had lived had not yet migrated to the new area. Therefore, students wanting protection formed these "vigilante-type" groups.

In the beginning of this stage of retaliatory conflict, all of the combatants were influenced primarily by revenge. Two examples, one indicating thought and the other action, are representative of newcomers' response to the renewed attacks on them by the incumbent group. The first example involved Brian, an African American attending Boston's Shawmut High School:

> Look here, we got to go after that guy Collin and his group for what they did to Collinda and Derek and the group. We can't let the motherfuckers get away with this shit, we got to act fast and make them pay. I don't care how much trouble we get into for this, we're going to hurt them like they did to Derek and Collinda![54]

Five days after making this statement, a group of African Americans attacked Collin and four other Irish American students while they were eating lunch in the school cafeteria. No weapons were used, but Collin and two of the other Irish Americans needed medical attention. Brian was the leader of the nine African Americans who attacked Collin, and two members of the African American group also received medical treatment for cuts and bruises.

The second example involves Raphael, a Mexican American attending Oakland's Kaiser High School. Raphael and two of his friends had been walking home from school, when they were surrounded by a group of twelve African American students and told they were going to be made examples for what would happen if they did not cooperate with paying "rights of passage fees" (i.e., money) to and from school. They were then attacked and beaten up by the group. Raphael had a broken nose. After this incident, Raphael and a group of fifteen Mexican American students cornered three African American members of the group that had attacked him and assaulted them, leaving all three with cuts on their faces, arms, and backs. Two days after the attack, Raphael was back at school saying to a group of twenty students, "If the fucking *mayates* [derogatory term used for African Americans], attack us, we're going to pay them back! So it's up to them to stop attacking us."[55]

During this stage, the individuals who directly participated in the retaliatory attacks overcame their fears of being injured by drawing on four beliefs: that their parents had a right to buy a home in the area, that they themselves had a right to live and go to high school in the area, that the incumbent ethnic group had behaved unjustly toward them and that they had a right to take revenge on members of the incumbent group whenever this occurred. The fact that they were being attacked for reasons that had no apparent connection to anything they were doing seemed to nearly all the new students in each of these schools grossly unjust. Such feelings should not be discounted, for they have been shown historically to be critical in stimulating participation in social movements of rebellion.[56] An example of such feelings can be seen in the comments of Julius, an African American who was attending Boston's Paul Revere High School:

> Them crackers [white Irish students] is trying to beat us and shoot us [there had been a shooting a couple of weeks before] for coming to their school and it ain't even our fault. We don't want to come to their fucking school either! They should be fucking pissed at the white judge who said it has to happen and not us, but they too fucking stupid to figure that out! So, we ain't putting up with their shit 'cause it is fucking not right. We got a right to go to whatever school there is in this country. . . . If I see any them fucking with us about this [going to school], I swear I'll put them down and I don't fucking care if it's for good.[57]

Eleven days after Julius made these statements, he and two other African American male students were detained for a fight they had had with three Irish American students, one of whom suffered a puncture wound from an object that was never found by authorities.

Further, there was a general feeling among the newcomers that they had a right to security, which they could achieve only if they retaliated every time they were attacked. A representative example of this can be seen in the comments of Tomás, a Mexican American attending Los Angeles's Tongva High School:

> No, you don't have to worry about getting the shit kicked out of you because if that happens we will definitely go and kick the shit out a number of them until they get it that they are going to get attacked if they attack us.[58]

A month later, Eugenio, the student whom Tomás was talking to, was one of three Mexican students who got into a very intense fight with four African American students that culminated with two of the combatants becoming injured and requiring medical attention. The conflict began when a Mexican student was pushed to the ground and kicked by four African American students on the school grounds near the football field during lunch hour. When the Mexican American student ran back to the cafeteria area and told a number of Mexican American students what had happened, Eugenio and six other students ran to the area where the Mexican student had been attacked. The student identified the African Americans who had attacked him. Eugenio and the six other students waited at the edge of a building until the African Americans walked by to go to class, and then they attacked with vicious blows, using both their fists and a wooden baseball bat that had been sawed off just above the trademark. One of the group of Mexican Americans pulled a rubber comb from the back of his pants and in a swiping motion ripped the African American's shirt and opened a cut on the upper arm near the shoulder. The African American flinched and shouted, "He's got a knife!" At this, another of the African Americans pulled off his belt, which had a very large buckle. He swung it at another Mexican American, hitting him multiple times, including on the side of his face near his jawbone. Eugenio, using a piece of wood he had gotten from his woodshop class, hit the African American he was engaged with multiple times. Another Mexican American picked up two handfuls of stones by the side of the building, threw them at the face of an African American, and then charged him with his belt. He hit the African American in the back of the head so hard that the African American grabbed his head and started to retreat. At that moment, a number of the school's security aides and a police officer came running and apprehended all the combatants, taking them to the principal's office on campus and then transporting them to the city police precinct for processing.[59]

At this stage of the conflict, the leaders as well as the rank-and-file Mexican Americans believed that retaliatory violence was the most important way to prevent attack. The newcomers, acting as individuals or in groups, would usually retaliate after members of the incumbent group had attacked one of them. The intensity of the counterattack signaled an escalation to the violence. One could observe a determined intent to inflict harm and if possible leave some physical mark on the body of one's opponent; and this was substantively different from engaging in defensive violence to protect oneself. For example, in an incident at L.A.'s Chumash High School a group of four male Mexican students attacked two male African American students at a bus stop. The Mexican students divided up, with two fighting with each African American. The African American students were physically bigger than the Mexican students, and in one fight were able gain a draw, but in the other the Mexican students got the African American on the ground, and as one held him down the other quickly approached him with a broken beer bottle and said, "Don't keep messing with us or this is what you'll get" and went to cut the African American's face. The African American moved quickly and the bottle ripped his shirt cutting his upper arm around the shoulder, but he was able to free himself and get to his feet when police sirens sounded increasingly close. Alerted that the police were about to imminently arrive, all the combatants fled, even the African Americans who had been attacked.[60]

Like the other stages of ethnic violence that have been discussed, this one had a distinct pattern that was based on the desire for *retribution* that had evolved from the interactions in the other phases. During this period in which retribution was dominant, any rumor of an "out-group" attack on a member of the "in-group" generated a call for pay-back on the part of a significant number of individuals who felt this injustice deserved a similar response. Usually during this phase of the violence a rumor that an injustice had been committed against someone in one ethnic group required that a witness substantiate it to justify retaliatory revenge, but this would not be required for retaliatory revenge to occur in the next stage of violence.

A COUNTERINTERLUDE

While these stages in ethnic violence were taking place in four of the six schools in the present study, there were two other schools in the sample where no violence occurred for the entire three years of the research. What was different about those schools, the students, and circumstances in them that produced this situation? The two schools were De Neve High School in Los Angeles and Ohlone High School in Oakland. Three main differences between them and the other four high schools in both cities inhibited violence from occurring. First, even though these schools, and the neighborhoods of which they were a part, were multiethnic, with the first group being white, the second African American, and the third Mexican, the overwhelming majority of families that lived in each area were socioeconomically middle class. The home prices ranged between $300,000 and $900,000, numbers that in California would be considered standard middle-class housing prices, though in other parts of the country they would be upper-middle or lower-upper class.

Generally, each of the families had moved to these areas for the tra-ditional reasons of providing their children with greater educational opportunities (because the schools were considered excellent), and taking advantage of increasing home values in the area. So most of the families knew that whoever bought homes in the area needed to have a certain level of capital regardless of their ethnicity. This proved to be the case as new owners arrived and home values increased. More than anything, these economic considerations relieved most homeowners from feeling economically vulnerable (on account of the equity in their homes) or unable to move to another location if they wanted. Thus the area was stabilized and homeowners did not engage in the frenzied selling of homes to avoid economic risk that has plagued other urban areas.[61] In contrast, the families whose children attended the four schools where violence took place were working class or had incomes near the poverty line. Most of them felt economically trapped because they did not have the money to buy in areas that would improve the value of their homes.[62] The comments in a conversation between Oscar, a middle-aged Mexican American father of three, and Rob, young thirtyish-looking white father of two, express their rationale for buying in their middle-class neighborhood:

> *Oscar:* Well, I'm just like you [one of the other fathers who had just finished talking]. I got a new job with one of the financial loaning agencies in Los Angeles, and my new salary allowed me and my wife to think about buying a new house. We were both making good money now, and the new house we wanted to buy was larger and less money, but it was in a neighborhood that was old with so-so schools. So we decided that the best long-term bet for us was to move into our present house, which was a thousand feet smaller than the other one, but the schools for the kids were excellent and it was in an area that a lot of people want to live, and this makes it good for increasing our equity, which will help when we will need to borrow against it to send the kids to college.

> *Rob:* Plus, if anything goes wrong and housing prices start falling we can get the hell out and not lose money 'cause we already made a good deal in equity. . . . Yeah, well, the first year we worried about making the payments, but now we know it was the best thing we did.[63]

The second difference was related to the nature of the schools. In the middle-class schools, an individual student's clique was determined by his or her interests and the social status he or she had accrued from the peer group and not by familial social class standing or ethnicity. Social groups were both interclass and interethnic. Thus it was common for students from working-class families to mix easily with the middle-class students because they were such a small minority within the school. The comments of Connie, a Mexican American attending Los Angeles's De

Neve High School, are representative of the prevailing attitudes and behaviors concerning social groups in the school:

> Yeah, it's so different from [the previous high school] I attended. You guys let anybody that you like hang out with your group, but at [my previous high school] you could only hang out with your own [ethnic group]. I like it so much better this way because you feel like you're appreciated for being who you are as a person and not other stuff.[64]

The bottom line here was that middle-class culture dominated the school environment. Students from working-class families adapted to "fit in," supporting the existing criteria for determining social cliques and networks that were based not on income or ethnicity but on whom one associated with and what their interests were.[65] Ethnicity was not particularly important in these schools. Students not only were trying to assimilate with their peers but were encouraged to do so.[66] The most salient attributes for acceptance into one clique or another were subjective ones like attractiveness, academic success, athletic skills, material possessions, clothing, congeniality, and what boy or girl one was dating.

The third difference had to do with the norms of the middle-class parents and students about how to handle conflict. Middle-class students at these schools did experience conflict that could be quite vicious, especially the symbolic type that can lead to psychological harm and even suicide as a result of bullying.[67] However, in the present study, when middle-class students experienced conflict, they were overwhelmingly inclined to use a third party to aid in mediating it. The third party was either another friend whom they would ask to talk to the person they were having a dispute with or the various officials within the formal authority structure that included teachers, school administrators, law enforcement, and the legal system. What most parents did not want was for their children to handle the conflict themselves using any kind of physical force. This was not only discouraged but as close to being forbidden as possible. In addition, if any parents felt that some level of physical force was necessary in a dispute, the message to their children was that the parents would be the ones to use it and that their children should not become involved. The comments of Noah and Ricardo are representative. Noah was an African American attending Oakland's Ohlone High School:

> I was just telling my mother last night about these two guys that I knew who were kicked out of high school for getting into a fight with two Mexicans

about something they said, and my mom just goes off and starts with how dumb that is and guys that do this are just losers because they can't figure out that the only thing fighting can get you is kicked out of school and jail. . . . I wasn't even talking about doing anything myself, since I haven't gotten into a fight since grade school, and my mom went off about how she didn't care if it wasn't my fault, fighting was not going to help me get to college. . . . Oh, she's said that to me too: "Don't get into trouble, if there's trouble then tell me [his mom] and I'll handle it, not you."[68]

Ricardo was a Mexican American attending Los Angeles's De Neve High School:

My brother and I were watching the news where there was trouble at one of the schools in L.A. and my dad says, "See how stupid those guys are. They fight and think they're real bad, but just risk getting hurt or killed and for what?! Nothing! If you guys get into trouble, just walk away and me or your mom will handle it. Just don't try to handle it yourself and make it worse!" Me and my brother have heard this so much that we just say "Yeah," 'cause were not going to be stupid and get into a fight, but if we say more than "Yeah" he will go on and on and on.[69]

In sum, the schools that were dominated by middle-class families, regardless of the ethnic mixture, not only were free from interethnic violence during the time of the field research for the present study but have remained that way for ten years. This highlights the importance of the factors discussed in chapters 2 and 3 as those setting the stage for ethnic violence in schools. In addition, a comparison of these schools to the low-income schools described in other chapters shows that the types of violence mobilized (i.e., the resources people deploy (bodily or discursive) vary by social class context, and that the target of the violence (group or individual) varies by social class context. Therefore, in lower-class schools the individual is a proxy for the group, while in middle-class schools the individual is targeted as an individual alone.

SOME CONCLUDING COMMENTS

When conflict between students from differing ethnic backgrounds occurs, it is fueled by a sense of injustice that is shared by both the aggressors and the victims, although their points of reference are often different. This sense of injustice involves both past struggles as a group to realize the hopes and dreams for a "good life" and the group's present experiences with hardship. However, the formation of groups and their actions during this period of the ethnic conflict escalate the violence because although the groups are quite small they reinforce the idea that violence based on ethnic identity requires a collective response, not an individual one.

During the initial phase of conflict, violence develops as a sequence of actions that includes aggression, resistance, and counteraggression by the students of each ethnicity. Further, while one finds normal adolescent development during the high school years to include individuals acting out in impulsive ways, the evidence concerning ethnic violence in high school points in its initial period to planned rather than spontaneous behavior. Finally, the evolution of violence during this period is certainly influenced by the adolescent drive to be attached to a social group (i.e., a clique) and to seek status through group approval of one's actions. Therefore, in the beginning phases of ethnic conflict in high schools individuals tend to seek out peers who share their feelings about the presence of new students (to them) from a different ethnic group,[70] as well as a sense of how to deal with them, and a commitment to cooperate with other individuals from their collectives.

Collins theorized that tension and fear more often than not inhibit individuals from engaging in violence, but that once individuals overcome these feelings they are caught up in hysterical entrainment involving an altered state of consciousness that leads to a "frenzied" mode of overkill behavior. Collins called this dynamic a "forward panic."[71] In the present study, internal issues, like fear, inhibited some individuals from engaging in violence, and some emotions, like feeling violated, caused others to become violent toward students from another group. Some of the violent incidents discussed in this chapter followed the "forward panic" dynamic while others did not. Behavior that was consistent with a "forward panic" involved incidents where a person clearly felt trapped and attacked out of panic exactly the way a trapped animal would. Further, when individuals felt in a superior strategic position—either because they were physically larger than their adversary or because they outnumbered the adversarial group—their violence showed a "forward panic" dynamic. However, the majority of violent cases included a variety of emotions involving rage, resentment, identity formation, and self-defense, where the dynamic never evolved into behaviors resembling a "forward panic." In these violent incidents, behaviors switched from one affective state to another in various permutations but never evolved into Collins's "entrainment-type" dynamic leading to overkill.[72] In addition, most of the emotions present in a violent incident were incorporated in a collective context that brought additional group dynamics into play.[73] Thus, where Collins would reduce violence to something that is emotional and psychological, I observed numerous instances where violence was deployed rationally and strategically because that was the resource available. Therefore, while emotional/psychological factors may be present, the story of the "forward panic" cannot fully account for the variation in dynamics governing different cases of ethnic violence in high schools.

CHAPTER 5

Fire

The Maturation of Ethnic Violence

The phases of fire are craving and satiety.

—Heraclitus, *Fragments*, 500 CE

Ethnic violence in schools involves a process, a series of actions and reactions between individuals that evolve over time. The last chapter showed that stages within the first and second phases of violence constituted an evolving sequence. In the second phase (figure 4.1, P2, S1 and S2), various groups acted as teams for retaliatory purposes, eventually creating a form of "deterrence" between the ethnic factions and a quasi-lull in the violence.[1] In cases involving countries, violence often stops at this stage because the combatants feel that more violence is counterproductive to each of their respective interests. However, when it came to ethnic violence in the schools of this study, this "deterrence-producing lull" was temporary.[2]

The earlier lull in violence at the end of phase 1, associated with the deterrent conditions produced from phase 1's roving groups of individuals engaged in vigilante-type behavior, lasted no longer than a month in each of the schools of this study, with the exception of the middle-class schools, where no interethnic violence was reported and where I independently observed none while I was present for the entire research period. When this phase in the ethnic violence ended, phase 2 emerged, having two stages. In the first stage individuals aggressed because of personal reasons. Yet students, family, and residents of the neighborhood interpreted those incidents as episodes of ethnic violence. In the second stage significant numbers of students reacted to such individual confrontations in very intense "team-type" interactions. This chapter looks at the factors that influenced violence to go beyond the team-type interactions that dominated phase 2 (i.e., armed skirmishes and engagements, to use a geopolitical metaphor) and to become more destructive by involving even larger numbers of people (i.e., to go from "battles" to "war").

INDIVIDUAL VIOLENCE AND GROUP UNDERSTANDINGS

As has been previously mentioned, after the second phase of ethnic violence in the schools, when parties arrived at a limited "standoff," there was a lull in violent incidents. During this lull, students went about their normal routines, and most appeared to behave as though the time of violence had never happened. Some students from the two ethnic groups had friendly conversations with each other and even socialized during lunch or on the way to and from home. However, this period of apparent "normalcy" would break down within a five-week interval when individuals from different ethnic groups became involved in an incident related to one of three actions: a dispute, an insult, or an outright act of aggression resulting from certain individuals' internal psychological disturbance, manifested as one or more abnormal behavioral responses to various physical and social stimuli.

Disputes

Disputes (i.e., disagreements or arguments over an issue) are a normal occurrence in life. The most common at each of the schools arose when individual students violated social etiquette generally accepted by the other students: for example, talking in a language other than English (e.g., Spanish) when all members of the group did not understand it, or making fun of members of another person's family and in the process insulting the honor of that family. When an etiquette violation occurred among members of the same ethnic group, little if anything happened, but when the situation involved members of the rival ethnic group it produced two general responses: emotional arousal and a public verbal declaration that an action or statement was unfair. (See the Introduction and Methodological Appendix for method used in identifying emotions.) When the objection to a rival's behavior was expressed loudly, it alerted everyone, including the perceive violator(s), that a formal social dispute was being initiated. In these cases the dispute became public and the accuser and accused would confront each other. This confrontation involved accusations and counteraccusations, which in no more than three minutes created a situation that challenged the identities of the participants—that is to say, their sense of integrity as "men or women," members of their ethnic group, or both. There were occasions when women engaging in these confrontations with other women did physically fight with each other, but most often they would stand up for the rights of their ethnic group and perform the feminine role of emotionally supporting their male coethnics when they were in a physical fight. The comments of Tara, Wilma, and Sonia are representative. Tara was an Irish American attending Boston's Shawmut High School:

> No, you should just support the guys when they are fighting with the niggers, 'cause we girls aren't supposed to do what the guy's supposed to do, you know? I support what they're doing [fighting with African Americans], because they're protecting our community from them scum.[3]

Wilma was an African American from Los Angeles's Tongva High School:

> You know the boys here got it covered [fighting with Mexicans], and my mom is always telling me to avoid fights myself and act like a lady, and I got to agree, but that don't mean we [girls] got to stop supporting what the boys are doing, 'cause they just protecting our rights to have something of our own, you know? [All three girls verbally agree with here.][4]

Sonia was a Mexican American attending Oakland's Kaiser High School:

> I'm going to be careful about getting into fights with them [African Americans] when they get into it with the guys, 'cause I ain't a fighter and I don't think girls should be anyway. . . . I'll definitely support what the guys are doing, though, because they're protecting our rights to be here against them [African Americans].[5]

Disputes over space, time, and materials (i.e., cell phones, iPods, sneakers, baseball caps, basketballs, computer access, and sports facilities access) often created confrontations between opposing parties that led to violent physical exchanges. When this occurred two assertive moral positions were expressed. For those who were able to secure the desired space, time, or materials, the prevailing moral position was that they had the right to keep whatever they had secured in an equal and fair physical confrontation. For those who were deprived of what they desired in space, time, and materials, the dominant moral position was that they were the victims of cheating.

For all those who in some way felt deprived, this deprivation was not simply an inequity but an injustice. The assertion of these two moral positions led to a standoff requiring some other action to resolve the situation. When the situation was left to the competing groups to adjudicate, a physical altercation was generally the result. Three examples are representative of the *dispute-initiated fight*.

The first concerned space and occurred at Boston's Paul Revere High School. A group of African American students was standing in line waiting for lunch to be served, and three Irish American girls were in front of them. After a few minutes two Irish American boys came and started to talk to the girls and then proceeded to integrate themselves into the line ahead of the African Americans. This did not appear to make the African Americans upset, but a few minutes later three more Irish Americans came and integrated themselves into the line. The African Americans began to complain among themselves. So when three more Irish Americans came and started to talk to their friends in the line, the four African American students confronted the group of Irish Americans, who told them to mind their own business. This initiated the throwing of punches, and a fight involving all eight of the Irish American boys and five of the African Americans continued until the police security force arrived to break it up.[6]

The second example involved a dispute over both space and time. It occurred at Los Angeles's Tongva High School when a group of Mexican Americans were playing basketball on the school courts during lunchtime. A group of African Americans told the Mexicans that they had played long enough and it was their turn. The Mexicans said that they had gotten the court first and had been playing for only five minutes. They went on to say that they would yield the court when they were done with their game to 21, whereupon the African Americans rushed the Mexicans playing and started to swing at them. The fight escalated to eight Mexican American and seven African American students. It was ultimately stopped by school police and security guards.[7]

The third example was a dispute over purchasing goods at Oakland's Miwok High School on a very warm day. After school was out, a group of African American students approached a small pushcart where a Mexican man was selling cold treats, like popsicles and traditional Mexican-flavored shaved ice. The Mexican seller told everyone in line that he had sold nearly his entire product and had enough left for only four or five more. This irritated the Mexican American students in the line, who also wanted to buy some of the products and who felt that since the seller and the product were Mexican they were privileged to purchase the product before the African Americans who were ahead of them in line. They began to complain loudly and push toward the cart. The African Americans pushed back, and a fight started between six African Americans and seven Mexican Americans that was eventually broken up when the Oakland Police Department arrived.[8]

Compare this to an event at Oakland's middle-class-dominated Ohlone High School, where a Mexican concession was selling tacos and burritos at a football game. A group of Mexican students had been waiting in line behind five African American students to order when three African Americans came up and started to talk to the five students at the front of the line. They then joined the original five, and one of the Mexican American girls said, "Hey guys, we been waiting in line for a while now, and you'll need to get in line behind us." The three African American students said, "Yeah, you're right, there will be food for us when we get to the front," (this was not guaranteed, as this concession had run out of food in previous games), whereupon they left and went to the back of the line. There was no fight because there was no conflict between the groups, so etiquette, fairness, and aversion to trouble with school administrators prevailed. This type of outcome from a small dispute occurred regularly while I observed all the middle-class schools and was a function of class background and the desire to avoid personal trouble. As a consequence, conflict was minimal and rarely, if ever, associated with ethnicity.[9]

Turning back to the fights emanating from disputes in the lower-class schools, we see that they assumed a particular dynamic pattern. This dynamic started with a dispute over space, time, and materials in which the two parties were members of different ethnic groups, and it quickly took on the character of a clash between groups in which each group asserted its rights. Both parties to the dispute believed that they occupied the moral "high ground" and expressed this with a righteous smugness. The response of the party in possession of the desired good to the other party's wishes ranged from "passive-aggressiveness" (i.e., hearing the wishes expressed but simply smirking or making a gesture of annoyance and continuing doing what they had been doing) to moral outrage. Consequently both parties structured the dispute as "zero-sum," a framing that raised both the stakes and the emotions.[10] After the fight began, those watching kept it going, as much for entertainment purposes as for moral reasons.[11] The audience's loud encouragement of the combatants nearly always intensified the emotions and energy of the fight.[12] The comments of Matías, a Mexican American attending Los Angeles's Chumash High School, are representative:

> The blacks were always trying to take stuff from us, so we got into a fight about using the computers in the computer room. I was fighting and I kept it up because I didn't want everyone watching and yelling to think I was a coward or something, plus if I stopped the blacks would have just pounded me to mush![13]

All the fights that emerged from disputes continued until the authorities arrived to break them up.

Insults

The second situation that initiated violence in each of the troubled schools involved insults leveled by individuals of one ethnic group toward those of another. There were three types of insults. The first was name-calling, with one or more individuals in one group making a reference to one or more individuals of the opponent group that was meant to demean him or her. When this occurred the initial reaction was revulsion, contempt, and bitterness expressed in spitting at the perceived insulter, looking at the insulter with intense disdain (squinting eyes, frowns, clenched lips, and tight face), throwing an object at the insulter, calling the insulter derogatory names, and threatening him or her with harm. The response to anyone of these reactions was to retaliate with additional insults or start physically fighting, or both.[14] In a previous period, when the newcomers had recently arrived, insults directed at them would not have caused a fight. Feeling shy and vulnerable, as they expressed in statements of worry about being attacked, the newcomers would have simply absorbed the insults and avoided further contact with the aggressive group, but as different phases of interactions progressed the newcomers were no longer willing to put up with insults and felt confident enough to engage in a physical fight.

The second type of insult was the use of jokes to make fun of individuals in the opposing group. Public jokes were benign when they were done with no intended malice, but when individuals perceived that malice was involved, amusement faded and was replaced first by embarrassment and then by anger.[15] How individual students responded to the embarrassment was critical to the dynamic of violence that followed. Some individuals were inclined to resist carrying the confrontation to the next level where physical violence was probable, either because they feared for their own safety or the safety of others or because they felt it was not ethical or culturally appropriate to fight about such things. However, for others the embarrassment was so damaging to their sense of self or the group they identified with that the insult was a social stigma they could not ignore.[16] For these individuals the goal was to make the perpetrator feel the same discomfort that the joke had made them feel by physically attacking and hurting him or her.

A representative example comes from an interaction involving Doroteo, a Mexican American attending Oakland's Miwok High School. As he was sitting waiting for the bus to take him home, two African Americans who were also waiting for the bus asked him if he had a match so they could light their cigarettes. He shook his head indicating that he did not, and one of the African American students said to the other, "Did you hear the rattle when he shook that head? It was definitely full of Mexican seeds!" The other African American and two other African American students at the bus stop started to laugh. Doroteo immediately got up, took his backpack off, ran up to the student who had made the joke, and viciously hit him in the back of the head. Doroteo had obviously hurt the black student, who continued to hold the back of his head as Doroteo continued to swing his pack. The other African American started to swing at Doroteo, but everything stopped when school security arrived to separate the students and take them to the principal's office to wait for the police to arrive. All three students had scrapes to the head and were treated by the school nurse. No arrests were made, but all three were suspended from school.[17]

The third type of insult had to do with behavior that displayed a lack of respect. Examples included attempts by boys of one ethnic group to pick up girls from the other group while they were with their boyfriends or brothers, or to speak to or about these girls in ways that offended their dignity. Such behavior was considered an insult to the "manliness" of the accompanying boy and the moral dignity of the girl and her family. These types of insults nearly always produced a physical fight. The only difference was whether the fight occurred immediately or sometime after it was reported to male family members or boyfriends who were not present at the time of the insult.[18]

The dynamic in which an insult progresses to a physical fight starts with a statement or physical gesture that is intended to be, or is taken as, an affront to the person's positive definition of self. This statement or gesture elicits negative emotions about its content or its delivery or both. However, what is required for the aggrieved individual to act aggressively toward the person believed to be responsible for the social slight is a general change in emotions from disgust, to resentment, to ultimately hate.[19]

The aggression generally began when the slighted person responded with a retaliatory insult, threw an object at his or her perceived attacker, threatened the attacker verbally, moved toward the attacker, or overtly assaulted the attacker. A typical example of this occurred at Oakland's Miwok High School. A Mexican American student was walking home from school when, about a block away from the school, he walked by two African American students who were standing next to a mailbox on the corner. One of the African American students was using his cell phone while the other was just watching people. When the Mexican American student walked by, the African American student said, "What's up?" The Mexican American student simply kept his head down and continued walking. At this the African American student said, "What's the matter? Are you just dumb like an overcooked bean [*bean* being a derogatory reference to Mexican Americans]?"[20] The Mexican American student looked at the African American but kept walking, whereupon the African American student said, "I guess you're just dumb as a shoe." Then, as he continued to walk the Mexican American student looked back and spit at the African American, who responded by saying, "Just keep walking or I'll smash you into a refried bean." At this point, the Mexican American stopped, turned, and walked back toward the African American. The African American's companion was now aware that something might happen and stopped talking on the phone to watch his friend start walking to confront the Mexican American. When they got close, the Mexican American student kicked the African American student in the leg and started to swing, and the fight was on. It lasted for five minutes until the Oakland police came to break it up.[21]

The Role of Psychological Disturbances

The role of psychological disturbances experienced by young people are an important cause for the start of violent incidents between individuals from different ethnic backgrounds. Young students, particularly from poor families, often experience social problems at home. These problems may arise from a variety of sources: having only one or no parental figure in the home; parental marital conflict; feelings of moral violation or emasculation coming from interactions with family members, such as verbal, physical, or sexual abuse; physical deprivations like a lack of sleep or balanced diet; neighborhood interactions with peers who instill feelings of inadequacy, shame, and stigmatization; or problems originating at school related to instructional insults from teachers or the prohibition from participating in valued extracurricular activities.[22]

Over time, for some students these emotional issues become a preoccupation that influences their moods and reactions to others. In most cases in the present study, these individuals were an element of the student body responsible for initiating physical aggression toward other students, and particularly students from other ethnic backgrounds, but they were not the main or only element. Students with these problems exhibited symptoms that seemed extremely odd: excessive quietness, withdrawal to the point of disengagement from educational activities, agitation. In many cases, these symptoms were so marked that teachers reported them to campus authorities in the hope that the administration would provide professional intervention to assist these students.

Other students with disturbances were unrecognized by school authorities. Although their teachers were not aware of the internal conflicts occurring within these students, they would present a passive-aggressive asocial personality that their peers described as a bizarre combination of social withdrawal and verbal expressions of extreme positions on moral subjects.

The dynamic of ethnic violence associated with a psychological disturbance occurred when the person with a disorder identified a member of the opposing ethnic group as the reason for his or her feelings of discontent and attacked that person, or found a person from the other ethnic group who was marginal to the conflict but appeared to be vulnerable to attack and proceeded to attack him or her.[23] Often these students say something after this pointless attack indicating that this action gave them relief from some distressing inner conflict, such as "Now that that's over I feel better and I'll be on my way," "This felt so so good," or "Hey, just letting go some."

Regardless of the reason for these attacks, most of which were unrelated to the present ethnic conflict occurring in the schools and neighborhoods, members of both groups interpreted them as ethnic violence and not simply as related to individual issues. An example involved Anthony, an African American student at Los Angeles's Chumash High School who was with a group of four students talking about how a cat had made one of the girls feel uneasy. He said, "I felt that way too, but after I burned a cat alive in a brown paper bag I didn't have those feelings anymore." His fellow students just looked over at him and one girl said, "Sick! That is really sick!" whereupon he simply looked away and shrugged his shoulders, and the conversation continued.[24] Later, Anthony attacked a Mexican American student on the way to school, repeatedly hitting him on the head and causing significant injury. He was identified by a witness and was placed on probation. Evidence emerged that Anthony had endured severe physical abuse from his step-father, had been placed in foster care by Child Protective Services, and presented consistent symptoms of anger management problems to the school authorities. Three months after the incident that led to his pro-bation, Anthony was involved in a group fight in which he used a rock to hit one of the Mexican student combatants who was lying on the ground. The blow caused significant bleeding. He stopped only after he was interrupted by police sirens and ran away. His involvement in this incident was never brought to the attention of authorities, but in an incident two months later he was identified as one of a group of African Americans brawling with a group of Mexicans; and in that fight he had used a metal rod to attack other students. As a result of this incident he was expelled from school.[25] What is important about this example is that each event was talked about in the school among both Mexican and African American students as a "black-Mexican incident."

The Progressive Dynamic of Fights

Once a fight began, three emotions kept it going at an intense level. First, satisfaction from delivering blows to the opposing combatants seemed to provide an incentive to continue; the more these blows found their mark, the greater the expression of satisfaction. Such observations were consistent with research suggesting that the experiential deliver-ance of pain to another person can be cathartic by releasing built-up feelings ranging from anger to rage. This can be seen, as discussed above, when individuals with psychological disorders strike others and talk to them or an audience about these blows "evening the score" for the recipient's misdeeds.[26]

The second emotion was often observed among the African and Irish American students who blamed the other group for their personal as well as their group's misfortune. An example for each involved Henry, an Irish American attending Boston's Shawmut High School, and Aaron, an African American attending Los Angeles's Tongva High School.

Henry: Do you like this [blow to face], you nigger?! So you want to take our schools and leave us with shit like yours?! . . . This [a blow to the head] is for doing them rich bastard Prods' [reference to White Anglo-Saxon Protestants] job of trying to keep us poor and with nothing![27]

Aaron: You fuckin' little brown slime! Tell your fucking dad this [blows to the face and stomach] is what taking our jobs gets him—-a messed-up face for his kid . . . .So this [blows to the face] is for leaving us with no jobs, fucker![28]

It is important to mention that aggression toward members of another ethnic group to release built-up frustrations with one's present predicament was not observed among the Mexican American students for two reasons. First, many of these students were immigrants themselves or children of immigrants, and they were excited about a better future and not disappointed and frustrated. Second, those Mexicans who were disappointed, frustrated, and worried about the future would have blamed the recent immigrants from their own ethnic group for their present perceived misfortune. However, because they were in conflict with African Americans who blamed the Mexican ethnic group for their misfortune, their present situation did not lend itself to expressing their frustration with Mexican nationals.[29]

A third emotion that kept fights going was irritation with one's opponent for not fully engaging in the fight. During the exchange of blows, the more aggressive combatant interpreted the other's reluctance as a sign of fear and personal weakness, which he found so revolting that he became more aggressive to punish it. An example of this can be seen in the behavior of Jayden, an African American student at Oakland's Miwok High School. Jayden was in a fight with a Mexican American student who seemed scared, offering little resistance to Jayden's blows to his body. Jayden kept baiting him to fight back by calling him a "fucking coward" and a "worthless piece of shit." The more he kept shouting things like "I fucking hate people like you who are so gutless; don't you have any self-respect?" the more the Mexican student remained passive, and the more aggressive Jayden became in delivering blows to the Mexican's body. Even as the Mexican student began to bleed from the corner of his eye, Jayden kept hitting him harder.[30] Jayden finally stopped and ran off when he heard police sirens.[31] The police treated the Mexican student and took a statement from him regarding the incident, but Jayden was never identified.

To summarize, in the beginning stage of the second phase of ethnic violence in each of the schools the confrontations were between individuals from the different groups. Yet each of the encounters was interpreted by participants, witnesses, and those who heard about it second- or thirdhand not as a dispute between individuals but as part of the ongoing conflict between the two dominant ethnic groups. In the second stage of the second phase, individuals working as makeshift "teams" would confront and fight members of the opposing group in a show of force and resolve, creating a form of mutual deterrence.

GROUP VIOLENCE

The next phase of ethnic violence (phase 3 in figure 4.1) involved group action. The previous discussions focused on the factors initiating violence between individuals from different ethnic groups and the consequences of these encounters. Generally, ethnic violence involving a few individuals progresses to include ever larger numbers.[32] If there is one group behavior in schools that causes significant concern for parents, school professionals, and the general population, it is the form of ethnic violence that has been termed "a riot." For the purposes of this study, a riot will be defined as an unrestrained public disturbance involving a large number of individuals acting en masse in physically attacking objects and people and/or taking material items, fully aware that their behavior is illegal in one or more ways. This group action is dominated by a desire to target specific objects (human and material) for the purpose of expressing dissatisfaction, dislike, or disdain and involves some form of aggression leading to injury and destruction. In the present study, riots involving students did not occur often, nor do they in general, but when they do they cause significant property damage, bodily injuries, and disruption to educational schedules, all of which attract the attention of school officials, parents, the media, and the general public. Thus riots are unnerving events, in part because they are somewhat rare, along with the fact that they involve many people and destroy a significant amount of public property. Because school officials are particularly sensitive to the occurrence of riots, primarily out of a concern for protecting students from injury and avoiding the bad press that failure to do so would generate, a heightened vigilance often occurs for behavior signaling a riot, producing a tendency to misidentify other forms of collective behavior as riots. However, a variety of group actions generally associated with riots actually have diverse and distinct behavioral patterns. Collective violence generally proceeds through a series of stages, each with its own set of initiators and accelerators, suggesting the need to reconceptualize collective violence in general to better understand both who participates and the dynamic sequences that take place.

In the natural progression of collective forms of violence in high schools, a confrontation between two individuals was followed by a fight between them; then the fight was joined by other individuals from the ethnic groups of the combatants in a show of solidarity against the aggression of members from the opposing ethnic group. Thus these conflicts not only involved larger numbers of individuals but switched the participants' focus from an individual grievance to a group grievance. The evolution from individual acts of violence to group violence established a social psychological condition in which nearly every student felt that it was possible to be attacked by a group and that this could happen at any time. This generalized anxiety permeated each school's campus; individuals were constantly vigilant for potential outbreaks of violence that could draft them into being a combatant regardless of whether they were, or wanted to be, involved in fighting. It also led to the belief that acting in concert with one's group was a necessary requirement to protect oneself. Ultimately a social pressure cooker environment developed in which individual acts and their justifications were no longer individually focused (How should I act as an individual in this situation?) but group focused (I must follow what I understand the group to be doing).[33]

The circulation of "rumors" stimulated "ethnic collective violence" (not the "individual ethnic violence" discussed previously) within the schools.[34] Rumors are verbal depictions of past, present, and future events that may or may not have any evidence to support them. Rumors' "truth" or "validity" has no necessary connection to their power to influence behavior. Rumors are empowered by their ability to summon in the imagination of their audience the conviction that some part of what they report is possible. In the schools in this study that were experiencing ethnic violence, rumors helped create a situation where members of one or more groups were put on alert that conflict was or could be imminent. Lorenzo, a Mexican American student attending Oakland's Miwok High School, described this atmosphere of vigilance:

> Oh man, it is crazy around here. You never know if there is going to be a fight right next to you or down the hall or at lunch or wherever. You know it's going to happen, just don't know when. You just feel like you got to be looking all the time, and let me tell you, it ain't no fun.[35]

The Stages of Collective Violence in the Schools

Within each school's atmosphere of heightened anxiety, the first stage of collective violence (figure 4.1, P3, S1) started when a rumor that a student of a particular ethnic group was being attacked stimulated students to assemble as ad hoc combatants and rush to where the conflict was reportedly occurring. After arriving, either they would see that a fight was indeed happening and they would immediately join in, or their mere arrival caused members of the rival group to think they were going to be attacked and immediately to attack the new arrivals. In both cases there was a fight that involved groups in what would be generally described as a "brawl."[36] (See table 4.1 for a description of each type of violence.)

An example comes from Los Angeles's Chumash High School. A group of Mexican students heard that a group of African Americans was attacking two Mexican students, and this galvanized them to run to the site. When they arrived, there was no fight to be seen, but when the fifteen or so African Americans who were on the site saw a large group of nine Mexican students coming toward them, they immediately charged the arriving group. Pairs of combatants swung and kicked at one another in an uncontrolled manner. Some of the students used weapons such as rulers, compasses, combs, sticks, and clothing (curled and used as whips); and injuries did occur, although none life-threatening. This particular brawl lasted for eight minutes before the school police and security guards arrived and arrested all the participants.[37] (See figure 4.2 for a summary of the average durations of each form of violent encounter.)

After becoming involved in the initial "brawl," students from both sides found themselves in a dilemma. Should they become involved in future brawls? The ones who decided that they would offered two reasons for doing so. Some said that they felt that if they did not many of their coethnics would view them as cowards and would express public contempt for them. Others feared that if they did not support their coethnics they could not expect to be protected from attacks. Two typical comments came from Reginio and Bartley. Reginio was a Mexican American attending Oakland's Kaiser High School:

> You got to fight when the blacks is attacking anyone of us because if you don't you just be considered a coward, and when that gets around no one is going to respect you. You might as well be dead because everyone, and I mean even the girls, won't have anything to do with you.[38]

Bartley was an Irish American attending Boston's Shawmut High School:

> Hey, when them five blacks came running I just turned with the other guys and started to get it on. I don't really like that stuff 'cause I'm small and can't really fight that good, but if I don't do it then when the blacks jump me some time nobody will be there for me. So there ain't much choice but to fight whenever one of us is fighting the blacks.[39]

Another factor that influenced students to become involved in brawls had to do with feeling vulnerable to attack simply because they were a member of one of the ethnic groups involved in the conflict. For example, when a group of students were engaged in a brawl there was no time to determine if someone close to the fighting was a combatant, simply a passerby, or a spectator. Thus fear of being attacked as a legitimate target overtook some individuals to such an extent that they simply decided to join in and start fighting. The comments of Orton and Lucas were typical. Orton was an African American attending Boston's Shawmut High School. Immediately after school was dismissed and the students were leaving through the front door, a fight broke out. He was in the fight and was taken into custody by the police for participation. After he returned to school he said:

> When that big fight started at the front door after school I just started to fight when one of the Irish guys came at me. I ain't really going to say I like fighting, but I might as well because all them white guys just see a black dude and attack. So the best way to defend yourself is that when a fight starts, just start attacking; and if it happens again, I'll do it again.[40]

A similar representative situation involved Lucas, a Mexican American attending Los Angeles's Tongva High School. He became part of a fight that started between three African Americans and three Mexican Americans after someone spilled a soda over the meal that one of the combatants was eating. Within two minutes the fighting had come to involve nine additional combatants who aggressively went to aid their coethnics. This brawl lasted seven minutes and was broken up by school police and security guards. While in the assistant principal's office Lucas said:

> I was like fighting this dude and he fell down, so I looked to see who was around to hit and started to hit a guy that was a couple of feet from me. Everything was wild and it was like crazy, but not scary because nobody had guns and stuff like that, so I kind of thought it was sort of fun too. . . . Yeah, at first I was like concerned 'cause the *mayates* [pejorative for African Amer-

icans] were bigger than us, but then as we got going it was whatever, and you was just throwing punches and stuff.[41]

Reginio, Bartley, Orton, and Lucas all became involved in subsequent brawls. Afterwards each explained that he did so because either he felt a responsibility to aid a coethnic in trouble, or he sensed that he might be mistaken for a combatant and be attacked by those in the brawl anyway. In addition, and equally important, direct participation in brawls was generally dominated by male students, but female students did participate. During fights involving male students one would observe girls intervening to aid a male (or another female) coethnic and in the process becoming physically entangled in the fight, whereupon they would begin swinging and screaming. This generally intensified the fight between the boys as the screams were taken as a sign that one or more of their female coethnics was being hurt by their adversaries and needed additional help. A typical example involved a fight in the courtyard at Oakland's Kaiser High School. It began when an African American accidentally bumped into a Mexican American, causing him to drop his bag of Frito Red Hots on the ground. Instead of apologizing for the mistake, the African American said nothing. The Mexican American understood this as the African American's deliberate move to entertain his friends, who were all laughing at what had just happened. The Mexican American said, "You think I'm some kind of fucking clown to be laughed at?" and then attacked the African American. A few seconds after the fight began, Elena, a Mexican American student, tried to get in between the two combatants. She was trying to support her coethnic, who was outnumbered by a group of African American boys. She was restrained by two of the African American boys who were watching the fight. Immediately after they touched her she began to scream, "Take your hands off me, don't touch me!" Within two minutes eight more Mexican Americans had arrived on the scene and started to fight with the African Americans, who had up until then been simply watching the fight. Although the female Mexican American received a bloody nose and a swollen eye, she was not seriously injured. Only one of the Mexican American male combatants had an injury, a cut to the corner of his eye that did not require medical attention. Of the African American combatants, two received minor injuries (a cut lip, a bleeding ear from being scratched), and a third got a severely bruised ankle from having been kicked. After the fight was broken up by school police, the Mexican American girl told the school dean, "The blacks were trying to mess up one of us and I'm not going to let that happen, so I tried to stop it, and I'll do it again!"[42]

Another type of collective violence that occurred in schools had to do with quasi-organized "vigilante" groups roaming the campus and the neighborhood looking for conflict. When these groups heard that a conflict was occurring, they rushed to the site and immediately became engaged in aggressive fighting. Conflicts involving these types of groups often appeared to be simply "ad hoc" brawls like the ones described above. However, the engagement of these groups in conflict would not have satisfied the criteria established for confrontations involving ad hoc groups. One, and possibly more, of the groups who participated in these fights did not, as an ad hoc group would have, react spontaneously as individuals to aid a coethnic they thought was being beaten by members of the rival group. Rather, they reacted as part of an existing organized vigilante group for the express purpose of retaliating against rivals who had initiated violence toward members of their ethnic group.[43] Although defensive in public ideology, they would use offensive aggression in their efforts to protect members of their ethnic group, and while they did engage in "ganging behavior" they were not part of the formal youth gangs in the neighborhoods, nor would they become gangs.[44]

In the case involving Elena mentioned above, minutes after the word spread that there was a fight, a group of eight Mexican Americans, a vigilante-type group established to protect other Mexican American students, ran to the location of the fight. When they arrived at the site they immediately split up and started to physically fight members of the African American group, who were mostly, with the exception of the two trying to restrain Elena, merely watching the fight. This group fight was definitely a brawl, since a brawl is defined by its chaotic nature: group members do not plan coordination of tactics, and individuals fight with little if any information about, or regard for, whether the specific individual they are fighting harmed members of their ethnic group.

When the brawl is in progress, one can observe a student fighting another student and then switching and fighting yet another. Although the brawl is chaotic, the underlying pattern of this chaos creates a structured encounter, but not one that resembles a coordinated attack of any kind. Take the comments of Felipe, a Mexican American attending Oakland's Kaiser High School:

> I just was coming from my gym class with a group of guys who hang together to help other Mexicans from getting beat up by the blacks, and someone says there's a fight at the lunch line, so when we get there and there's about fifteen

guys fighting, and I told my friends "Now's the time to help" and so we all just ran into where they were fighting. I started to hit one black guy in the back of the head, then I turned and hit another black guy who just hit me in the side of the head. Everyone who was fighting was hitting whoever was in the other group that was closest until the police came, and now we're waiting for what they're [the police] goin' to do next.[45]

In these "vigilante-type" encounters gang members were involved but were almost exclusively acting as individuals and not as part of their formal gang organization(s). This was supported not only by my direct observations but by circulating rumors, and later by gang members' own admissions that they were just acting to help the vigilante group that had formed for retribution purposes.

FROM BRAWLS TO RIOTS

Immediately after a period of numerous brawls, a second stage of collective violence began (figure 4.1, P3, S2). This stage is best characterized as riot behavior. During the three years of research there were not many riots, but when they did occur they caused considerable property damage, injured students, sometimes seriously, and resulted in the loss of a substantial amount of instructional time. Three types of riot behaviors were observed. The first, represented in table 4.1 as "riot type 1: protest oriented," involved individuals rioting out of frustration with a current situation that created a sense of injustice.[46] In this situation, members of the incumbent group were unhappy with a rapid influx of students from a new and different ethnic group and sensed that no one was helping them to confront the social change that these students were bringing to their environment. Take two very typical examples of this perception, one expressed by Katy, an Irish American student at Boston's Shawmut High School, and the other expressed twenty-six years later by Jade, an African American attending Los Angeles's Chumash High School.

> *Katy:* They just decided to send the niggers to us 'cause they didn't want them to screw up their life. Them rich fuckers don't care about us whites, they think we're trash, but we had enough of their bullshit, and so we ain't taking them niggers in our school and changing everything. We're going to stop school the way they want it and they better not try to stop us or they're going to get hurt![47]

> *Jade:* Them fucking Mexicans keep coming and coming; and they're changing everything in the school just by just [*sic*] being here! Ain't nobody helping us keep what we had and liked, so we got to send a message that we ain't fucking putting up with this shit! We going to walk out, and if

they [school authorities] try to stop us, they're going to see we mean business. So they better look out if they get involved.[48]

Protest-Oriented Riots

Now, let us turn to the actual behavior of the students during what I have labeled type 1 or "protest-oriented" riots. In the case involving Los Angeles's Chumash High School, the African American students decided on a protest "walkout" from school at the predetermined time of 1:30 p.m. As that time approached and they began to leave their classrooms and move toward the school exits, some school authorities (mainly teachers) who did not know about or want to heed prior warnings tried to prevent the students from leaving their classrooms. The students reacted by aggressively pushing them out of their way and attacking a number of physical objects in the school to show their displeasure with the general situation in the school and the administration's management of it. They broke windows, turned over chairs and desks, and destroyed instructional equipment (video apparatuses and screens, computers, books). Some of the teachers were punched and pushed to the ground. Thus, out of a calm mood of protest there emerged a riot caused by school authorities disrupting the protest's established social order and resulting in the student protesters' undisciplined reactions toward all the symbols of school authority that they viewed as treating them unjustly.

Bryce, an African American attending Los Angeles's Tongva High School, provides an example of this motivation. While engaged in a riot at that school he said to one of his friends running next to him, "Hey, we'll show the motherfuckers [school authorities] that we ain't putting up with them helping them wetbacks [Mexicans] anymore!" Within a half minute of saying this they both picked up chairs and threw them through a window, then kicked over a number of computer monitors in a classroom they entered. These protest riots lasted on average about fifty minutes before law enforcement was able to restore order.[49] There are times when these events are reported in the newspapers, but most often they are not. I will discuss why later.

Entertainment-Oriented Riots

The second type of riot that I have labeled "entertainment oriented." This kind of riot began the same way as the type 1 "protest-oriented riot." A walkout was planned for a certain time. At that time students started to leave their classrooms to exit the school. As this was occurring, one or more of the students began to destroy and steal objects merely because it was against the law and they found pleasure in violating a prohibition. The comments of Cooper, an Irish American attending Boston's Shawmut High School, exemplify this:

> I threw that fucking chair through that class window that everyone likes and you saw how it just smashed it all to smithereens. Let's do this again at this window 'cause this is fun and we ain't going to be able to do this all the time with the fucking police everywhere.[50]

The selection of targets was based on the students' assessment of the object's value to authorities and how convenient it was to being taken or destroyed. What was most clearly observed about students' participation was their joy and excitement in behaving in normally unacceptable and illegal ways. For example, while the riot was occurring there was steady chatter among the participants and a constant display of amusement in marauding through the building(s) and throwing objects into windows, turning desks upside down, knocking computer screens and typewriters off tables, plugging up toilets so that they would flood floors, turning over vending machines, and stealing school supplies from the classrooms. The students generally expressed their pleasure by smiling, laughing, and excitingly pointing to additional objects that they wanted to attack.[51]

When students are rioting like this, one finds that ethnic antagonisms have been quasi-suspended because members of each group are having fun. An example of this occurred at Oakland's Kaiser High School when African American students planned a protest walkout to begin immediately after lunch because they believed Mexican students were receiving more educational assistance in the classroom than they were. On schedule, when the first period following lunch bell rang indicating that instruction was to begin, the African Americans began to leave their classrooms and head for the exits. As they were moving, someone hit the fire alarm and everyone started to run. As they ran, a large number of students started to throw things at the lights and windows. With the growing noise and commotion, the Mexican students got up and started to leave the classroom as well. As they were leaving, they joined African Americans and began to throw things and tip garbage containers upside down. Not only was there no fighting between the Mexican and African American students, but there was joint laughter and playfulness in their joint destructive behavior.

Animosity-Oriented Riots

Probably the most ominous type of riot behavior, which I have labeled type 3 or "animosity oriented." It involves elements of what Donald L. Horowitz has called the "deadly ethnic riot." Riot participants target individuals from a rival ethnic group for the express purpose of injuring them.[52] There was never a time in the schools of the present study that a riot completely fit Horowitz's description, partly because the riots that I observed in schools never involved the great numbers of people that he described for the Indian riots he analyzed, nor was the availability of lethal weapons of the same magnitude. However, there were times when the riots I observed exhibited some of the characteristics that Horowitz described.

The behavior most resembling that of the "deadly ethnic riot" was the targeting of individuals from the opposing ethnic group with the intent to administer bodily harm. Although there was never a fatality, a significant number of students were severely injured as a result of being attacked by members of the opposing group. It was not possible to determine whether there was any intent to actually kill the people attacked, but there was evidence that individuals did look for students from the rival ethnic group for the sole purpose of administering harm. Once the riot started, packs of students, generally five to fifteen in number, immediately identified students from the rival group and aggressively attacked them. Not only did group members emphasize to each other that they should stay together and not individually veer off alone, but someone in the group would identify one or more targets and then summon everyone to collectively attack them. After attacking the target, and in some cases beating the individual severely, they would immediately set out to look for another target and attack that individual(s). These marauding groups involved gang members but generally included more nongang members. As in the preceding phases of school violence, those who were members of a gang were acting as individuals and not as part of their gang's formal organization.

Another difference between the riots in the schools that I observed and the riots that Horowitz described was that in my sample there was little evidence suggesting that the individuals who were attacked had been chosen before the riot started, or that the riots had been initiated for the primary purpose of attacking specific individuals.[53] Rather, in the highly tense atmosphere among the students in which each group identified the other as the reason for bad relations, once a dispute occurred and a fight broke out, a general riot began with marauding groups attacking others from the rival ethnicity. The pattern within this type of riot situation involved a combination of groups. First, a large number of students who were acting as individuals simply trying to exit the school for the purpose of seeking safety were intermixed with other groups of students who had known each other before the riot and had banded together to retaliate against individuals from the rival ethnicity.[54] The intermixing of students with different motives for participating in the riot provided those who were intent on administering harm a considerable amount of protection from detection. As a result, the students who wanted to inflict injury were provided the perfect environment to continue in that pursuit.

In describing their motives, the participants of the marauding packs were remarkably consistent in what they said before, during, and after they attacked. They generally understood their actions as retaliation for an injustice perpetrated on their group by members of the rival group. The injustice could have occurred the same day or sometime in the past. Either way, it had to be brought into the ongoing situation.

When ethnic conflict in the schools had been present for months, any single event that involved a perceived injustice was treated as though it were part of an ongoing pattern of attack that required retaliation for moral, personal identity, and physical self-protection purposes.[55] An example of this occurred at Los Angeles's Chumash High School when African American students began to leave their classrooms in a prearranged "walkout" to protest school authorities' punishment of three African American students for attacking two Mexican American students. As the "walkout" was starting, Trey and Kurt brought together ten other African American male students for the purpose of attacking Mexican American male students in retaliation for an incident that had occurred two weeks earlier when Mexican American students had attacked two African Americans on their way home.[56] The group of twelve African Americans began by randomly attacking the very first group of male Mexican Americans that they encountered. After hitting and kicking their targets for four minutes, Trey or Kurt hollered out, "Let's go get some more," and the group stopped fighting and moved to a new location where they attacked a new group of Mexican Americans. These attacks initiated a panic among the majority of Mexican Americans, who started to run in an unorganized manner toward the exits of the school. However, various small groups of six to twelve Mexican Americans began to randomly attack African American males in retaliation. The result of this situation was a general riot on campus, with numerous police units called in to restore order. When the riot ceased and calm was restored, Trey and Kurt, as well as members of the various Mexican American groups that were involved in the violence, all voiced moral indignation for having been victims, as well as moral righteousness for striking back.[57] The comments of Trey, an African American, and Max, a Mexican American, express this rationale.

> *Trey:* Okay, we jumped a number of them Mexes and hurt them 'cause they went and did the same to two brothers [African Americans] a couple of weeks ago; and we ain't going to let that shit go. They ain't goin' to fucking come here and think they own the school and think they can mess with us. We fucking own this school, and we going to punish them until they know that.[58]

> *Max:* They been kicking our asses for months and we fucking ain't taking it anymore! We going to kick some ass ourselves, 'cause them blacks is just fucking rotten assholes! Them worthless fuckers will know we're in this school to stay and we ain't afraid of them.[59]

Although the justifications used for having engaged in violence were generally predicated on an event interpreted as an inexcusable act against a coethnic(s), the event itself might have occurred either sometime in the past, or immediately before the melee. As it turned out, the event that Trey and Kurt used during the "walkout" to recruit the ten African American male students for attacks on Mexican Americans was found to have no evidentiary basis. However, because emotions were heightened during the "walkout," accurate rumors were not required for the individuals to attack.

Female Participants in the Riots

Most examples of violence to this point involved male students, and they indeed participated far more often in violence than did female students. Nonetheless, there were riot situations during which female students also engaged in violence. In the overwhelming majority of cases that I observed, it was young women from the incumbent majority ethnic group who were most apt to form a group and attack rival young women—for example, Irish American girls in Boston attacked African American girls, and African American girls in Los Angeles and Oakland attacked Mexican American girls. The pattern of engagement in all the schools during these riot situations started with a fight. This was followed by the word spreading that newcomer girls had been attacked by girls from the incumbent group, which in turn led the girls from the newcomer group to band together as they tried to move to a safe place. However, as they attempted to do so they were sometimes confronted by girls from the incumbent group, and in these situations the girls from the newcomer group who were feeling threatened unhesitatingly lashed out by punching and kicking any of the girls who appeared to them to be blocking their movement to a safe place.

A representative example of this occurred at Los Angeles' Tongva High School when a riot broke out and rumors spread that male and female Mexican Americans were being attacked by male and female African Americans. In response, a group of Mexican American girls assembled to protect themselves from what they feared would be an attack by African American students. As they moved from the second floor to the first floor in an effort to exit the school and avoid being harmed, a group of African American girls came up the stairs and one of them said, "There's a group." As the Mexican Americans proceeded toward the stairs, another African American girl said, "Where you in a hurry to?" This appears to have been taken by the Mexican Americans as a threat, with the result that one of the Mexican Americans, a straight "A" student with no record of trouble for any reason during her three years of high school, answered, "Fuck you, bitch!" and started swinging at one of the African Americans. Both groups of young women immediately began to swing, kick, and scream at each other. One of the African American girls had a large comb that she swung like a knife. It ripped the blouse sleeve of a Mexican American girl, cutting her on the forearm. As the melee continued, an African American girl used her purse to hit one of the Mexican American girls in the face, and one of the Mexican American girls used a small umbrella that she carried in her purse to strike an African American girl in the head while another Mexican American girl took one of the straight pins that she was using to hold her hair in place and jabbed an African American girl in the upper arm, producing bleeding. After this encounter ended, both sets of girls morally justified their actions by claiming they were the victims, their opponents were the victimizers, and they had the right to defend themselves. The comments of Litia, a Mexican American attending Los Angeles' Tongva High School whom I observed participating in the incident, are representative:

> I don't really get involved in fighting or stuff like that ever, but I had to this time because they [the African American girls who had confronted the group she was with] would have hurt us, and all we wanted to do was just leave the

school. . . . No, I didn't want to hurt them, I just wanted to swing at them so we could get out. They would have hurt us. I know it, so if they do that again I'll use whatever I got to stop them 'cause they are mean![60]

Litia's actual behavior during the fight was a little different from what she told the counselor. She had indeed swung at the African American girls as she said, but what she did not say was that she had removed a makeup mirror from her purse, broken it to make a sharp instrument, and swung it to keep the African American girls away. With one of her swings, she scraped one of the African American girls with the broken mirror. The cut caused some bleeding on the forearm, whereupon the African American girl withdrew.[61]

FROM RIOT TO STAMPEDE

The third stage of collective violence (figure 4.1, P3, S3) follows the first two and is best understood as a human form of stampede (see table 4.1 for a description). It appeared after the first two stages in the latter part of the second semester precisely because it was a reaction to the conditions established by the first two (brawls and riots). The first two phases of violence produced accumulated anxiety in the student body, making everyone very wary of being in constant danger. Although this was a reasonable and practical response, it carried with it a psychological predisposition to be hyperreactive to any action in the school that would resemble a brawl or riot. This hyperreactivity was focused on being ready to move quickly to a safe space away from physical harm. In the minds of the vast majority of students from the schools studied, that meant leaving the school's formal campus. An example of this thinking can be seen in the comments of Alfredo, a Mexican American attending Oakland's Kaiser High School:

> Well yeah, if we see students get in a fight, we know that it ain't going to be just between them. It's going to spread, and there's going to be a whole lot of people getting mixed up in it. So most of us just try to get as far away from it as we can, 'cause there's going to be a riot for sure, and the only thing to do is get out of the school, 'cause when it happens a lot people will get hurt.[62]

This form of collective behavior became a mass exit from the campus that I categorized a "stampede" and defined as a frenzied movement of a large number of individuals from one location to another for the primary purpose of achieving a greater degree of safety from physical or legal harm. During these occasions students in the school moved quickly en masse toward the formal exits, picking up more students in the process and becoming more limited in behavioral-direction options. That is, confined by the walls of the school's corridors, the limited staircases from one level to another, and the campus's entry and exit sites, students were structurally forced to follow in the direction that the students in the front decided to take. Thus, if the students in the front chose to turn right, the entire body was forced to follow because of the building's physical structure (i.e., corridor walls) and the group's density. Further, when the group's movement en masse was outside the school building in areas such as the outside court where lunch was taken, then the entire group's movement followed those who started to move first because they knew exit sites were limited. Later, after the stampede was over, students said they followed those in front because they were preoccupied with getting out of the school quickly and thought that the students at the front would naturally choose the most expedient direction for exiting the campus fast. An example of this thinking comes from Ivan, a Mexican American attending Los Angeles's Chumash High School:

> When it [the stampede] first started, everyone just got out of their seats and started to walk fast down the hall. But when everyone was doing it, the halls just filled up and we all just kept walking until we heard a big, big bang, kind of like an explosion, maybe not an explosion, but something really loud that scared everyone into running, and as we were running people just followed who was in front, 'cause they could see the best and they were obviously going to pick the quickest way out of school.[63]

Denise was an African American attending Boston's Paul Revere High School:

> I was just opening my locker between classes and I heard all the noise and there was shots fired and we all just started to run for the school exits. It was crazy with everyone, whites and us, all just racing for the door. We were all packed against the walls [of the corridor] like sardines and we just followed whoever's in front. Me and my friends was kinda in the middle, and we just figured that we would follow the people in front 'cause they could see where the closest exit was.[64]

As I previously mentioned, these stampedes occur because students want to avoid physical harm as well as possible legal jeopardy. When students heard of an altercation, or heard a noise that sounded like gunshots, some of them moved quickly to avoid being injured. Others were concerned about avoiding the legal trouble they might incur if they were caught up in any altercation involving students who were breaking the law or who had previously participated in violence. This concern can be seen in the comments of Omar, a fifteen-year-old African American student from Oakland's Kaiser High School:

> If trouble breaks out and you're where it is with a number of dudes that always get into trouble with the law, you get the hell out of there because if the police get there and they see guys that is in trouble a lot, they just arrest everyone that's close to these guys and then try to see who did the shit. I don't get in trouble, so I run like hell to get out of wherever these guys are 'cause they're trouble if the police arrest you, then you got to pay money for a lawyer and shit. Then your lawyer could be no good and you go to jail for something you didn't have nothin' to do with. It can be that fucked up![65]

In sum, within the schools of the present study, stampedes had their origins in individual students' joint reactions to a fight, brawl, rumor, or noise indicating to them the presence of danger, and their attempt to remove themselves to safety. However, once the stampede began the collective movement of students assumed a momentum that produced both physical damage to the campus and injuries to some students involved. The behaviors of individuals in these stampedes differed from those found in the various riots in that they lacked any instrumental intentionality, and thus any bodily and physical damage that occurred was unintended.[66]

PATTERNS IN COLLECTIVE VIOLENCE'S PROGRESSION

In the present study violence proceeded in discrete phases and followed a progressive pattern over the school year, with different types becoming prominent at different times (see figures 5.1, 5.2, and 5.3; the same data are presented in tabular form in the Methodological Appendix). The general pattern in school violence began with conflict between two individuals from different ethnic backgrounds and widened when individuals not involved in the initial conflict intervened to aid a coethnic who was being dominated by a member of the rival ethnic group. I labeled these groups "ad hoc groups" because the students intervened as individuals, and the group that they formed during a particular fight was temporary.

The appearance of ad hoc groups in the ethnic conflict of the schools in this study acted as the intermediary phase connecting individual-level to collective-level violence. Thus the evolution of collective violence in the schools began at the elementary level of individuals forming "ad hoc groups" to manage a particular situation, and extended to the forming

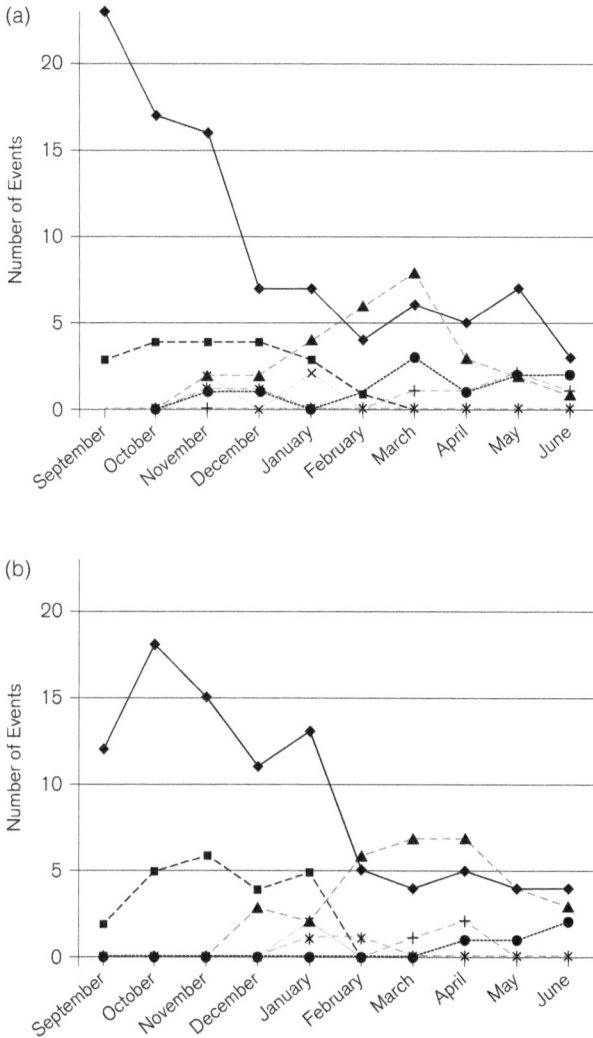

FIGURE 5.1a–c *(continued on page 134)*. Violent episodes over
school year 1. (a) Boston schools, 1974–75. (b) Los Angeles
schools, 2000–2001. (c) Oakland schools, 2000–2001. These
numbers come from my field notes. Obviously I could not be in
every place that the events occurred, so the numbers of events
tabulated are not the total numbers but only those that I observed
and recorded—except in the case of riots and stampedes, where
the data from my field notes has been supplemented by reports
from school authorities that such events occurred while I was not
present. Two administrators, two teachers, two students, and two
security guards were given the definitions for a stampede and for
each type of riot and then were asked to assign the event for
which I was not present to one of the categories. The agreement
was between 87.5 percent (seven of eight were in agreement) and
100 percent (eight of eight were in agreement).

(c)

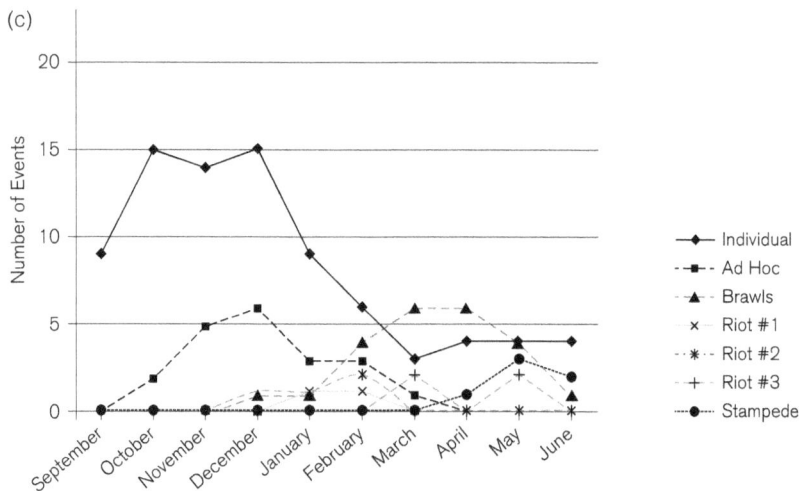

FIGURE 5.1a–c *(continued)*

of permanent groups for the primary purpose of inflicting harm on members of the other group. Sometimes these permanent groups acted in an unorganized way such as a "brawl," and this phase created the predispositions required for increased numbers of individuals to become involved in violent behavior. The most common form of collective violence to emerge from participation in brawls was the riot. Participation in this type of violent action was characterized by three progressive forms. The first was rioting to protest perceived injustices toward one's ethnic group, the second focused on the opportunity to be entertained and have fun, and the third focused on inflicting physical retribution on members of the rival group(s) seen as the perpetrators of their ethnic group's woes.

This progression in types of violence was also associated with specific time periods in the official school instructional calendar (see figures 5.1 and 5.2). The pattern was the movement from individual-level violence at the start of the school year, to "ad hoc group" violence, to collective brawl-type violence toward the end of the first semester of school (December). Then with the start of the second semester, in January, the riot form of collective violence began: first type 1 "protest-oriented" rioting, then type 2 "entertainment-oriented" rioting and type 3 "animosity-oriented" rioting from February to April. Collective violence ended with the stampede during the second semester's final two months of

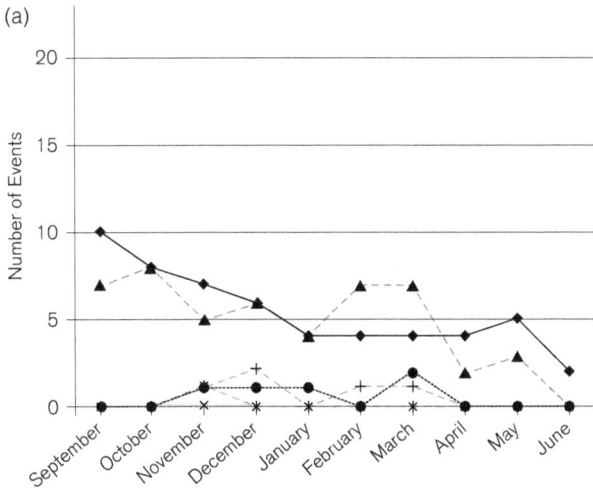

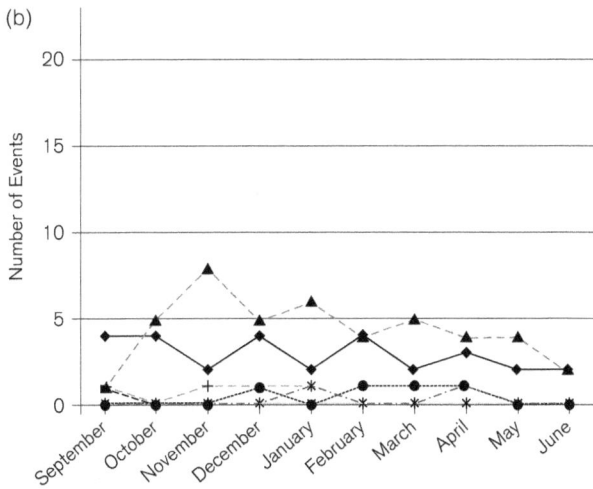

FIGURE 5.2a–c *(continued on page 136)*. Violent episodes over school year 2. (a) Boston schools, 1975–76. (b) Los Angeles schools, 2001–2. (c) Oakland schools, 2001–2. The data were sourced and categorized as in figure 5.1a–c.

(c)

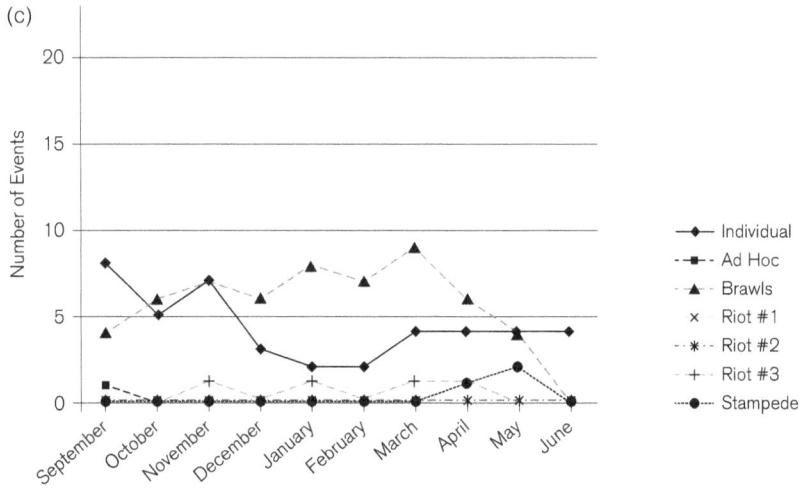

FIGURE 5.2a–c *(continued)*

May and June.[67] For the second and succeeding years of the research project the pattern of declining individual violence over the year continued, but aspects of the collective form appeared in the first semester instead of the latter part of the second as they had in the first year (phase 4; see figure 4.1, P4). This was because there was a carryover from the year before. With the start of the new school year, much of the student body was conscious of how the last school year had ended and the collective forms of violence that had occurred. This made them much more prepared to engage in violence when that seemed the appropriate response to disturbances like ad hoc group fighting or brawls. We see that in the second year all but one of the schools experienced not only brawls but at least one type 3 "animosity-oriented riot" in the first semester, whereas in the first year all of the schools experienced these only late in the second semester. Even the one exception experienced a type 3 "animosity-oriented riot" early in January when the second semester had just started instead at the end of the semester, as had been the case in the first year.

The third year of the research project, which involved only the Los Angeles and Oakland schools, saw violence generally waning. The violence that did occur happened in the first semester and was mostly of the "individual" and "brawl" types; the only form of collective violence was the stampede, which occurred twice. By the second semester of the third year there was no violence at all.

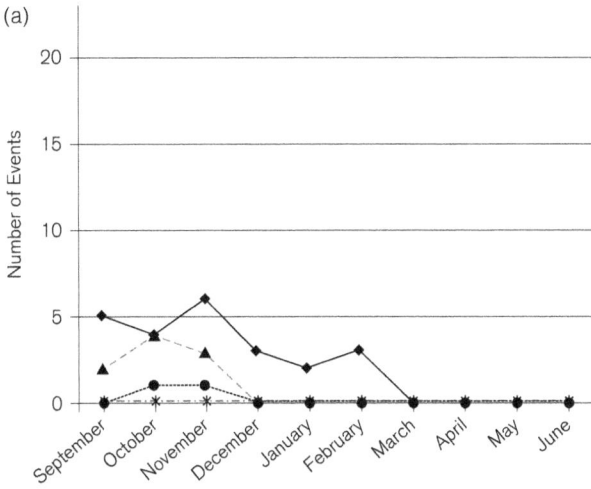

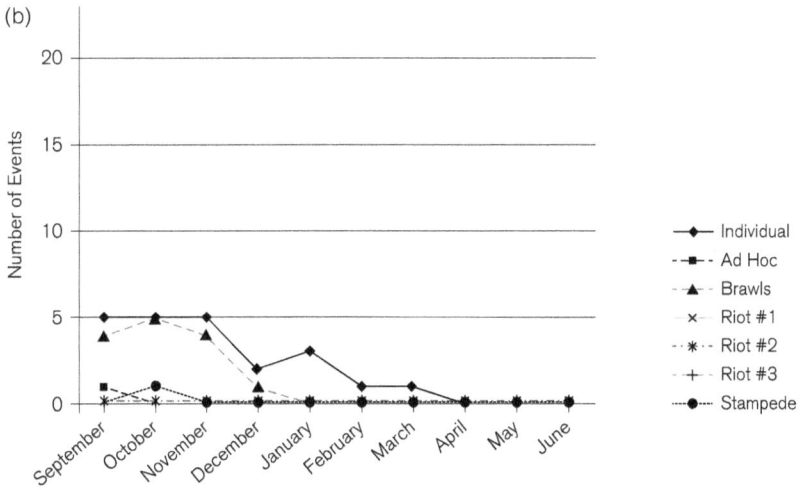

FIGURE 5.3a–b. Violent episodes over school year 3. (a) Los Angeles schools, 2002–3. (b) Oakland schools, 2002–3. The data were sourced and categorized as in figure 5.1a–c.

SOME CONCLUDING COMMENTS

When collective violence occurs in schools, especially involving members of different ethnic groups, it can easily be misunderstood as simply a riot event. However, as this chapter has indicated, students in this study engaged in many forms of collective violence, and these were not all riots. Nor were they instigated and carried out mainly by youth gangs. In fact, gang members played a rather limited role as compared to other members of their respective ethnic groups during this stage.

Collective violence is in many ways a somewhat vague term. It is understood as involving more than one person, but even though acting in a collective manner is fundamental to the definition, the exact number of people involved varies considerably. This chapter provided a number of observations into the nature of collective violence within the schools studied. First, the role of various grievances, the emotions of fear and revenge, and especially the role of punishment in restoring collective identity were particularly important as initiators and energizers of collective violence. In brief, they provided a foundation for shifting the focus of violence from a quarrel between individuals to a quarrel between groups. Second, the acts of mimicking and emotionally reacting to insults played critical roles in maintaining violent confrontations in the schools. Third, the various forms of ethnic school violence followed a general progression from violence between individuals to more collective forms of violence fueled by hatred, revenge, opportunities for status gain, frustrations that had nothing to do with ethnic relations, and protection of others considered vulnerable to being hurt. This fuel provided the energy for initiating and sustaining the succeeding form of violence. Fourth, the progression in violence corresponded to different time periods within the academic year. In this regard, violence at the beginning of the school year started with individuals, and as the semester proceeded the violence moved toward group violence involving larger numbers of individuals. Further, the second year in which violence was present in the same schools saw the same pattern, with the exception that the sequencing between stages quickened.

Some of this chapter's findings support Randall Collin's theoretical postulate concerning the importance of "interaction chains" in the violence process, particularly the finding that a progression of events influences the onset of the next set of events.[68] There are also findings consistent with his theoretical postulate concerning the "forward panic," whereby individuals who experience a buildup of tension that overcomes their inhibitions so that they begin to act violently are entrained in a frenzied trance until the interaction is complete. Yet data in the present study do not fully support his postulate that the "forward panic" is the *primary* dynamic experienced by individuals engaging in violence. I say "do not fully support" because it is difficult to definitively determine what is occurring in the mind of every individual while he or she is engaged in violent acts. Some individuals, after violent confrontations, described feelings that could be consistent with Collin's "forward panic" definition, but it would be impossible to fully know what was happening in their minds while they were engaged in the violence. However, I observed significant numbers of individuals involved in violence whose body language and verbal articulation of measured reactions intermixed with exhilarating flurries of physicality suggested that the "forward panic" dynamic may not be the sole or the primary dynamic involved in violent confrontations, at least those involving ethnic conflict among adolescents. There was evidence that some individuals used a calculus of deciding when, where, and even how to fight while being engaged in a physical confrontation. This would be quite different from the concept of entrainment that Collins advances as part of the "forward panic" dynamic. Further, there was evidence that group dynamics strongly influenced the initiation, form, and duration of individual participation in violence. Here again, one must be cautious and simply acknowledge that several social-psychological dynamics may be at work among those directly engaged in any type of violence. Nonetheless, the present study emphasizes that when collective ethnic violence in schools occurred it was fueled by multiple factors. Some, but not all, sprang from the internal dispositions of individuals with psychological problems; others from the emotions surrounding the social problems created by the influx of new students from a different ethnicity; others from attempts to have fun, find safety, or do justice; and still others from group dynamics such as acquiescing to the perceived preferences of the group and/or thoughtlessly following (i.e., mimicking) the behavior of the group. Most importantly, we see that collective ethnic violence in the schools follows a particular progression, moving from conflicts between loosely associated individuals, to conflicts between more strongly associated groups, to the collective engagement of large groups of students in such mass behaviors as riots and stampedes.

PART THREE

Embers

CHAPTER 6

Dousing and Suffocating the Flames

Violence Suppression

And one day man's hatred burns itself out.
—André Malraux, *Man's Hope*, 1938

As with many aspects of the social sciences, we know more about what causes violence to occur than what causes it to end. The implication is that once the factors causing a social action to occur are identified and analyzed, their absence will cause the action to stop.[1] Some theories concerning fighting look at the inner workings of cognitive structure that lead individuals to become involved in violence;[2] some address the structure of social circumstances like the limiting of life chances;[3] some point to the inadequate functioning of critical institutions;[4] and some examine the structure of interactional dynamics that produces violence between individuals.[5] Of course, the obvious answer to the question as to why violence stops is that the elements involved in initiating or maintaining it, such as those just referred to, are no longer present. However, in some cases the factors that initiated it and those that maintained it require analytic separation, as it is possible for violence to end even when some factors that initiated it are still present, while those that maintained it no longer exist. For example, sometimes ethnic violence ends and the original precipitating factors, like a breach of etiquette, a violation of space, or envy of material possessions, still exist but the means to ameliorate the conflicts related to them have expanded to incorporate nonviolence. Likewise there are times when the prejudice and hatred that would ordinarily maintain violence still exist, but the necessary leadership and group participation at the scene of a violent event cease to exist. As a result, potentially violent incidents can be averted, or if a the fight does erupt it ends very quickly. So to understand the "full" process of the violent dynamic as it relates to ethnic conflict in schools, particularly how it stops, it will be necessary to recognize that violence does not stop merely when the initiating and maintaining factors are gone; rather, the "endings" to violence have their own history. Consequently, I will first analyze how fights stop between two individuals, or between combinations of multiple individuals (e.g., one against two or three, two or three against five or six), and then move to analyze what causes a consistent pattern of violent incidents as clusters to stop. As will be seen, what stops violence between individuals acting independently and acting as groups during a specific incident, as well as what causes violent incidents to continue, has very little to do with the elimination of those factors responsible for starting and supporting it in the first place. Rather, violence ends when factors responsible for causing it to start and continue, which may still be present, no longer operate as they previously did.

HOW INDIVIDUAL VIOLENCE STOPS

This section focuses on individual violence (combat between people who act and see themselves acting as individuals), as opposed to group violence (multiple individuals who act and see themselves acting as part of a group) and will begin with violence between two people. Violent interaction between individuals begins for a number of reasons that have already been discussed, but for each combatant it is centered on the goal of inflicting bodily injury on the foe or avoiding being hurt and injured oneself, or both. While the fight is in progress a number of emotional factors, such as fear, rage, and excitement, act to maintain the engagement at various levels of intensity. However, in the present study four conditions caused the violent interaction between individuals to slow and ultimately end.

The first of these occurred when one of the combatants so dominated his or her opponent that the opponent was no longer considered a threat. In this situation the fight's level of intensity began to fade as the number of blows delivered and the force of the blows declined. Once combatants determined that they were dominating their opponent there was a very brief period of time between reducing the intensity of the fight (the number of blows delivered) and their decision to fully stop fighting. This brief interval usually lasted no more than three minutes and acted as a step in the process of disengagement. The winning combatant had time to emotionally unwind from the intensity of physical combat and to receive public acknowledgment for having won the fight. Ironically, during this brief period of "emotional decompression" the intensity of each blow delivered increased as the absolute number of blows decreased. In addition, during this transition period the winner of the fight would perform two symbolic acts to indicate that he or she had dominated the fight. The first was intended to send potential adversaries the message that they should not try to hurt him or her in the future or they too would face such a beating;[6] the second was to revel verbally and physically in "the earned right" to bask in the glory of having won the contest.[7]

Two examples of this follow. One incident took place in Boston's Shawmut High School when a group of seven Irish American boys were taunting an African American by calling him "nigger" and telling him to "go home so the air smells better." The African American gave them "the finger" and called them "beer-smelling white trash." After this verbal exchange, the African American moved forward toward one of the Irish students. As soon as he did, another of the Irish Americans attacked him with a club he had smuggled into the school. The African American was beaten down to the ground. Once there, he was quite vulnerable, but instead of fully stopping the attack because he had clearly won, the Irish American delivered two more intense blows to the African American with his club. After the first blow the Irish American said, "You fucking niggers ain't nothing but shit, just like I thought you were!" and then struck him again with extreme force. As the crowd of Irish Americans watching yelled their approval, he held up the club in symbolic glory of his victory and said, "Yes! Don't fuck with us!" Within a minute of celebrating with the combatant, the crowd started to disperse quickly as the state police rushed in to arrest the Irish American who had been involved.[8]

The other incident occurred in Los Angeles's Chumash High School. A Mexican American female student was walking toward a lavatory when three female African Americans at the top of the stairs poured some water down on her and started to laugh. She was upset and shouted, "You fucking dirty fuckups!" She used the lavatory and walked back to class. The African Americans were waiting for her, and as she passed them one of the African Americans bumped into her. The African American combatant was taller and much heavier than the Mexican American and quickly hit her multiple times with force, knocking her to the floor. The Mexican American was completely helpless and her face was hurt quite badly. At this point she was not capable of resisting any of the blows delivered by the African American. Once the African American saw this, she proceeded to forcefully kick her three times to the ribs and genital areas, saying, "Don't fuck with me, you brown whore!" The other two African Americans said, "Tell her what's up" and then raised their arms and slapped hands in a congratulatory "high five" gesture. After their celebratory ritual, they walked away to class, and the Mexican American stayed behind in pain until a hall monitor making rounds saw her and called for aid. The Mexican American student's injuries consisted of a severely bruised rib cage and minor bruising over the face and arms. She was never capable, or willing, to identify her attackers, so no arrests or suspensions were made. However, she harbored a considerable amount of resentment and in a later act of retribution she would release this resentment by ferociously attacking one of the African American girls that had been a part of the group who watched her being beaten with amusement.[9]

The second condition causing a violent fight to end was the physical fatigue of one or both combatants. In such situations, both combatants generally understood that neither had won the fight and that there was an immediate need to discontinue fighting to avoid any injury associated with being on the losing end. Thus, while the combatants seemed willing to continue fighting, their bodily engine was not cooperating because of fatigue. In some of the situations that I observed, one of the combatants was so tired that he could not raise his arms to either deliver or defend against a blow. Other situations were slightly less obvious, as when an African American student attending Oakland's Miwok High School was in a fight with a Mexican American student on the way home from school.[10] The African American student, physically much larger, was beating the Mexican American student severely. Although the Mexican American was bleeding from the corner of his mouth and nose, he just kept fighting back. After eight minutes of blows delivered and defended, both fighters were breathing hard. The African American said, "Did you have enough?" The Mexican American answered, "If you had enough." Whereupon both fighters, whose arms were so tired that they hung at their sides, walked away and the fight was over. I observed many similar violent situations in which the combatants were using some rational calculus while fighting and not merely responding to emotions.[11]

After this type of incident, respect increases for the participants among their own group but does not increase between combatants.

This is because combatants need to feel that their enemy is less capable than they are. Whenever individuals doubt their physical superiority to their enemy, they make concerted efforts to avoid fights.

The second example involved a Mexican American and African American in a fight on the way home from Oakland's Kaiser High School. The African American, physically much larger and much quicker, dominated the fight. The Mexican American received many punches to the head and side of his body for about four minutes. After two punches by the African American, the Mexican American student coiled and let out a groan. The African American kept punching, but the Mexican American neither fell to the ground nor said he wanted to quit. The fight was now in its eleventh minute, with the African American remaining dominant. However, in the twelfth minute, it was apparent that the African American's arms were starting to tire, and he stopped to rest his arms in an downward position before delivering more blows. During the entire fight to this point the Mexican did nothing to swing back. He simply tried to block the blows. At the fourteen-minute mark, the African American's arms were so tired that he stopped and let them drop to his side to rest them. The Mexican American seized the opportunity to run away, thereby ending the fight. From the appearance on both combatants' faces, as well as an absence of verbal expressions of dissatisfaction, it was clear that both were relieved that the fight had ended.[12]

A third condition that ended fights was associated with the combatants' inability to get the approval from their peers for it to continue. When a fight started between individuals from different ethnic groups, it was often initiated by resentment, fear, and retribution related to some sense of injustice felt on the part of one or both combatants. However, once the fight began it was often fueled in part by the support of ethnic coethnics who were present and witnessing it.[13] Therefore, when verbal encouragement was slowly retracted by a decline in the number of times it was offered or the verbal force with which it was delivered (i.e. decibel level and emphasis), combatants would begin to withdraw from fighting and the clash would cease.[14] To better understand this condition, one must appreciate the cultural factors influencing these adolescent combatants. As was described in previous chapters, many combatants thought they were making a commitment to their ethnic group by fighting, and this was often reinforced if coethnics were present while a fight was in progress.[15] For many of the combatants, the desire to avoid being labeled either a "coward" or someone lacking appropriate concern for their ethnic group's negative position in the school and neighborhood was a critical factor influencing their involvement. The importance of peer approval, particularly of a valued clique, during the adolescent developmental stage was clearly a factor that intensified participation.[16] So when combatants who were obviously winning their fights found that their peer group coethnics did not support continuing the fight they invariably began to disengage. Once peer group approval, which had most often stimulated the intensity of the fighting, was removed, the "will" to continue fighting declined.[17] In other words, violence ceases when the factor(s) producing and sustaining it are changed to create a different and sometimes reverse result.

There were three reasons for peer group reluctance to support the continuance of a fight. The first was that members of the peer group thought that a fight based on ethnic identification alone was immoral. Often observers of these disturbances assume that there is complete solidarity within each group concerning the conflict. This is simply not accurate. In most conflicts involving ethnic groups, many believed that violence based on ethnic antagonism was just plain wrong, although they were often a minority and were shy and reticent about voicing their position for fear of being socially rejected. However, if they happened to be on the scene when a fight occurred, and were a majority of their ethnic group present, they would express their disapproval by withholding verbal support. The comments of Calinda, an African American student at Oakland's Miwok High School, were a typical example of this. While observing a fight that had started between two individuals on the way home from school I noticed that nine of the eleven African Americans watching the fight did not say anything to encourage it to continue. The African American combatant who was winning the fight clearly understood that there was limited support for this fight; he stopped suddenly and with a friend resumed walking toward a small store where he would buy some snacks. When one of the African American students who had been watching asked Calinda after the fight ended why she did not support the African American in the fight while it was occurring, she said, "I think the whole thing is stupid! I'm not for anyone fighting over race, it's not moral and that's what I believe."[18]

The second reason for disapproval was that coethnics thought that the initiating incident was not significant enough to merit fighting over. A typical example of this involved an encounter between an African American and a Mexican American at Los Angeles's Chumash High School. The school had a dispensary where students could purchase snacks in the afternoon like candies, soda, and fresh popcorn. A fight started when a Mexican American student who had been standing in line bought the last bag of popcorn and an African American student who had also wanted popcorn got frustrated and began to call the Mexican American derogatory names. When the fight began, the African Americans who were watching were conspicuously quiet, and many were shaking their heads. Both responses were quite unusual for an interethnic fight. After the African American delivered a few blows to the much smaller Mexican American, one of the African American male students that was watching said, "It's just popcorn, man." The African American hit the Mexican American on the side of the shoulder and then stopped and walked away. One of the African Americans watching the fight said to the other, "Hey, it ended fast, 'cause the dude [the African American] knows everybody thought that it was stupid to fight about fucking popcorn! Was that stupid or what?!"[19]

A third reason for peers' disapproval of the continuation of a fight was that one or more of their coethnics had gained the upper hand and in their opinion did not need to deliver any further punishment. In these situations, peers of the dominant fighter believed that inflicting additional pain on the opponent was not merely unnecessary but inappropriately cruel.[20] A typical example occurred at Los Angeles's Tongva High School. A fight started on the way home from school when eight Mexican American students were confronted by an African American who said that one of them was looking at him "funny." The fight started slowly, but as the two were rolling on the ground, the Mexican American used some object to stab the African American in the side. As the African American stopped and grabbed his side, his opponent pulled up a stick used to support a newly planted tree and began to hit the African American with it. The Mexican American students watching were completely and unusually silent. After three swings with the stick the Mexican American abruptly stopped and left quickly with the others, who continued to say nothing. Evan, a Mexican American who had been at the scene, mentioned the fight to two other students at lunch the next day. "The black dude shouldn't have tried to mess with him, but Germán went way too far, and he stopped because he knew we all thought that." David, another Mexican American that was part of the group, said, "Yeah, Germán told me that he quit because everybody thought he did enough."[21]

Thus disapproval was an important factor in curtailing violent encounters between individuals. Disapproval could be communicated by silence, but it could also be verbally indicated. Usually this was done with statements like "That's enough, you hit him enough!" or "Stop before we all get jumped [attacked] here," "Stop, this is bad for us now," "Just back off and let them go before there's more trouble."[22]

Peers could also show disapproval by means of facial expressions, comments, and leaving the scene. For example, in a fight at Oakland's Miwok High School, the African American student who was dominating the fight pulled a knife from his pants and brandished it at his Mexican American opponent. Two of the African American students watching said to him, "Put the knife down, you hurt him enough." However, the African American swiped at his opponent, who jumped back to avoid being stabbed. Immediately after this, five of the African Americans waved their hands to indicate that they were finished supporting the combatant and then turned and left. Seeing them leave, the African American combatant stopped, put the knife away, and walked fast to catch up with them.[23]

When displeasure with continuing a fight was communicated by observers, it was rarely misunderstood or ignored. The object of this disapproval would generally begin to end the fight. The disengaging combatant generally would make sure that if he continued to hit his opponent the blows would not inflict pain. Thus the combatant wanting to disengage used the symbolic action of swinging lightly to communicate to his or her opponent the desire to stop fighting.[24] This was followed by a short statement indicating a willingness to end the fight such as "So now you know I ain't playing," "I let you know what's not going to go down," "Is things clear to you now?"[25] However, before the opponent had a chance to respond, the winning combatant would warn that any form of verbal disrespect or physical movement in his or her direction would be considered hostile, would cancel the deal, and would be subject to immediate aggressive retaliation. Examples of warning phrases were "Don't fuck this up, or it's going to get worse for you!" "Be cool and we can walk away, don't be cool and I'm going to fuck you up!" or "You be okay with this and we can move on, get stupid with your mouth and stuff, and you're going to be hurt bad!"[26] The usual response signaling a willingness to end the fight on the part of the person who was losing was silence, generally understood as an acceptance of the overture. At that point the combatant who had been winning would walk away from his opponent to rejoin the group that had signaled its displeasure with the fight continuing.

The final condition influencing the cessation of an individual violent event was the arrival of a group of students from the rival group who were prepared to intervene in support of their coethnic. Sometimes a fight between individuals stopped because one of the individuals, even if he or she was winning, saw a group coming to the aid of the opponent and decided to stop and retreat to the protection of his or her own group.[27] Sometimes the entire group of supporting onlookers would retreat if the opponent's group quickly arrived to offer support. The only time that this did not occur was when an additional group representing the other ethnicity arrived at the same time; then a brawl immediately began.

HOW GROUP VIOLENCE STOPS

A Brief Prelude

As discussed earlier, groups of actors engaged in multiple forms of violence. The first of these is what I labeled "ad hoc group action" because a number of individuals came independently to the aid of a coethnic in danger of being beaten by a group of their ethnic rivals. In this case individuals temporarily constituted a group, but the fight was between individuals and not between organized units. After the incident, the group almost never became a formal group.

The second form of violent interaction between groups of individuals is what I labeled a "brawl." It involved a conscious "group action" even though there was no formal organizational coordination of this action. Thus brawls consisted primarily of a mixture of individuals who had coalesced into semiformal "self-defense" or "vigilante" groups and were intending to confront their rivals, and individuals who happened to find themselves besieged by a group of antagonists and were forced to engage in a fight alongside the more semiformal groups. Most salient is that both types of "group actions" (ad hoc and semiformal self-defense/vigilante groups) formed middle links in a progression from individual violence to the group-oriented violence associated with riots and stampedes.[28] The question addressed in this section is, What factors caused group-oriented violence to stop?

Cessation of Ad Hoc Group Violence and Brawls

Four factors caused the cessation of ad hoc group violence and brawls. The first was the *verbal warning* by a student from either ethnic group that the authorities were due to arrive imminently. When this warning occurred, some of the combatants would immediately disengage and quickly leave the area. After two to three of these encounters, along with the circulation of information that arrests, suspensions, and expulsions had occurred, combatants made an increased effort to avoid detection. The result was that members of both groups used one or more individuals as "lookouts" for authorities and made sure that they were in place during the fighting. The "lookouts" became quite adept not only at notifying the participants of the impending arrival of the authorities but also at hiding their group's combatants before the authorities arrived. A representative example of this occurred at Boston's Shawmut High School when six individuals composing two ad hoc groups of African and Irish Americans became involved in a fight. The fight was in the hall between classes, and as soon as one of the Irish American students called out that the police were on their way the fight stopped and all the students ran to their next classes. None were caught because the students watching the fight gathered together to conceal the participants' retreat and because none of the students said they could identify who was fighting.[29]

The second example involved a brawl that took place between two temporary mobile classrooms on the campus of Los Angeles's Chumash High School. Twenty-one Mexican and African American students were directly involved in the fighting, but as word spread more than thirty other students ran to watch it. The brawl was going for six minutes when an African American student acting as the "lookout" shouted, "The police are on their way!" The combatants immediately stopped, but instead of running they began to mingle among members of their group, all of whom pretended that everything was normal. When the police arrived and asked what had occurred, the students they interviewed told them versions of the following statement made by Jessica, a Mexican American: "There had been some pushing around, but it was really nothing because it stopped and people just went on their way."[30] Thus the warning that the authorities were coming, as well as information that if the combatants were caught they would face stiff penalties, caused these two types of group-violent events to stop.[31] The warning "The cops are coming" was not sufficient to stop a one-on-one fight because usually the police were not immediately called, or by the time they did come school security guards had already been summoned and had broken up the fight. However, when it came to brawls too many students were involved for the security guards to intervene, so they would wait until the police arrived.

The second factor that ended ad hoc group violence and brawls was the arrival of the police and security personnel, who immediately separated and detained students. They used a variety of techniques and equipment that included physically restraining students, holding/wrestling individuals to the ground (mostly done by security personnel) and handcuffing (mostly by police), or striking, shocking, and immobilizing students with nightsticks, tasers, and occasionally pepper spray. A representative example of this occurred at Oakland's Kaiser High School when a group of twenty-six students were brawling just outside the school campus. Between twenty and thirty Oakland police surrounded the students and began to use their nightsticks to break up each fight by striking the fighters in the legs and shoulders. Once they separated the combatants, various police managed to handcuff some of the them. They were unable to handcuff all combatants because there were incidents where they did not have enough handcuffs. Further, in some situations the police could not effectively intervene because the combatants were so engaged in fighting that the police could not secure their hands. When this occurred, police would use nightsticks to pry fighters apart. Once they separated the combatants, the police used nightsticks to push them into groups and then physically surrounded each group. Because the police actions were executed with precision and resolute force, they managed to stop even extremely intense fights where the students were so intent on injuring members of the opposing group that they resisted the police's initial verbal demands to stop.[32] Ultimately, these "group hostilities" would end with the arrival of official vehicles in which combatants were loaded and transported to the police station for questioning and processing.[33]

The third factor stopping a violent incident associated with both ad hoc group violence and brawls was a group's loss of confidence that they could prevail in victory and escape serious injury. As more individuals felt insecure about their group's ability to win the fight and their personal ability to avoid injury, they began to flee from the fight in a panic mode.[34] An example of this comes from a brawl between fourteen African and Mexican American students on their way home from Oakland's Miwok High School. Julio, a Mexican American student, began to lose his strategic position in the brawl as his opponent continued to hit him in the head, while Orlando, another Mexican American, started to lose his fight with his African American opponent and suffered a bloody nose and a cut on the side of his face. Although these two individuals were on opposite sides of the brawl, they realized that no improvement in the immediate situation was probable and they became unnerved and started to panic. Both started to throw wild punches that rarely managed to hit their opponent while simultaneously retreating at an increasing pace until they simply stopped swinging and ran away. One of Julio's coethnics, Miguel, who was on Julio's left, turned and said, "Julio, what the fuck are you doing?" Julio answered, "They're winning." Miguel, who had given his opponent a bloody lip, was now faced with a different situation: Julio's opponent was free and started to come at him. As Miguel tried to fend off both opponents, he was increasingly hit on the side of his head until he too panicked and ran away from the fight. The other five Mexican Americans noticed this and they too stopped fighting and ran. This type of situation highlights how a loss of confidence can give way to fear, panic, and ultimately a breakdown in whatever solidarity and order was established in the fight, causing it to end.[35]

Cessation of Riots and Stampedes

When a riot or a stampede was in progress, the authorities usually established some areas that would be protected with a massive presence of police but that allowed the students to move in the general direction of the campus's exit.[36] The riot or stampede was ended when members of the groups who had been participating in these actions began to feel that there was no further need to engage in this behavior. Two examples, one a stampede and the other a riot, follow. The first example occurred in Los Angeles's Chumash High School, where tension between Mexican and African American students had been building for two days. A fight broke out during lunchtime and the word quickly spread. The Mexican students, having heard about the fight, took this information as a warning and started to exit en masse toward the school's back parking lot. The African Americans, observing the Mexicans' exit behavior, began to depart through the front door. Once each group recognized the other's preferred exit strategy, a clear separation reduced further conflict between the groups. Nonetheless, the exiting was essentially a stampede to get out of the school as quickly as possible. The police were called, and the school authorities, who generally stayed in their classrooms or offices to guard against property theft and destruction, simply watched the students leave. After the students exited the building they continued their stampede behavior for another half block from the campus, then stopped, saw no need to continue, milled around for ten minutes, and broke up into small contingents to proceed on toward their homes.[37]

A second example involved an "animosity-oriented" (type 3) riot (see table 4.1) that occurred at Los Angeles's Tongva High School. One morning, rumors circulated that there had been a fight the previous night involving African and Mexican American gang members and that there might be another fight involving them at school. Within minutes of a fight breaking out between members of these gangs, groups formed to either attack their adversaries or defend themselves from being attacked. The riot that was occurring had both groups, the vast majority with no gang association, engaged in fistfights with each other, as well as students exiting the building in an effort to avoid being injured by the fighting. It ended when the combatants who were actively fighting switched to joining the students who were filing out of the building because they no longer felt the desire to fight in the absence of a clear and present need for such behavior.[38]

In sum, the cessation of riots or stampedes was due to group entropy (see chapter 1). Riots and stampedes ended when the group dynamic changed and its intensity dissipated. The stampeding and rioting students ran out of the will to continue acting with the same destructive intensity and ultimately even to participate. Returning to the fire analogy, riots and stampedes sometimes ended because the direction of the wind changed so that it was now blowing in the face of the fire, so that the fire turned on itself, and other times ended because the wind stopped blowing and the fire had little energy to continue.

HOW PARTICULAR PHASES OF VIOLENCE END

The last section discussed what causes a cessation in any single individual- and group-oriented violent event. This section focuses on factors that caused the cessation of particular phases or clusters of violence (see figure 4.1). Violence occurs in cycles, and each phase in the cycle includes various forms of conflict ranging from individual-level and ad hoc group violence to brawls, riots, and stampedes. The phases not only last for differing periods of time but also include variations in the amount of time between each, so it is instructive to understand the factors that affected the variations in the duration of each phase and the duration of the periods between phases. I found that the same four factors influenced both the amount of time of a particular phase and the length of time between phases.

Removal of Leaders

The first factor that proved to be salient in temporarily suppressing the violence was the removal of students who had assumed a leadership role in the conflict or who might have become leaders. Three sets of actors removed the leaders. The first set involved law enforcement, which included state, local, and school police, as well as local probation/parole officers, who arrested them. Probation and parole officers were particularly effective. In Los Angeles, those who had an office within the schools and worked there for some part of each day could be summoned quickly to the scene of a disturbance and asked to determine if any of those detained were on probation or parole. If they found any who were, they would immediately start the process of revoking probation or parole and return these students to a formal detention facility. In Boston and Oakland, police had to call and alert parole officers that a parolee had been involved in an incident. While this procedure would produce the same result, it was not as efficient and thus not as effective as the system found in some of the Los Angeles schools.

A typical example of the system of calling in offsite parole officers involved two African Americans, Marcus and Dallas, and a Mexican American named Enrique, all of whom had been apprehended by police for participation in a very aggressive interaction during a walkout at Oakland's Miwok High School that turned into a riot. Weapons involving a shank (i.e., a makeshift stabbing instrument), a club, and a metal pipe were used by each of the three in attacking each other. Although Enrique was facing both Marcus, who had a shank, and Dallas, who had a metal club, he proved very adept at dodging blows and using his club made from bamboo. He was able to hit Marcus flush in his ear, which made Marcus drop to his knees and grab his ear in agony. Enrique then made a very acrobatic move in which he dodged one of Dallas's blows and in one motion struck Dallas with all his force on the side of the knee. This caused Dallas's leg to buckle and he fell onto one knee. At this point Enrique finished the fight with three blows, two to Dallas's back and face and one to the side of Marcus. Both Marcus and Dallas lay in pain when the police arrived. Enrique was on probation, and in a fight four days before this incident he had injured another African American student quite badly when he struck the victim's genitalia. After the police investigated the incident involving Marcus and Dallas, they notified Enrique's probation officer, who immediately revoked his probation. Enrique was apprehended and sent back to the state juvenile detention facility. This did prevent

Enrique from engaging in further violence, but had there been a system in place like that in Los Angeles, Enrique would have been removed from school within a day of the incident where he had struck a student's genitalia, and this would have prevented him from becoming involved in the fight with Marcus and Dallas.

The second contingent of actors who removed leaders consisted of the various school authorities (principal and assistant principal), who would identify individual leaders that had been involved in violent incidents and either expel or transfer them to another school. Leaders were very important in getting more people to be involved in the school's violence through both positive and negative incentives. The positive incentives involved using their charismatic influence to get individuals to emulate them as "group soldiers protecting other members of the group." The negative incentives involved intimidating individuals to become soldiers for the group by calling into question their commitment to the welfare of the group or their courage. An example of this involved Ricky, an African American, and Matty, a Mexican American, both of whom attended Los Angeles's Tongva High School. Ricky, along with two other African Americans, and Matty, along with three other Mexican Americans, were involved in a brawl a block from the school just after they had left for the day. All four were arrested, but Ricky and Matty were processed and detained for having used weapons in the fight. Ricky used a metal shank that he had been hiding in his pants and stabbed a Mexican American in the arm, while Matty used a knife and sliced the backpack of one the African American combatants before police arrived and took everyone to the station for processing. When reviewing the case, the administrators (principal, assistant principal, and a dean) decided they needed to remove both students from the school. Matty would be expelled and Ricky would be transferred to another school. Their decision to transfer Ricky was based on his record of having been suspended for being in one other fight in which no weapon was involved, having a "B" average in most of his academic courses, and missing only two days of school during the semester. Their decision to expel Matty was based on his record of having been suspended twice for his role in fights, in one of which he had used a plastic comb to cut another student. He had missed sixteen days of school during the semester and was passing only two courses (physical education and history with "Cs").

Whatever the rationale used for removing the student(s) from the school, it was the removal itself that proved to be especially decisive in retarding the violence.[39] Removals accomplished two things. First, they deprived the rank-and-file students in a group of those individuals who gave them psychological security by supplying plans for dealing with imminent threats; arranging and coordinating fights, brawls, and walkouts; guiding students to safety during walkouts, certain types of riots, and stampedes; and presenting an example of how to fight. Second, the removal of these types of individuals made it more difficult to persuade new individuals to join the group as soldiers for future violent incidents.

The third contingent was the parents of leaders who intervened with school authorities to have their children transferred to another school in an effort to protect them from being arrested or expelled. An example involved Toby, an African American attending Los Angeles's Chumash High School. Toby had been involved in two brawls, both of which included the use of a weapon. In the first incident he was charged with assault with the intent to commit bodily harm. The charges were later dropped because the object that he was accused of using was a ballpoint pen. While one of the combatants had a severe puncture wound in his forearm allegedly inflicted by Toby, there were no witnesses willing to say he had used the pen to stab the other student, and the pen was never recovered. The second incident found Toby again detained for allegedly using his comb to cut another student during a brawl. In this case there were two witnesses, but because Toby had been cut by a rival combatant's razor blade there was insufficient evidence as to who the aggressor was and who was acting in self-defense. Nonetheless, after the second incident the assistant principal decided to suspend Toby and the others involved in the brawl for two weeks. Toby's parents were required to accompany him to school when the two-week suspension ended. During their meeting with the assistant principal they requested that Toby be allowed to transfer to another school because his two best friends were acknowledged leaders among the African American students. His parents thought it was only a matter of time before he would be arrested for participating in another brawl and sent to a juvenile detention facility. Toby's case is interesting because he was a good student with over a 3.0 grade point average, but he was also a physically imposing figure. He had been a leader in three of the brawls that had occurred during the month, so the likelihood that he would have continued in trouble was quite high. The parents were successful in getting him transferred to another school, and when he left, the vigilante group he had been associated with also disbanded.

Dissension within Ethnic Groups

A second factor that proved critical in ending school violence was the emergence of dissension within one or both ethnic groups. Members' competing ideas about how to proceed undermined the consensus to continue a particular phase and diminished the pace and intensity of conflict. In some of the schools there was a split among the most active participants within a phase as to how much effort should be put into attacking individuals in the rival group. This division greatly reduced the number of violent interactions because while some of the groups' most active members favored greater numbers of violent attacks, a significant number wanted to reduce or even stop the violence and return to the "normal" school activities of learning. This internal division created bickering and frustration within the leadership that led to accusations of "cowardice" or "craziness" levied against those holding the counterposition, which in turn increased internal conflict to a point that the broad participation necessary to maintain a concerted offensive toward rival ethnic members could no longer be generated. A representative example occurred among Irish American students in Boston's Shawmut High School. During one period of violence between the Irish and African Americans students, the leaders of a large group of Irish students met at one of the local community centers to talk about what they wanted to do about a recent event where five African Americans had ganged up on two Irish Americans on the way to their homeroom, repeatedly kicking them while they were on the floor and taking their money. The seven leaders at the community center consisted of five boys (Tom, Floyd, Roy, Burt, and Vic) and two girls (Cynthia and Ellen), and they took seats around a small table that was usually used to play a board game.

The group was divided about what to do next. Vic made an emotionally charged suggestion that they should contact Whitey Bulger, the kingpin of the local crime syndicate, and ask him to provide a hit man to shoot one of the African American students, but such statements elicited reactions like "Oh come on man, even if we wouldn't mind if one of the niggers was wasted [killed], we do that and nobody will support us." This response acknowledged the reasonableness of the expressions of outrage at what occurred but exhibited the awareness that it would be way out of proportion to what had occurred and had a good deal of risk associated with it. The conversation switched to whether there should be a general walkout to protest African Americans' being in the school or whether some of the group should ask a number of the bigger male students to retaliate by attacking an African American. Tom, Vic, Burt, and Cynthia were for getting a number of Irish American male students to attack individual African Americans using small metal umbrellas and, as Cynthia said, to "make sure that they are in a lot of pain when we leave." Roy, Floyd, and Ellen, on the other hand, were for a walkout and then a boycott of school for two days. Tom said, "Walkout! That does nothing! If you don't hurt the niggers, they're just going to keep up this shit. We need to fucking punish them real bad!" Ellen said, "If we do that then we'll just get more police here, more arrests of our students, and then we start this all over again." Floyd said, "I agree with Ellen, we've been attacking each other and now we should get the police to arrest the niggers responsible and take them out of school." Burt then said, "That is so fucked up! You're acting like a bunch of fucking gutless worms! No wonder we still got trouble with fucking cowards like you guys!" This was followed by Floyd saying, "I don't think we're cowards, we supported fighting them in the past, it's just now with what you guys are saying it would just get us in more trouble. So I ain't agreeing to do what you want with more fighting, and I ain't helping or asking any of my friends to help either." Both Ellen and Roy agreed, and then Vic and Cynthia got up from their chairs to leave, with Vic saying, "This was a big fucking waste of time! The next time one of us gets jumped, you guys are to blame because the only thing niggers know is force."[40] The meeting ended, and for the next two weeks there was no retaliation. The police worked to arrest the individuals who had attacked the Irish Americans, and violence throughout the school was reduced to one incident in three weeks.[41]

Another situation that produced dissension and a lack of consensus had to do with individuals that people refer to as "troublemakers."[42] These were individuals that found fighting or hurting other individuals appealing because they were consumed by hate, suffered from some form of psychopathology like sadism, or sought the social status that their peers often gave to individuals for fighting.[43] The fact that these individuals either started a fight or immediately ran to engage in one that had already begun inspired students to admire their bravado and established them as acknowledged leaders. Coethnics looked to them as a conflict ensued, depending on them for support and protection.[44] As Gilberto, a Mexican American attending Los Angeles's Tongva High School, said to a friend during a class break: "Hey, just follow Jesse when the fight starts and you'll be okay. We all do that because he knows how to battle, and I ain't kidding."[45] However, these "trouble-makers" would inevitably engage in activities that in a previous phase of the conflict many students had looked to with envy and awe but that in the current situation were considered unacceptable or detrimental to the group's interest. This produced a reluctance to follow whatever the "troublemaker" thought was the best course of action or even to come to assist him or her in a fight. In both situations, this lack of consensus about who to follow and what to consider a "reasonable" violent act against the opposing group compromised in-group solidarity and contributed to the steady decline of violent acts within each school, as well as to the ending of one of the more violent phases in the conflict.

Reconsideration of Personal Risks

A third factor leading to the cessation of a violent phase was a reconsideration, among subsets of members in one or both ethnic groups, of the risks involved in continuing to fight, and concomitantly a breakdown in group discipline. One of the three risks students mentioned most was that of being injured or even killed in a melee. Two representative examples can be seen in the comments of Dixon and Danica. Dixon was an African American attending Oakland's Miwok High School:

> When we were starting off, I was for us getting into it [attacking] with the Mexicans because I really didn't want them in our neighborhoods, but I ain't for that as much now 'cause when shit is coming down it can fucking mess me and the rest of us up, you know? I mean, what if one of them shoots us or we get arrested or some shit like that? That would be fucked up, man; and then it ain't worth it 'cause we'd have more problems than having to fuck'n deal them [Mexicans], so I ain't getting involved in the violent shit anymore 'cause it just ain't worth it, you know?[46]

Danica was a Mexican American attending Los Angeles's Chumash High School:

> I don't want to keep fighting the blacks like a lot of the boys want to do 'cause the other day a girl student who was Mexican got into a fight and she got stabbed in the side of the stomach with a hair comb. They said it just missed something in her stomach that would have stopped her from having a baby. It's just getting too crazy, and someone's going to get killed, and I definitely don't want that to happen to me. [The three other girls she is talking to start to nervously laugh.] No, I'm serious, I'm going to try to avoid that shit because it is just getting too dangerous. [The other three nod in agreement.][47]

Another risk frequently mentioned was the chance of being arrested and having to endure court procedures with the chance of being convicted and acquiring a permanent criminal record that would further jeopardize one's chances of obtaining a job in the civilian or military sector of the economy. The comments of Cameron and Matías are representative. Cameron was an African American attending Oakland's Miwok High School:

> We should stop jumping them [the Mexican students] 'cause if we don't we're eventually going to get in trouble with the law. I mean, we're going to get arrested, and then if we get convicted for some shit like assault or something, I don't know, something that's a felony, then we'll have a record forever, and I definitely can't have that because I want to join the army and that will stop me from getting in. I'm just not going to do the shit I used to do in terms of fighting and stuff because I got to think about the future 'cause I'm graduating this year and I want to start in the army right after summer.[48]

Matías was a Mexican American attending Los Angeles's Tongva High School:

> No, I'm just out of this fighting now because it's getting more serious and I don't want to get arrested for some felony. Just think, if we get a felony who is going to give us a job? There ain't no place on any application that I filled out where you can explain why you got in trouble, plus they won't even care because they got lots of people looking for good jobs. So that's it for me. I really want to start working when I get out of here, and I don't want anything to get in the way of that.[49]

Still another risk was that of compromising one's academic goals. For those who wanted to attend college, reluctance to either become or remain involved in fights, brawls, or riots was based on their assessment that participation would take valuable time away from learning and would jeopardize their ability to gain the information and skills necessary to pass the exams at a level required by the college of their choice. An example can be seen in the comments of Doris, an Irish American attending Boston's Shawmut High School:

> No I ain't going to do all that walking out and stuff 'cause then I ain't in school, and if I want to go on to college I got to get more studying in or I won't be able to pass the college exam [the SAT] with high enough scores to get into one of the good ones. . . . I just think we got to fight less with the niggers or everybody will be able to graduate all right but not learn enough to go to college. So I'm stopping getting involved with all the fighting and riots and stuff.[50]

It should be remembered that although the students weighed the costs of continuing these fights, all these deliberations came after a considerable amount of time spent in risky violent behavior. These students had accumulated evidence from numerous experiences with violence that changed their outlook and commitment to further participation. This contributed to diminishing the level of violence in the schools.[51] Thus the utilization of a rational choice calculus could lead to both group solidarity and its dissolution.[52]

Personal Fatigue

Finally, students often lost their commitment to fight because of simple fatigue: they got tired of the fighting and the anxiety associated with it. Some of the fatigue was related to emotional excitement. There were students who said that fighting had once been exciting but had now become so normalized that it was not really exciting at all. These students went on to say that they had been less interested in planning and participating in staged fights, brawls, riots, and stampedes, or even rushing to become a spectator of them. Fatigue undermined the group solidarity that was so essential in maintaining a high level of violence in the schools, although its full impact was gradual as it grew over a two-month period.[53] A typical example of this thinking can be seen in the comments of Brandon and Malik, which were made twenty-seven years apart. Brandon was an Irish American attending Boston's Paul Revere High School:

> I just don't feel like walking out tomorrow to protest and start a riot. It's not that I'm for what we got here now [the situation resulting from busing], because I fucking hate them banana brains [African Americans], but I'm tired of leaving school and then having to make up the work and stuff. I ain't going to be doing all the stuff I done for all these months, I'm just not. I'm tired of it.[54]

Malik was an African American attending Oakland's Kaiser High School:

> Fuck this fighting all the time. We just need to cool it some, 'cause I just can't get excited about fucking up them turds [Mexican American students]. We been doing this for a full half year, and it's just a big hassle now and with the police and all. You know, it's just "old" having the police come and take you in and then let you go. I mean, I'm just tired of it.[55]

It is important to reiterate that all these factors emanated from inside the broad ethnic coalitions that were engaged in each school's conflict.

These internal factors slowly sucked the life out of the various forms of collective involvement that were so instrumental in fueling the school violence.

SOME CONCLUDING COMMENTS

Ethnic violence, even when it occurs in schools, is a very potent force, but it is not immune to conditions that will retard its momentum or bring it to a halt. The various factors analyzed here, some internal and some external to the groups of ethnic combatants, worked to siphon the energy from the interactive violence between the students and in so doing to decelerate its intensity.

To return to the fire metaphor, the external agents that had an impact on eliminating this violence—law enforcement, school officials, parents—were doing work like that of a fire department, preventing and extinguishing fires. The factors that were internal to the groups participating in the violence were similar to changing environmental conditions in a fire—factors that can be best understood as natural retardants that suffocate a fire's internal energy to persist.

CHAPTER 7

Monitoring the Embers

Keeping the Peace

In everyone, even the most fainthearted, it is natural for a
period of calm to follow a violent emotion, for even if our
feelings are boundless, our physical organs are limited.

—Honoré De Balzac, *An Incident in the Reign of Terror,* 1830

As described in the preceding chapter, both internal and external factors
caused violence in the schools to decline (phase 5), but during the final
phase of uneasy peace (phase 6) a delicate situation existed. Clearly
some of the conditions responsible for the violence had sufficiently
changed to put an end to it, but certainly not all of them had. Some
aspects associated with the past violence were still present in each of the
schools and were capable of destabilizing the newly existing peace and
calm. These factors consisted of emotional dispositions, weapons, and
organizations. In this chapter, I describe what contributed to maintaining peace in light of these remaining factors.

THE LAG IN EMOTIONAL DISPOSITIONS

During the new period of relative calm, students expressed the fear,
hatred, and resentment that were present during previous periods of
violence. This was a time of transition in which not only were all these
emotions still present, but there was a sequential order in when they
would be the dominant influence in social relations between members
of the rival groups. Probably the emotion most prevalently displayed
when the violence first stopped was *fear.* Two aspects of fear were most
widespread. The first was a carryover from the period of violence and
had to do with anxiety about being physically attacked and injured. The

second was the worry that a fight would break out somewhere on or off campus and would reignite a new period of violence. The comments of Janet, an Irish American attending Boston's Paul Revere High School, and Taylor, an African American attending Oakland's Kaiser High School, are representative:

> *Janet:* I'm glad that there is hardly any violence around school, but I always worry that some black will start something and I'm going to get caught in it; or a fight will start and then the whole back-and-forth of violence will start all over again. Don't you guys?[1]

> *Taylor:* Today I got to study in the class without having to get into a fight with the wetbacks [Mexican students]. It felt good, it really felt good, but you know you got to watch out because they're sneaky and they'll come up and jump you with about seven or eight guys. They can hurt you, you know? So you just got to see if we're really over this [fighting between the two groups] because maybe something will go down [another fight] and we're right back to the beginning with the fuckers![2]

Once the fear waned, *hatred* became the ascendant emotion among members of both groups. However, it was "controlled hatred": the students hated the other ethnic group, but this hatred was controlled by countervailing moral doubt as to whether it was appropriate for the present situation. The comments of Kim, an African American at Paul Revere High School, and Julián, a Mexican American from Los Angeles's Chumash High School, are representative.

> *Kim:* It is so hard not to hate them *crackers* [Irish Americans] for what they said and done to us over these two years. I mean, look at the shit we had to put up with. They called me and you dirty niggers every day. Even said we was from humans mating with animals! Then they'd throw things at the bus when we came. . . . Yeah, I really hate them, but my grandma says it ain't righteous to hate, and especially now that things is calm and they ain't doing nothing to us. So now I sort of feel kind of bad that I hate them, you know?[3]

> *Julián:* It was terrible to try to learn here when all the fights and riots was going on. They [the African Americans] just picked on us every day and especially me 'cause I live right where there is only them. . . . Yeah, I still hate them too, but now that things is calmed down it'll just make things worse to keep hating them, even though I still don't like what they did to us.[4]

Even though hatred was present among students from both sides of the conflict, as time moved on it was replaced by *resentment*. This was part of the process by which students were able to reconcile their strong feelings from the period of intense fighting and physical disruption (walkouts, riots, and stampedes) with the new period of relative peace and calm. The emotion of resentment that replaced hatred was based on the awareness that a considerable amount of time had been wasted on fighting and that this had been at the expense of learning, personal growth, and having fun. Of course, each group blamed the other for the problems in the school. This time of resentment was predicated on the idea that had the rival group acted as they were now, or had they not attended the school to start with, things would have been different and students would have been able to just learn, grow, and have fun. Though resentment permeated group relations, the end of fighting between the rival groups established an expectation that coexistence was possible and that learning, growing, and having fun were possible within the present "shared" social environment. The comments of Darcy, an Irish American from Boston's Shawmut High School, and Isaiah, an African American from Los Angeles's Tongva High School, are representative:

> *Darcy:* Yeah, I'm glad there's no violence right now, but I resent the niggers for coming here. I'm going to have a hard time getting into college now because the stuff we needed to learn to get into college went down the toilet with trying to get our constitutional rights back [resisting the busing]. The fucking judge just wasted all our fucking time! Even the niggers' time was wasted.[5]

> *Isaiah:* I think if things would be like this [no violence] all of us could've had fun at this school. I know we'd have learned a lot more because it was impossible when all the craziness was going on. I have these bad feelings [resentment] toward the Mexicans 'cause it was a waste of time while we were here [in school] and they started a lot of the fights. Now high school is going to be over and we could've had a lot more experiences if everything was like now. That's really, really fucked up![6]

Each of the emotions just identified led to a number of dispositions. The first was a lack of trust in the ability of members of the rival group to refrain from attacking a student from "our" group, or the ability of members of one's own group to refrain from starting a fight with someone from the rival group and renewing hostilities, or the ability of school authorities and law enforcement agencies to maintain the present peace. Two illustrative examples of this disposition can be seen in the comments of Nora, a Mexican American attending Los Angeles's Chumash High School, and Tad, an African American attending Boston's Paul Revere High School.

> *Nora:* Yeah, after all that's gone on, I hope it's finally over, but I just can't believe it because there is too much hatred between the groups. . . . Well,

I do hope it stays normal [without violence], but I just don't think they're [the African Americans] going to act right so it stays normal.[7]

Tad: They say that everything is good now [no more violence will occur], but then we had people saying shit like that and then all hell broke loose when Julius [an African American friend] couldn't keep it together and delivered it to [hit] one of the fucking Irish assholes. . . . Hey, do you see what I see? There is like half or less police as there used to be around here. So if anything happens it ain't going to get stopped and it'll be back to the same shit again [start of fighting]![8]

"Cautiousness" was the second disposition encountered during this time among the students in these schools. Students walked around looking for signs that violence was imminent. The experience of the past months, or years, had socialized them to believe that they were responsible for themselves and that if they were attacked it was their fault because they were not vigilant enough.[9] The comments of Tammy, an Irish American attending Boston's Shawmut High School, and Ricardo, a Mexican American attending Oakland's Kaiser High School, are representative of this disposition.

Tammy: Oh I don't know if them niggers is going to keep from attacking us. You better look out. I am always looking out when I get around them because they could jump us any time. Remember they did it before, and if they do it again we better be ready because we know what they're like, and then who'd we blame? Them? I don't know why, because we should know they'd do it.[10]

Ricardo: Shit, I ain't never looking the other way when them blacks is around 'cause they'll fucking jump you in a second if they be in a gang and outnumber you. So if they do jump me now it's 'cause I got my mind on something else, and that's on me. You understand?[11]

The third disposition, "guardedness," was critical in inhibiting the transition to a long-term commitment toward coexistence and nonviolence among the rival groups because it prevented students from being able to completely trust the overtures of "friendliness" offered by members of the rival group.[12] The students with this disposition hesitated to allow themselves to rely and depend on individuals whom they had considered enemies. Overcoming this disposition would prove essential for old rivals to begin to effectively work together. Two examples of this disposition can be seen in the comments of Andy, an African American attending Boston's Shawmut High School, and Inez, a Mexican American attending Oakland's Miwok High School.

Andy: Things are better now between us [African Americans and Irish Americans], but it's kinda hard to know what to expect. I get along with whites [Irish Americans] that I been working with in drama class, and we're practicing [acting] together in this play, but again I don't really expect that they want me here and in a play, they just got to put up with it. So, I just take what I get and that way I ain't disappointed. You know?[13]

Inez: It's just like you say for me too. All the blacks I been around are nice to me now since the fighting and stuff stopped. It's been totally different and I like it, but I don't think any of us [Mexican Americans] should think that all the blacks like us though because that's not going to happen.[14]

THE CONTINUED PRESENCE OF WEAPONS ON CAMPUS

In addition to the emotional factors just discussed, school authorities found themselves having to deal with two other "lag conditions" (i.e., persisting spillover effects that retard the shift to a new condition). The first of these was the often ingenious means that the students had developed to bring weapons onto the campus or have weapons available to them as they walked home. School authorities implemented a number of initiatives to limit weapons on campus, but the students still thought up ways to get around the rules. Smuggling weapons or objects that could be used as weapons was one way; the other was to make objects already available on campus into usable weapons.

Although the students used a large variety of objects as weapons, I will simply mention four as examples. Combs could be brought to campus. Those used by African Americans to groom the "Afro" hairstyle of the time had long metal prongs that were both sharp and sturdy. Students in all the schools I studied used these "picks" as weapons and could inflict serious injuries and even fatalities with them if they happened to penetrate a vital organ. Another type of comb made from hard rubber that could be either tapered or straight in form was employed as a weapon with a slashing motion to cut opponents.

In each school, the police had tried to have the combs with prongs longer than three inches banned from school, but this proposal was always successfully resisted by either school authorities or the lawyers for various public interest groups who argued that the mere fact that a comb could be used as a weapon did not mean that it would be and thus that imposing such a code would violate an individual's rights.[15]

The second object employed as a weapon, primarily utilized by female students, was a razor blade. Latinas were more likely to use razor blades and would generally conceal them within their hair. In schools that had metal detectors, students would usually place the blade deep within their hair immediately behind a hairpin or barrette so that if they had to go through a metal detector and the alarm indicated a metal object they would point to the hairpin and attempt to explain that it had set off the alarm. In the morning period this was an extremely effective ploy, as the security staff was quite stressed to get all the students past the checkpoint and on to their first class before the first bell rang for instruction to begin.

A third object employed as a weapon was the compass instrument used to draw arcs in geometry and "woodshop" courses. This instrument, as well as ballpoint pens, could also be used to create puncture wounds during a fight. Therefore, efforts to relegate their use solely to the classroom were virtually impossible.

Further, the students creatively took objects made for other purposes and reconfigured them into weapons. Some examples included finding a piece of wood or metal piping and using the sidewalk, a woodshop lathe, or a nonpointed fingernail or woodshop file to sharpen it into a pointed object; gathering the plastic knives, forks, and cups found in the cafeteria and using scissors to cut pointed edges in them;[16] inserting metal objects like nails or buckshot into hollow metal/plastic tubing and then configuring it into a crude zip gun[17]; or using a strong rubber band as a slingshot to hurl sharp objects at rivals.

Thus, after the violence had stopped for a few months, weapons based on this crude technology remained available to those who might want to start fights for reasons having nothing to do with ethnic conflict. School officials were aware and vigilant about this, as well as proactive in their efforts to prevent individual-oriented violence from being misinterpreted and redeveloped into ethnic-based violence.

AVAILABILITY OF ORGANIZATIONAL RESOURCES FOR VIOLENCE

Some organizations could facilitate additional rounds of violence between students from different ethnic backgrounds. Two types of groups posed threats to the existing peace. The first was street gangs. Although they were not a factor in the Boston schools, they were significant actors in the violent periods of each California school and thus remained a threat to the existing peace.

In Los Angeles and Oakland, youth gangs were active long before there was ethnic violence in the schools, but once violence did break out they slowly became an integral part of the violence in each school. It should be remembered that gangs, as formal organizations, were initially not active when violence first began because they were not represented in the first wave of new ethnic students to the school. It would take a year before the number of gang members from the ethnic group migrating to the neighborhood and school was large enough to establish an "official" gang presence. Thus, in the beginning of the ethnic violence those students who were gang members became active in the violence as individuals and not agents of their formal gangs. However, as violence evolved into its later stages, gang members became very active because their gangs were often asked by other students for help in defending them from attacks by members of the rival ethnicity,[18] and they consented out of a sense of ethnic identity and obligatory allegiance to defend members of their besieged community.[19] The comments of Nestor, a Mexican American gang member attending Los Angeles's Chumash High School, and Tito, an African American gang member attending Oakland's Kaiser High School, are representative:

> Nestor: We will definitely be up for defending our people. We definitely ain't going to be laying down and letting them *mayates* [derogatory word for African Americans] mess with us whenever they want . . . and we'll do it [defend other Mexican Americans] as long as the *mayates* mess with us.[20]
>
> Tito: I don't care what the conflict's about, we're [his gang] from this neighborhood and it's for us to control. So, we'll [his gang] protect the blacks in the neighborhood because, as I said, this is our hood, and no fucking Mexican is going to fuck with us![21]

Gangs also became active in the schools' ethnic violence because they saw an opportunity to expand their organizational numbers by using the violence to recruit new members more easily than during nonconflict times.[22] In all of the Los Angeles and Oakland schools studied there was a strong gang presence among both African and Mexican American students, and these gangs became stronger while the conflict was at its height because they were a source of protection for the general student body representing their ethnic group. When the conflict had subsided gang numbers did not immediately decline. Thus, even during months when no ethnic violence was reported, they remained a source that could open another round of violence.[23]

The other organizational group that was present in the schools of Boston, and in other schools that had no significant presence of youth gangs before the ethnic violence began, was the "vigilante group."

Vigilante groups were "ad hoc groups" that grew out of the developmental process of violence found in each school.[24] These groups formed to defend members of their group and attack members of the rival group as they deemed necessary for both protection and the ability to "right" a moral injustice inflicted on members of their ethnic group. Although vigilante groups always started with a loose association of individuals acting collectively in "ganging" behavior, as time progressed they produced a leadership and rank-and-file structure.[25] During periods of persistent violence this structure provided members with status and identities that proved functional to themselves and to their coethnics. However, the situation became more complicated when the conditions that had originally given rise to vigilante groups disappeared but the vigilante groups themselves still existed. This presented authorities with an ongoing threat to the recently established peace in the schools and forced them to engage in surveillance and intervention to prevent ethnic violence from reigniting.[26]

Thus both students and administrators felt wary during the initial period of peace. Administrators understood that the existing condition of peaceful coexistence between the groups required them to manage each of the factors just identified if they were to reduce the probability that violence would again arise. The initiatives included approaches usually described as forms of "deterrence" and "public health," with more being said about them in the succeeding sections of this chapter.

SECURITY INITIATIVES

Given the fragile state of affairs just discussed, security remained the primary concern of school officials. Three steps were initiated to provide security during this period, a period that generally started the semester following the riots and stampedes. The first involved the police, who formed the foundation for maintaining public order by using a traditional deterrence approach. Boston, Los Angeles, and Oakland each used different police contingents to provide security. For Boston, primarily the state police with the aid of the local police were assigned to each school to prevent violence from breaking out or to stop it once it started. For Los Angeles, this responsibility fell on the Los Angeles Unified School District Police Department as well as the city police and the county sheriff's department; and for Oakland it was the sole responsibility of the local police.

In their role as peacekeepers, the police in each city would use car patrols to observe the primary routes taken by the students traveling between their homes and school, and while at school they would use foot patrols. Although school officials were well aware of the need for a police presence to keep the peace, the fact that there was both a large student population and a substantial amount of territory to cover presented the police with a logistical challenge. The standard strategy was to have six to ten officers outside as well inside the school one hour before classes started and one hour after they ended, and then to have one or two remain in or around the school while classes were in session. This strategy was predicated on the belief that since the school was now peaceful students were more willing to control their behavior, especially while school was in session. This belief turned out to be accurate. Having police present on campus did act as a deterrent during this time, and the comments of Junior, an African American attending Los Angeles's Tongva High School, and Sybil, an Irish American attending Boston's Shawmut High School, were typical of those who found the police presence effective.

> *Junior:* Naw, I ain't into fighting them [Mexican American students] right now because everything got cool. Plus, if I get into it with one of 'em there will be a policeman there in no time 'cause they're hanging around all the time. . . . Yeah, I ain't about to get in fights now 'cause if I get caught it's just on me 'cause everybody's done with violence and they'll say, "He's just fucking crazy, lock him up!"[27]

> *Sybil:* There's still police everywhere, but before no one cared, and if someone started something there were all kinds of people that'd join in. I know my brothers would do that [join in] all the time. Now, though, there are so many police that if you're in a fight they're going to be there in a second and arrest you on the spot. Then you got real problems! I know my brothers said they're not going to fight now 'cause everything is quiet and the police are in better places to arrest people.[28]

In addition, during this period of uneasy calm, the police and school officials worked closely with the county's probation department to locate, apprehend, and reassign individual students who were found to be involved in aggressive assaults.[29] In the case of Boston and Oakland, the police would generally contact the probation department to locate or process a particular individual for assaulting another student either on campus or en route to and from school. However, in Los Angeles, a probation officer was physically present on each school's campus for some portion of every day, and while there they would actively monitor the behaviors of those students who were on the officer's "client" roster. The use of agents to monitor individuals who were either on probation or on parole and thereby to deter them from becoming involved in violence was an integral part of the overall strategy to establish social control, not only for this new period of peace but for the longer-term maintenance of the peace as well. This strategy was aggressively pursued and proved particularly effective in deterring violent episodes within the schools because information permeated the student body that individuals who were on probation or parole and became active in violence on the campus would be hunted down and remanded to the custody of the correctional system.

Law enforcement working closely with probation officers could not only remove from campus those individuals who had violated the peace but also provide additional agents to monitor potential threats to the peace. The various probation officers in Los Angeles's schools met with their assigned cases on a regular weekly basis during the school day, a practice that constantly reminded individuals on probation that they were being closely watched and that any violation would end with the immediate suspension of their freedom. The comments of Dorisha, an African American student attending Los Angeles's Chumash High School, and Mateo, a Mexican American attending Oakland's Miwok High School, were representative of the students' concerns about participating in violence at school.

> *Dorisha:* No sister, I ain't been involved in that mess yesterday. I'm staying clear of that shit now 'cause they been using probation to take everything away if you get into trouble. . . . Well, you know I had my go with them Mexicans, but that's got to be over for now 'cause I'm in the system [she was on probation] and I ain't about to fuck around and go back to juvy [a juvenile detention facility].[30]

> *Mateo:* Some of the blacks is messing with us, but you really got to watch it because now the cops are all around. If they get you they're going to check to see if you're on probation, and if you are, they're going to call your officer to get it revoked immediately! I know me and Omar is staying out of things now 'cause we ain't about to get sent back to juvy.[31]

The next factor that influenced the newly established peace between the rival ethnic groups was the increased use of security guards in the school. During most of the previous periods of violence the presence of security guards had proved ineffective in deterring physical conflict. Most of the security guards were from either the immediate geographic area of the school or one in close proximity. The vast majority had not been trained in conflict resolution or self-defense strategies and were liable to be the object of legal action if a student was hurt by them while they were executing their duties. These conditions left them feeling vulnerable to physical and social retribution from their community members and to legal problems from the larger community (via the courts), and they believed that the pay was too low to compensate them for the risks. This made them reluctant to become aggressive in stopping fights. However, when new guards were hired who were not from the immediate area and were provided additional training in violence suppression, they felt more comfortable about intervening quickly and aggressively.[32]

The increase in security guard numbers and effectiveness in executing their duties was particularly important in deterring violence because the students interacted with these security guards every day, making identification and police apprehension more efficient. A typical example of this involved Arland, a thirty-four-year-old security guard, Ricky, an African American student, and Lester, a Mexican American student, at Los Angeles's Chumash High School. The incident began during a gym class where the students were playing a basketball game. Ricky drove to the basket, and just before he was able to release the ball toward the hoop Lester slammed into him, trying to block his shot. Ricky was in the air and, losing his balance, fell to the court. He scraped a large area of his forearm and hip in the process, causing surface bleeding and requiring him to go to the school nurse for some minor medical attention. In an everyday conversation with Arland, one of Ricky's friends insinuated that Ricky and some friends would retaliate against Lester after woodshop class for what had happened that day. Just before the end of the woodshop class, Arland went to the door where Ricky and a number of students were exiting and told them that he knew what they were planning and that he did not want them to do it. They told him that it was only right that Lester pay for what he did to Ricky. Arland told them that he would tell the police and principal who was involved if anything happened to Lester. They protested, but Arland said, "We got peace now, and they [school administrators] told me that if violence started to break out on our watch we'd be let go because there's a lot of people that want our jobs, so I ain't going to lose my job for this. You got it?" Ricky and the others left and they must have decided that the matter was not worth getting arrested or expelled for, because an attack on Lester never did occur.[33]

In sum, after more than a year of violence the combination in each school of a newly established calm and security guards' more proactive role (encouraged by a firmly stated directive from school officials regarding the consequences of ineffectiveness) prevented new outbreaks.

Probably the least effective and efficient mechanisms used to manage student behavior were the installation of metal detectors at the main entrance(s) of the schools and the performance of random searches throughout the day. Of the schools I studied, only those in Boston used metal detectors. Schools in Los Angeles and Oakland occasionally tried them but usually decided that the costs of installation and the logistics necessary to manage them were not worth the benefits they would provide. In Boston, as well as most other schools throughout the nation, the procedure was to have the students line up for machine scanning of themselves and their property when they were coming into school through one of the main entrances. The machines could detect a number of weapons or potential weapons such as guns, knives, shanks, brass knuckles, letter openers, scissors, nails, retractable electronic aerials, pepper spray, mace spray, and nonlethal acid (used to throw at an opponent in order to inflict a burn) and prevent them from entering the Boston schools.

The random searches in Los Angeles and Oakland found students possessing wooden objects sharpened to a fine point, fingernail files, metal hair combs, hairpins, sharpened plastics, and razor blades. Although both procedures detected large numbers of these objects when the violence was rampant, the number of students who continued to bring them during the period when the everyday violence had ceased steadily declined. Usually, the students who did try to bring weapons into the school did so out of a concern for protection rather than to renew attacks on the rival group. The policy to remove any potential weapon from campus contributed to the success of establishing a new climate of safety. However, there were some glitches in the system, and these generally revolved around delays for students in getting to class on time or classes not having enough students present to start on time. The comments of Gerry, an Irish American attending Boston's Shawmut High School, and Eugenio, a Mexican American attending Los Angeles's Tongva High School, exemplify how much metal detectors and random searches could deter students from bringing any object that could be used as a weapon to school.

> *Gerry:* I didn't want to be taking any chances that the niggers were going to jump me, so I brought a long pair of scissors in my backpack and the metal detector went off and they took them from me. They kept me in the office for a while and then I was late for class and got in trouble for that. So I'm just going to let it go until there's some new trouble with the niggers and then I might try again.[34]

Eugenio: My sister was stopped by the security guards checking everybody when they came into the school, and they found a long hairpin and some razor blades, so they took them away and took her to the office to talk to the dean. Man, they had my mom come to talk to them before they would let her back to school, and my mom was real mad, so I decided not to bring one of the plastic strips that I sharpened to use if the *mayates* started something again. It's just not worth it right now when there's nothing going down [violence occurring], and plus if they do find something then they're always stopping you and you get late for classes all the time.[35]

Finally, several school officials tried to enlist other influential professionals—teachers, reporters, and politicians—to help maintain the peace. They wanted teachers to be more proactive in creating and maintaining the newly established social order by providing reconnaissance, intervening to break up a fight, and calling for assistance from the administration, security, and police when violent confrontations occurred. This effort to more fully involve the teachers in peacekeeping was filled with challenges. The teachers were represented by a union, which had negotiated the work specifications of their employment, specifications that were somewhat incompatible with the administration's desire to have them act as quasi-security agents. Although significant numbers of teachers in all the schools were willing to provide information about a potential disturbance in order to maintain a peaceful environment, teachers often refused to assume a more direct role in stopping fights. They believed that this confused their role as educators with the role of police, was physically dangerous for them, and risked their being judged as culpable for injuries that might occur while they were trying to intervene.[36] The comments of Jared, a history teacher at Los Angeles's Chumash High School, and Cynthia, a science teacher at Oakland's Kaiser High School, were representative of this line of thought.

Jared: Yeah, I can't believe she [principal] wants us to stop fights when they occur. It's just not my job to do that. I don't have any training in that sort of thing. A lot of the students are just pure fighters, so what's a guy like me going to do breaking up a fight they're having? This is just insane and I am not going to do it! I'm contacting Charles [the union representative] to have him get involved here.[37]

Cynthia: Just yesterday I was going to my next class when a Mexican and black student got into it [a fight]. I reported it, but what I understand from the meeting this morning is that the administration expects us to try to stop these fights. That's just crazy. I know this is not part of our contract, and I'm glad June [another teacher] interjected that this is not part of our contract. To think that I have to teach and be a security guard too is crazy because I'm trained in one and the other I'm not. I'm just not doing it![38]

The second group of professionals targeted by school officials for cooperative assistance was the various media reporters assigned to cover educational issues within the district. The media's primary role was to report events and provide investigative coverage of them. As was mentioned earlier in the case of Boston, the local radio talk shows were especially instrumental in reinforcing the convictions of white parents, activists, and students that they were morally right in resisting the busing of African Americans to their schools and in giving the impression that this opposition was supported by a majority of Massachusetts's citizenry. On the African American side it was not the local talk shows that had the most impact in reinforcing their convictions but the local newspaper and TV news shows that bolstered their beliefs that they held the moral high ground over white resistance and were supported by a larger number of the Massachusetts's citizenry. Twenty-six years later in Los Angeles and Oakland the local newspapers and the various local television stations unintentionally influenced many of those participating and/or supporting the violence in the schools to continue their activities.

Although the local media were simply reporting the events that had occurred in the schools, by making these events "visible" their reporting provided those involved with a degree of personal notoriety, and this helped create a "contagion effect" that encouraged further student violence. The media's influence on events was evident in the constant discussions occurring among the students in the affected schools. In most cases, a significant number of students found something personally exciting about the coverage even though it was not necessarily flattering. This did not go unnoticed by the school administration, which, when the violence stopped, decided to make an effort to reduce the media's potential to encourage the restart of violence.

The approach taken by officials in all three cities to minimize the unintentional impact the media might have on restarting the ethnic violence in the schools was to control the information concerning violent episodes or the conditions that promoted them. They did this in a number of ways. First, they attempted to control how the events were reported by creating categories like "disturbance" in place of "fight" that would provide a different, or softer, impression of an incident.[39] Second, they would use phrasing like "a number of people," "a group of students," or "a relatively small bunch of students" to describe participants in an effort to disguise which and how many individuals were involved in the violence.[40] There was evidence that this strategy had an immediate impact in deterring students from participating in future violence. Three examples of this can be seen in the comments of Kerry, an Irish American attending Boston's Shawmut High School, and Carla, a Mexican American attending Oakland's Kaiser High.

> *Kerry:* There's nothing going on here now, you know, no fights; and the *Herald* [local *Herald-American* newspaper] ain't had nothing in it that there's been fighting at the other schools, so there ain't no reason to start stuff with the niggers right now. . . . Yeah, if stuff starts happening at the other schools, then yeah, we'd start up too because this is [name of school] and we're the leader in resisting this busing shit! [There had actually been a number of fights in the other Boston schools that had not been reported.][41]

> *Carla:* I'm glad things is good now and we don't have to worry about fights all the time. My mom told me that the paper said there was a disturbance among a few people at Chumash High, but nothing important like it had been reported anywhere else. I told her the same stuff goes on at our school, but it's different from before. It's usually gang stuff or between two people. [The incident she is referring to at Chumash actually involved about twelve people and was more like a brawl.][42]

The third way in which authorities tried to control the media was to have the school district's community relations department work with reporters from the commercial stations on how and when the coverage should be done. In some cases, the department would focus, not on the actual violence that had occurred, but on what school authorities had done to bring order back to the school. This strategy was an effort to stress the positive and minimize the negative. Further, if violence was reported, this was done a few days after its actual occurrence. For example, after more than two months of peaceful relations between the students in Los Angeles's Tongva High School a brawl broke out between twelve African and Mexican Americans. The brawl lasted about nine minutes until police reinforcements arrived to break it up and arrest the individuals who were still fighting. This particular episode was not reported in any of the media that day, and neither were the brawls that occurred the next day, or another brawl that occurred two days after that. Only after the fourth episode was there a small story in the newspaper, and it was placed in the middle of that day's edition. When I called and asked one of the reporters who had previously been covering the violence in schools why the other brawls had not been mentioned in the media, he said, "I guess it's fair to say we [in the media] don't want to be responsible for creating more violence, especially if it is just another story of the same violence that's been presented numerous times before. There's really no enormous incentive for it [to carry the story]."[43] Although no direct information surfaced indicating that school authorities and the various media directors had reached some agreement, I observed a significant reduction in the reportage of school violence in each of the schools during the period when some level of civility in interethnic relations had been established.[44]

REINVESTING IN INFRASTRUCTURE

Investing in physical projects to improve the school campus's infrastructure had a positive influence on maintaining the newfound peace in each school. Usually this involved athletic facilities, classrooms, or the various commons areas of the campus. Such projects were efforts to marry the social and physical environments to create the idea that a totally new environment and time had come, a time in which all students could pursue their education unimpeded by concerns of personal safety. An example of this occurred at Los Angeles's Tongva High School, where construction to improve the deteriorating physical condition of the campus began within sixty days after the violence between the ethnic groups had stopped. The school's athletic facilities were greatly upgraded, as were the configuration of classrooms, some new equipment was installed, and furniture was added to the cafeteria area. In addition, the custodial staff increased its efforts to maintain a very clean campus. These improvements made the school a more appealing place to be for six to eight hours of the day, and as the school became more appealing, students were more inclined to control their behavior for fear that if they did not they would be suspended, transferred, or expelled from a place that they now liked. This internally controlled behavior significantly eased the animosity among students and contributed to the maintenance of peaceful ethnic relations within the school. Examples of this can be seen in the comments of Nigel, an African American attending Oakland's Kaiser High School, and Sergio, a Mexican American attending Los Angeles's Chumash High School.

> *Nigel:* I do like the new gym floor and cafeteria that they put in the school. It was a piece of motherfucking shit before, and now it looks great and feels great to play on too. School is definitely better now, and you can have fun. . . . No, I ain't getting into shit [violence] anymore, 'cause like I said I like hanging at school, and if I smack a Mexican now I'm definitely

out of here to some school that's shitty like it was here before. So I ain't messing around with the Mexicans like I did before.[45]

Sergio: Yeah, I like coming to school now that everything is getting remodeled and stuff. It used to be such a mess, but they really improved it. The new classrooms are so much more bright, and I like what they did to the cafeteria too. . . . Shit, if I mess up like I used to and get into another fight they'll get rid of me, and I don't really want to go to another school now that the fighting is over and this place is getting nice.[46]

DEMOGRAPHIC AND SOCIAL CHANGE IN THE PEACE PROCESS

Despite all the efforts to create and maintain peace in the schools discussed thus far, there was still a period of uncertainty as to whether violence might rise up again. Two additional factors would prove instrumental in solidifying the peace that had been established. In the case of Boston, even though violence had been significantly reduced, it was the structural changes that proved decisive. The decision to eliminate forced busing removed one of the rival groups, and peaceful relations based on the old social order returned.

However, in the cases of Los Angeles and Oakland, it was the continuing increase of Mexican American families moving into the area, accompanied by some of the African American families moving out to other suburban areas, that helped to maintain civil relations among the students. The demographic change of increasing numbers of Mexican Americans in the area, and thus in the schools, forced the African Americans to see that the neighborhood they were defending was inevitably going to change and that the only choices they had were to move away, quit school, or find a way to adapt. Thus many students resigned themselves to the fact that they must try to get along with the Mexican Americans because they were going to be a permanent part of the school's student population. The comments of Shirley and Cameron are representative. Shirley was an African American attending Oakland's Kaiser High School:

My parents ain't going to move because they don't have any money to do it. So I'm just going to mind my business and if they [the Mexican American students] treat me good, I'll treat them good. If they treat me like a friend, I'll treat them like a friend. The Mexicans is going to keep living here, so we got to find a way to live with each other.[47]

Cameron was an African American student attending Los Angeles's Chumash High School:

I'm glad the fighting has stopped, it was really getting to be a mess for everybody. I know there's some guys that wanted to keep it up with the Mexicans, but there ain't no use trying to get them to leave this school and this area, 'cause they're just going to keep coming. We just going to have to keep working to see if we can get along because there ain't no other way now.[48]

During this period of calm, some violence in the Los Angeles and Oakland schools continued, much of it between rival gangs. Since the gangs were ethnically segregated, this might seem to be a continuation of the ethnic violence the school had experienced, especially because gang members had in previous times joined their coethnics in fighting members of the rival ethnic group. However, during this new phase the violence between the gangs was over organizational interests (drug business, neighborhood geographic control) and not over ethnic issues. School officials worked hard to clarify this for the students, parents, and the broader community so that these incidents would not produce a resumption of ethnic conflict. The efforts of school officials were quite effective, and ethnic violence in each of the schools of this study did not begin again.

Finally, as time moved on, the violence between students in Los Angeles and Oakland became increasingly seen by the broad student body as personal fights that had nothing to do with them being Mexican or African American. Two examples can be seen in the comments of Dana, an African American attending Oakland's Miwok High School, and Omar, a Mexican American attending Los Angeles's Tongva High School.

> *Dana:* Did you see the two guys fighting in the hall? It was something fierce. There was blood all over the place. . . . I don't really know the two very well, but the African American guy said the Mexican was interrupting him in class or something. They both are stupid if you ask me because they're always talking to people in class and making it hard to concentrate. Maybe if they hit each other enough they won't act so stupid to everyone else. [The others in the group, which includes both African American and Mexican students, all laugh.][49]

> *Omar:* I didn't see the whole fight, but when I walked by it was going pretty good. Then the security guards came and broke it up. The two girls in the fight were fighting over some boyfriend. The Mexican girl said she was just talking to the guy and the black girl said, "I don't care, just don't get near him!" and then she went to start the fight again. Is that crazy? [The others who are both African American and Mexican American laugh].[50]

DEMOGRAPHIC CHANGE AND THE EMERGENCE
OF NONETHNIC CONFLICT

The period of peace (though technically phase 6 in the ethnic violence) was the start of a significant change in the way violence would occur and the way the students in the schools of Los Angeles and Oakland would interpret it. The case of Boston never saw the violence as associated with anything other than ethnicity. That was because mixing students from different ethnic backgrounds was the result of busing one group to the geographic area of the other. However, in Los Angeles and Oakland the student composition of the schools was the result of new families moving into neighborhoods and enrolling their kids in the local school. Thus it was the natural process of neighborhood change that would ultimately prove decisive in determining the nature of violence in these L.A. and Oakland schools.

As more Mexicans moved to the area, some of the African Americans who did not like this demographic change moved to other neighborhoods, or, in the case of Los Angeles, even other cities such as Covina, Pomona, and San Bernardino, to name a few. The African Americans who were left usually did not have the necessary capital to buy or even rent housing in another area, so they had to deal with the change. For example, some of the students that left the school had been active in the violence, leaving those remaining with the problem of finding a way to maintain a strong active core group of students that would consistently engage in violence toward the newcomers. As time passed and the numbers of Mexican students increased while the numbers of African American students decreased, it became clear to the African American incumbents that they were going to have to accept the change and try to get along with the Mexicans.

Once members of the incumbent group stopped being hostile in their dealings with the newcomers, a more positive and friendly relationship between the members of each group began to form. This increase in friendships across ethnic lines, along with the absence of the stigma that had sometimes been attached to them in previous phases, ushered in a new social environment that altered the character of violence. Fights did continue to break out, but they were interpreted by both the participants and onlookers as disputes between the combatants about something that had nothing to do with ethnic issues. A typical example occurred on a Friday at Los Angeles's Tongva High School when I ran to witness a Mexican American and an African American fighting in the hallway. After about a minute of fighting, the school police and two security guards broke up the fight and escorted the two to the police room on campus. After the fight ended, a group of Mexican students were walking away from having witnessed the fight and one said, "That was stupid to fight over a girl that is actually the girlfriend of another boy." Two of the others said, "Yeah, really dumb!" This incident happened in the morning, and during different times of the day I recorded fourteen other students (eight African Americans and six Mexicans) who gave the same account of the fight when passing information on to other students. There was no mention of ethnicity, whereas before there would certainly have been.

In sum, as time passed, the violence that emerged would arise from such causes as disputes between gang members, personal disputes over perceived individual insults, rivalries involving romantic relationships or social status within peer networks, or disputes over the theft of personal items. In essence, the demographic changes that had brought violence to the schools were now providing the basis for better relations between the groups, and they would be responsible for a general change in the nature of the violence that would occur in the schools. This "new" violence would be the kind considered by the general public as generic to low-income communities and schools that goes unreported in the media because it is seen as being so "normal" to these areas. Thus, while the form of violence changed, it did not go away because the structural and cultural conditions of lower-class life across ethnic groups encourage, or do not discourage, the physical use of force as a legitimate means of solving disputes. In part this is because the world of the poor is a physical world where the primary resource available to individuals without money is personal strength.[51]

SOME CONCLUDING COMMENTS

This chapter has focused on the factors and interventions that helped authorities establish a more amicable climate within those schools that had been racked by violent confrontations between students from different ethnic groups. These factors and interventions could not immediately suspend all the violence, but over time they did manage to create a civil climate. The two general approaches were "deterrence," using the physical force of law enforcement, and a "public health approach," combining strategies for conflict resolution with improvements to the campus' physical infrastructure. School authorities established social control by first imposing it from the outside and then creating the type of social conditions where order occurred as result of the students' internal mechanisms for self-control.

In terms of what strategies were the most effective, one would have to start with those that have been identified as deterrence. The presence and tactics of police and parole officers were initially most effective in reducing the violence and restoring social order. However, because the police could not be present all the time, the subsequent efforts to provide social support systems to address grievances, ameliorate disputes, and invest in the school's infrastructures would lay the foundation for sustained tolerance.

As time moved on, these strategies became more effective in changing the basic character of the violence. Violent incidents in all the schools continued, but they ceased to be over ethnic issues and to be seen by the student body as such. Ironically, the efforts by school officials had been successful in subduing ethnic violence, but as a result the violence that did continue reestablished the idea that violence was just "normal" for schools with many students from lower-income families because this was simply how students from lower-class families dealt with conflict resolution.[52] This view would appear to be a roundabout way of saying there is a culture of violence within the lower class, but such a conclusion would be wrong. A more accurate understanding would be that a more general culture among the lower class values physical strength and resolve and considers the use of physical force in resolving certain disputes reasonable and appropriate.[53]

Conclusion

Now in the cool of evening I catch
a hint of the forest, of that taking
of sudden breath that pines demand;
it's on my skin, a light oil, a sweat
born of some forgotten leaning into fire.

—Philip Levine, "Fire," 1989

This book has focused on ethnic violence in schools. Ethnic violence is a phenomenon that continues to be an active part of social life throughout the world. The United States is not an exception. Given that it is a nation composed of an inordinately large number of divergent ethnicities with resource disparities and competition falling along ethnic lines, this violence is likely to continue in the immediate future. In an effort to better understand this phenomenon, the book drew on two studies of ethnic violence in eight US high schools. I focused on violence in schools because school is not only a socially designated protected space where the next generation is being educated in the academic skills necessary to be productive, but a place where students are being socialized to become what society has determined are responsible, law-abiding citizens. Further, this book includes two separate studies of ethnic violence in schools conducted twenty-six years apart. This large gap in time allowed for a better understanding of the factors specific to a particular time in history that precipitated, maintained, and stopped various aspects of ethnic violence, as well as factors that were consistent over time.[1] The use of both studies provided an empirical advantage to draw some valuable sociological conclusions concerning the dynamics of ethnic violence in schools, violence more generally, and specific policy approaches to control them.

SOME SOCIOLOGICAL LESSONS

To begin, ethnic conflict in schools is likely to occur when the ethnic demography of a school is disrupted by significant numbers of newcomers. This can be seen in the events associated with Mexicans moving into certain South Central areas of Los Angeles and the conflict that erupted in the local high schools there, which included schools participating in the present study, as well as in subsequent events when the tables were turned and Mexicans attacked African Americans who had recently moved into what had been the exclusively Mexican areas of Hawaiian Garden and Cypress Park in greater L.A.[2] Whereas middle-class schools can survive such changes, lower-class schools become volatile environments for conflict to emerge. This is a result of structural conditions limiting the choices of lower-class parents as to where they can afford to live, along with some cultural factors regarding how conflict is to be handled. Human relations are such that it is difficult to find a situation where there is no conflict, but how conflicts are expressed and mediated varies. Students in middle-class schools are more likely *not* to use physical aggression to deal with conflicts they are having with other student(s) and instead to use aggressive language and psychological bullying, involving the tactics of exclusion, negative exposés via the Internet, or simple avoidance of the people with whom they are in conflict.[3] This is due to a combination of two primary factors: (1) a pervading belief among middle-class parents and students that using violence increases the chances of becoming involved with the legal system, which could jeopardize students' chances of transitioning to college and realizing their socioeconomic goals; and (2) the recognition that on those rare occasions when violence is threatened, or even occurs, middle-class families have access to third-party officials such as state law enforcement and lawyers to intervene in the social conflict.

Now, concerning the first point it could be asked, don't parents from the lower socioeconomic strata also value the school as a vehicle to realize the socioeconomic goals of their children, and don't lower-class kids know there are authorities that could help them avoid conflict? Certainly some lower-class parents do value education for advancing their children' socioeconomic potentialities, but far fewer of them have achieved financial success, feel strongly enough about the importance of school, or have the time to constantly monitor their children' behaviors. What is more, their children have far fewer material possessions and comforts that they risk losing by participating in violence.[4] In brief, there is substantially less to leverage as a deterrent to violence in lower-class families, and this is even without considering the presence of strong values that approve of physical aggression as a way to settle disputes.[5] Further, lower-class kids do know there are authorities, but the vast majority of these youth see them as the "enemy," always trying to control them but either not willing or not capable of protecting them from danger.[6]

In addition, it could reasonably be asked whether the difference is that middle-class kids learn the skills of avoiding conflict better than lower-class kids, or whether administrators of middle-class schools are just more effective in squelching conflict. In addressing the first possibility, it is important to point out that skills to avoid conflict are learned and used every day by students from both social classes, but these skills are needed far less in middle-class schools because so little violence in the form of physical aggression occurs.[7] As to the second, in general, administrators in middle-class schools are not more effective than those in lower-class schools, because violence in the form of psychological bullying occurs more often in middle-class schools than in lower-class schools, and some of this psychological bullying is so severe that it leads to suicides. Further, rampage shootings, which have more often than not been directly related to bullying, have occurred more often in middle-class schools, even though there are procedures in place and these procedures are followed.[8] So, the answer still lies in the social class culture of the schools. That is why, when observing the behaviors of lower-class kids attending middle-class schools, I would see them consistently behave like their middle-class classmates. Basically, middle-class culture permeated these schools and averted the forms of ethnic violence seen in lower-class schools.

The case of lower-class kids is different. If they do not like the changes occurring in their school, they do not have the luxury of voicing their displeasure with the school to their parents and expecting their parents to be capable of making the adjustments necessary to correct the situation. Their parents generally lack the financial capital to move and the social capital, confidence, time, or will to intervene. Thus, the lower-class students have to acquiesce to these changes or fight to resist them; and, as has occurred in cases across the United States, they generally fight as a first option.

A second conclusion has to do with the development of the violence itself. A number of theories describe how violence occurs. In general, they focus on frustration-aggression, psychopathology, social learning, relative deprivation, or group dynamics,[9] but the occurrence of violence is not always the result of a singular process, as many of these theories would indicate. This would also include the theories of Collins and Horowitz, which, because of their relevance, have been consistently referenced throughout the book. No doubt, a significant number of violent events occur as the result of an internal buildup, as both Collins and Horowitz claim, and once the violence has been initiated individuals often become immersed in the immediate action. However, there is considerable variation in how individuals respond to the same stimuli, and this is dependent on the immediate situation with which they are confronted. Therefore, both of these theories are inadequate as stand-alone explanations of ethnic violence in American schools.

Theoretically, Collins's idea of "entrainment" is also present, although never explicitly stated, in Horowitz's theory of group actions within riots. Using some form of the "entrainment" concept to explain every violent incident, including the "deadly ethnic riot," misses some important distinctions involving the ethnic violence that occurred in the schools studied here as well as violence more generally. First, a great array of violent actions occur in both what I have called "individual-oriented" and "group-oriented" violence. Contrary to both Collins's and Horowitz's hypotheses, individuals have often become involved without any immediate emotional buildup, or, once involved, without being consumed in some trancelike experience until the violence has ended. Rather, the results from the present study indicate that participation in violence can be part of an instinctual response to being in the wrong place at the wrong time, part of a calculated plan to attack another person, the result of an immediate decision to come to the aid of another person, or simply the result of mimicking the behavior of another participant caught in the melee. Thus, the concept of "entrainment" is limited to specific events because there are occasions when emotional buildup is not present and individuals are fully calculating their moves in starting, participating, and ending their involvement. Consequently, "entrainment" plays a significant role in the violent process, but it is not sufficient to explain the range of observed behaviors presented in this book.

From the current study we learn that violence is a response to the specific predicament that individuals find themselves in, given the context of the larger social environment. Ethnic violence in the schools manifests in a variety of actions influenced by the ethnicity of the combatants, but the etiology of this violence will be quite varied, and the intensity of the actions taken will depend on the specific interactions of the fight and any information the combatants have concerning previous fights like the one they are in. In other words, how violence manifests itself depends on the prior experience of the combatants with fighting situations that they have observed or been directly involved in, as well as the immediate circumstances of the present encounter. However, notwithstanding the great variation in the causes and kinds of violent acts, ethnic violence in school will have its origins in the existing conflict of the local community, and like that conflict it will be intense (i.e., violent) because in practice ethnicity is a fundamental part of an individual's belief system and attacks on it, like attacks on religion, evoke a passionate reaction.

The third conclusion is that, regardless of class background, no specific ethnic group is, because of some cultural trait, more prone to being victims or victimizers. This can most clearly be seen in the actions of African Americans in the two studies of this book. In Boston they were more victims than victimizers, whereas in Los Angeles and Oakland they were more victimizers than victims. What is most critical in establishing the victim/victimizer position are the circumstances in which members of a particular ethnic group find themselves. If they are resident incumbents of a neighborhood, they are likely to aggressively resist newcomers' intrusion into their world; whereas, if they are the newcomers, they are likely to become victims of violent reactions to their presence.

A fourth conclusion has to do with the course of ethnic violence in high schools. Once ethnic violence emerges in schools it will have a natural history. This history presents itself in phases with different stages, and as I have described in this book, these phases have a starting point and an ending point. Left unattended, each phase will proceed to the next until there is a significant "official" intervention or until student resolve to continue has diminished. It is because of this natural history's content that I have found the metaphor of fires useful, for as in the case of fires, prior conditions set the stage for them, and once they begin their intensity and duration will be determined by the environmental conditions that feed them.

A fifth conclusion has to do with whether ethnic violence in schools is really just an extension of the "culture of violence" that already exists in the neighborhood. The ethnic violence that erupts in schools is not part of any existing "culture of violence" in the schools. It is linked to structural conditions within the broader social environment in which the students live. Although this form of violence is brought to the schools from the outside, once it appears on the school campus it is influenced by the specific conditions inside the school, such as the schedule of classes, the organization of students and curriculum (i.e., tracking of students), and the physical structure of classrooms, corridors, building entrances and exits. All of these influence the interactions of students and provide opportunities for violent encounters. They also affect the duration of a violent incident when the distance that authorities must travel to intervene is significant, or its intensity when, as in the case of riots and stampedes, the masses of students find limited options for exiting the school building.

It is true that after the ethnic violence ends in the schools, violence in each continues, but this violence is not driven by ethnic antagonisms. In this study the nonethnic violence that returned to the schools was clearly associated with the general norms that I had previously observed in other lower-class communities where physical force was valued and where there was a general approval, or at least not disapproval, of the use of violence in resolving disputes over personal respect and honor, possessions, and money.[10] Nonetheless, this general sanction for the use of violence to settle disputes does not mean that lower-class students approve of all forms of violence for all occasions. For example, they generally disapprove of the use of a gun in the following situations: when one of the combatants is unarmed, is physically smaller, and has not shown any signs of aggressing toward the individual with the gun; when the gun owner continues to use force, and in particular a weapon, after achieving dominance in a particular fight; or when the gun owner uses violence against random individuals. In brief, although violence is more likely to be approved of as an acceptable tool to manage some conflict situations in lower-class communities, it is also understood within these communities that violence is not universally applicable to all conflict situations or extolled as part of a generalized "culture of violence."[11]

POLICY CONSIDERATIONS

As in any case involving violence that causes physical injury and psychological distress, there must be a general strategy for managing the problem, and this strategy must include both deterrence and public health approaches. The exact proportion of each approach to be utilized by authorities will depend on both the conditions of the conflict, the time it occurs, and the capabilities of the authorities. When violence is occurring on a regular everyday basis, there is a need for an immediate and prolonged deterrence approach to reestablish order on the school campus. The vast majority of parents, students, teachers, and school authorities support such an approach. However, once social order has been reestablished, public health–oriented policies can be implemented in an incremental and progressively deliberate manner. What follows are initiatives that can be effective in managing the local community's ethnic antagonisms that students bring to their social interactions in the school, by reducing bullying behavior that expands into outright ethnic violence and by impeding fighting between individuals that can expand into more virulent forms of collective violence.

Deterrence Initiatives

Deterrence begins with school officials learning about the social conditions in the students' neighborhoods. Basically, school authorities need to do reconnaissance of the neighborhoods they serve to determine whether these neighborhoods are experiencing social change in their ethnic composition, class composition, or both. Problems associated with ethnic violence among students usually occur when new residents to a neighborhood, or a school, as in the case of Boston in this study, are from the lower class of a different ethnic group. In the present study the social class of the families in the neighborhoods from which students were drawn was a critical factor in determining whether there would be ethnic conflict and violence: the "control schools," which had the same ethnic groups attending them but no overt antagonism or violence between the two factions, were predominantly middle class.[12] Thus, knowing that changes are occurring in the neighborhood and what the demographic nature of those changes are will prove vital in constructing an effective policy to prevent or minimize both destructive behavior and a disrupted learning experience.

Once there is evidence that changes are occurring in the neighborhood and that there are reports of antagonisms between the new and incumbent residents, school authorities should begin to think of how they will use the assets at their disposal to deter violent behavior. Hiring more school security guards will be essential, but two other policies must be initiated as well. The first is a more thorough training period for prospective guards in skills as conflict mediators as well as agents of intervention to stop violent interactions once they have begun. What I observed in the schools of this study was that the security guards were usually drawn from the neighborhoods around the schools. Thus, they were vulnerable and ineffectual in performing their duties because they had a tendency to identify with the ethnic group they themselves were from, yield to social pressure from neighborhood coethnics to support the ethnic group they were from, or be fearful of injury in stopping a violent incident. In essence, administrators must upgrade personnel charged with providing security for the students and teachers by selecting individuals from a broad geographic base, training them better in both dispute mediation and self-defense, increasing their pay to strengthen professionalization of the job, placing them in schools that are not in the area that they live in, and instituting a formal review process concerning the execution of their duties.

It should be emphasized that security guards form the "front line" for school safety because they closely interact every day with the students and can hear what the issues are among the various segments of the student body. If the information they receive is passed on to school authorities, this information can better prepare officials to be on the alert for problems. This will significantly lessen the need for additional police support.

The various departments of law enforcement form the next group of agents needed to deter ethnic violence in schools. When there is a school district police department as there is in Los Angeles, additional officers must be assigned to be present in schools where there is evidence of increased ethnic tensions. In cities where the local police are solely responsible for public safety, school officials must communicate to police officials the need for a greater presence to deter and break up violence between students from the rival ethnic groups. The presence of police at the school, as well as an increase in police surveillance of the primary routes taken by the students going to and from school, will help reduce the initiation of violence or, if unable to deter fights from starting, then lessen the time of each confrontation. It should be remembered (see chapter 4) that the time involved in violent acts is quite brief, so being in position to intervene quickly will be very important. This is likely to reduce the number and extent of physical injuries connected with each episode.

The use of agents from the probation and parole departments of the state judicial system is also an effective means of deterring violence. There is no question that having parole officers present in schools experiencing ethnic violence, or any kind of violence for that matter, had a positive impact in lessening the violence. Even when no parole officer is physically present on the school campus, if the local office is alerted to the problem so that it can act quickly to stop the violator, this effectively disrupts the contribution of formal organizations in perpetrating additional violence, as many of the individuals removed assume some type of leadership role. Often the state can be a force for reproducing inequality, but in the case of ethnic school violence the social stability provided by state agents, Weber's "armed men with guns," is preferable to ethnic warfare. Therefore, the use of these law enforcement departments is particularly important for effectively deterring ongoing and future ethnic violence in schools.

Some schools, like those in Boston and New York, have installed metal detectors. Generally, there is some question about their overall effectiveness because the machines are not particularly sophisticated in detecting all the objects that can be used as weapons and students have found ways to get weapons into the schools despite the machines. There is the additional logistical problem during the morning of efficiently processing all the students who have to go through the machines so that they can get to class on time. Further, although students have found ways to make weapons available for use, it is not clear whether they are able to circumvent the machines or whether they simply find an alternative way to sneak weapons in. Thus it is best not to rely on metal detection devices before there is evidence that ethnic violence has become a consistent occurrence. Using metal detectors sparingly at specific times when violence is present on the campus will avoid the concerns of some educational critics that such devices create a mood of insecurity and negatively affect the overall educational climate of the schools, thereby producing the very outcome they were intended to prevent.[13] However, once violence has developed into an everyday occurrence, metal detection machines can reduce the number of weapons on campus and thus make some modest contribution toward reducing the severity of injuries from violent incidents.

Various institutions outside the school itself have been shown to have an impact on violence. One of these is the media. The media have generally proceeded to do their job and report violent events that have involved relatively large numbers of students and caused injuries. The reporting has included the "normal" recording of events, as well as more in-depth "magazine" or "feature" stories. Each has had the unintended consequence of contributing to the violence by appealing to some adolescent needs for attention and fame. Thus, school officials must clarify with the reporters and editors that coverage of such events is more helpful when the stories simply recount the known facts and when the more in-depth stories that identify specific individuals are eliminated.

Local politicians representing the district where there was ethnic conflict were another faction found to have had the unintended effect of promoting the violence in the schools. They all attempted to represent the interests of their districts and by extension their own positions within the various polities. They tried to avoid blaming and demonizing their community members by justifying those who were involved at the ground level of the conflict, a position as it turned out that was often interpreted by participants in the violence as supportive of their actions. Therefore, when ethnic violence begins school officials must quickly contact local leaders to request their assistance in condemning it, and at the same time encourage them to use any influence they have with local families and provide any incentives they have to stop local youth from participating.

Finally, many times during the present research, teachers either verbally supported the students of their own ethnic group or simply stayed silent about these students' participation in violence. Students inevitably interpreted their silence as support, and this assisted in furthering the violence. In addition, teachers' fears of being physically injured as a result of any efforts to intervene to stop the fighting, or fears of being attacked after school as punishment for intervening in an earlier altercation, often inhibited them from consistently intervening to quell the violence. The upshot was that teachers' actions, or inactions, were counterproductive in impeding the violence. Clearly, some of the teachers' inhibitions were associated with both their own and their union's reluctance to assume any role in providing security because they were hired to be educators, as well as their reluctance to risk becoming the target of legal proceedings if someone were to be injured as a result of their intervention. Therefore, it is imperative that school officials work with teachers and unions to seek their support in informing school officials, formal security guards, and police of impending student fights, brawls, riots, and in identifying individuals involved (both leaders and participants) in all of these after they have occurred. This would be a reasonable substitute for direct intervention and could contribute to reducing future violence. Certainly a case can be made that providing this information is not a violation of an educator's formal duties because at some level teachers are official agents of the institution. However, if school administrators are successful in recruiting teachers to provide this information, security must be heightened to ensure their maximum safety from retaliation while they are on the school campus. This would require that police and/or security guards be on duty until all the teachers had left the campus safely.

Public Health Initiatives

I have spent a good deal of time on initiatives designed to deter ethnic violence in schools. A public health approach to eliminating violence is related to the idea that if officials want to sustain a peaceful climate they must invest in the social environment of the school itself. Much of what I will suggest is likely to have little impact on deterring the violence once it gets started. However, it can help prevent violence from getting a significant toehold in a particular school or, once the peace has been restored, can help create a climate of tolerance and amity.

The primary intent of a public health approach is to create a new violence-resistant environment. The first step in this approach is to invest in the physical structure of the campus. Building new structures, or remodeling existing classrooms and activity facilities, is important. So too is purchasing new electronic and athletic equipment. This not only provides the students, most of whom are from low-income families, with a new view of their social environment but also creates a greater desire to be in school because school is a place where, along with learning, one can have fun. Certainly the schools that began to remodel facilities while violence was still in an intense phase found that it had an immediate influence on switching the students' attention away from fear, anger, and revenge to an interest in what was being created and how it would look. Thus renovating the physical environment can be particularly valuable.

On the social side, a number of associations must be developed and nurtured—as much as possible, at the same time. One of these associations must involve parents, who should meet formally and regularly to discuss problems and to make recommendations about educational and safety issues at the school. The parent organization could also serve as a place to explain to parents what is occurring in the schools and how they might reach out to other parents to assist school officials' attempts to suppress violence on campus. Usually there exists, on paper at least, a school PTA (parent-teacher association) that can be revitalized and used for this purpose, but if community parents view the existing PTA as obsolete or irrelevant a new organization can be established for the primary purpose of controlling violence.

A second extremely important association should be composed of a specific number of students selected by members of their high school class to represent them. These representatives may be formal officers elected by each school class (i.e., class president, vice president, treasurer, and secretary) or individuals that students select informally, or a combination of the two. Such associations can assume a number of roles, for example, a fact-finding commission concerning student discontent, antagonisms, and conflict that passes on its findings and recommendations to school officials or a quasi-court that adjudicates student conflicts by recommending to school officials penalties for violations of school rules of conduct.

Third, there should be a faculty association to advise faculty on professional conduct, explaining expectations of them as teachers and agents of the school district. Teachers should be clear about their role in education and the monitoring of students' sexual harassment and aggressive behavior (bullying, threats of physical violence, and assaults) that they observe in their classrooms and other public spaces on campus. This would aid in dealing with not only ethnic violence but conflict and violence in general.

One of the vital strategies of a public health approach to violence is to generate and disseminate information. In this regard, the formal educational curriculum should be expanded to include in humanities and social studies courses the histories and cultural attributes (morals, values, and beliefs) of the various ethnic groups attending the school. These new inclusions should discuss the way that different cultures understand jokes and slights, as well as what each considers the proper response to them. This is essential in reducing unintentional interpretations perceived as violations of respect or honor and seen by those offended or humiliated as calling for a physically aggressive response that can initiate a round of interethnic violence. Further, the school should integrate into their rules of conduct, as well as the teaching curriculum, a clear and precise definition of what constitutes bullying, extortion, battery, assault, and hate crimes. As I indicated earlier in the text, often students will ignore these types of efforts, but that is not a sufficient reason to dismiss them because they can contribute to student self-control by giving them some guidance as to whether to participate in what they now know is an officially prohibited action.

A telephone hotline for parents, community residents, and students to anonymously report occurring or impending violence is very helpful to officials in their efforts to intervene quickly and effectively. The protection of callers' identities may encourage more students to monitor violence and participate in peace efforts because they need not worry about retaliation and physical injury.

Finally, an effective policy is much less dependent on its design than on its implementation.[14] Implementation is the most critical element to the realization of any policy's goals. In brief, the effectiveness of the initiatives I have just advanced will be predicated on believing in the policy, committing to its operationalization every day, and regularly evaluating its progress. A policy that does not build in an evaluative component is operating in the dark.

TOWARD A COMPREHENSIVE PLAN

I have suggested that ethnic violence in schools can be understood through the metaphor of fire, and fire protection for the future does not rest solely with the fire department. It requires a more comprehensive plan that includes other agencies like landscape architects to design an environment with plants that make for a healthier and more fire-resistant ecosystem. However, as a society we find it much more challenging to both our moral and value orientations to commit to such an approach. For example, we as a society find it extremely difficult to aid people who have violated the existing laws, no matter what circumstances may have justified their actions, because of a pervasive and intensely held belief that everyone has opportunities and difficulties that they alone are responsible for managing.[15] Thus it is the publicly accepted norm that, whatever troubles individuals experience, they and they alone must resolve their problem or face society's disdain and possible punishment.[16]

The logistics that would be required to implement a comprehensive approach to violence in schools (deterrence and public health) present yet another challenge. For example, a number of years ago, in an attempt to solve the youth gang problem confronting many communities throughout the nation, the US Department of Justice developed a comprehensive program called the Weed and Seed Program. This program recognized that if law enforcement was to effectively confront the gang problem it needed both to establish and maintain safety and social order and to invest resources in rebuilding local communities' economic and material infrastructure to produce an environment more resistant to gang development. This idea of getting rid of the weeds and reseeding plants that were more productive and resilient to the regrowth of weeds was simple, but it proved too complicated to implement because the logistics of "weeding" involved merely one federal agency (the Department of Justice), whereas "seeding" required the coordination of multiple federal agencies (e.g., the Departments of Health and Human

Services, Commerce, Labor, and Housing and Urban Development) who lacked the legislative authority, the necessary lines of communication, and the integrated budget to manage this segment of the policy.[17] Thus there has been a constant need to fix logistical problems associated with the policy's design.

Finally, those interested in creating a social environment that will control violence in our inner-city schools, and not just ethnic violence, will need to employ both "weed" (i.e., law enforcement/deterrence) and "seed" (i.e., public health/investment) approaches no matter how difficult the exercise. Of course, no policy can assure the elimination of ethnic violence, as the examples of ethnic riots in Los Angeles and ethnic conflict in New York can attest.[18] Nonetheless, such an approach can create conditions presenting the individuals who lived through it with the opportunity to use the experience as a resource to rise like a phoenix from the ashes into a community that is both tolerant and cooperative.[19] This has occurred in numerous sections of Los Angeles, Oakland, New York, and Boston that have experienced the intense ethnic conflict described in this book. However, a critic of the comprehensive approach I have suggested could point out that ethnic violence ceased in the schools I studied without a great deal of seeding by government, and that observation would be accurate. Nevertheless, and this is most important, nonethnic violence remains a serious problem in all of these schools, and for that matter in most public schools where the majority of students come from low-income families, and this is directly related to the fact that little seeding has been done in these communities. What is most important is that a comprehensive program implemented before any outbreak of ethnic violence stands a much greater chance of reducing the probability of its starting and of reducing the amount of destruction in student injuries, education, and property damage that it will cause once it begins.

The violence that occurred in the schools of this study effectively destroyed civil relations between the students much as a fire destroys a forest, but such disasters need not spell long-term doom. The fire analogy helps us to understand this point. It has the advantage of demonstrating how after such intense violence social relations between the previous antagonist ethnic groups within each of the "problem" schools are currently (2015) quite amicable. This was the result of a combination of efforts by a variety of groups to create (i.e., seed) a healthier new environment. First, the students who had been in the heat of the fighting decided that they no longer wanted to continue or no longer approved of violence. Second, the state (law enforcement and school authorities) took action to both weed out those individuals who wanted to maintain the violence and begin a seeding process to improve the physical and pedagogical infrastructure. Third, with the arrival of a new generation of students who had not experienced any of the violence, and whose families had not experienced the same social and economic tensions associated with neighborhood change, there began a slow but steady regrowth of amicable social relations between the groups.

Methodological Appendix

The goal of the study was to examine how ethnic violence in high schools works. To understand this it was necessary to observe the violence firsthand as it was happening in the schools. Thus the first task was to pick schools that would allow for as full an investigation as possible into the conditions that precipitated the violence, how the violent actions between individuals took place, and what caused the violence to subside and stop.

DRAWING A SAMPLE OF SCHOOLS

The first step toward creating a sample was to draw up a list of schools throughout the United States that had reported experiencing ethnic violence. The list was constructed from news reports and a survey of the reports on violence published by the state departments of education in the fifty states. A total of 119 schools were identified as reporting ethnic violence, 84 of them in the state of California. The data indicated that while a variety of ethnic groups were involved in these schools' conflicts the overwhelming majority of the conflict was between Latinos and African Americans. Given that the largest number of schools reporting violence were in California and that they overwhelmingly involved the same conflicting ethnicities (Latinos and African Americans) as found in other parts of the nation, it was determined that the study's sample should be drawn from California schools. Of the 84 California schools reporting ethnic violence, all were found to be in areas experiencing ethnic demographic change. For this reason it was decided that a stratified sampling frame would be used that would include one list of schools experiencing ethnic violence related to neighborhood change and another list of schools in neighborhoods experiencing ethnic change but no ethnic violence. To determine if a school's social class composition had any impact on whether there would be ethnic violence, I decided that an additional stratified frame should be used. I took the list of schools experiencing ethnic change with no ethnic violence and divided it into two sublists, one composed of schools with the majority of their student body coming from middle- and upper-income families, and another composed of schools with the majority of their student population coming from families with working-class or low incomes.

I did not use census or Current Population Survey data to track neighborhoods undergoing ethnic demographic change and from that data identify the local schools that potentially could have been sites for violence because these data generally cannot provide an accurate identification of the most current changes occurring in neighborhoods and because some census tracts do not match the school district's geographic areas where the residents' children are assigned. Thus I decided to create what became my primary sample pool of seventy-three California schools by canvassing the school districts in the five largest metropolitan areas of California and asking them to identify which high schools were experiencing ethnic changes to their student populations and also ethnic violence and which of these schools were experiencing ethnic change but no ethnic violence. Canvassing the school districts provided a more current and accurate pool of schools experiencing ethnic change and violence.

Once the lists were formed, I entered them into a computer program file, and from that file I asked the computer to randomly draw two names from the list of schools that had reported violence. One of these was from Los Angeles and the other was from Oakland. I then selected four schools from the list where ethnic change was occurring with no ethnic violence. I randomly selected two schools that had the majority of their student populations coming from lower-income families and two schools with the majority of their populations coming from middle- or upper-income families. The final sample consisted of three schools from the Los Angeles area, one that reported ethnic violence, another that reported no violence and that drew its students from lower-income families, and a third that reported no violence and drew its students from middle- and upper-income families. In addition, the sample included three schools from the greater Oakland area, one that reported ethnic violence, one that reported no ethnic violence and drew its students from lower-income families, and another that reported no violence and drew its students from middle-income families. The total number of schools in this comparative sample was six. All of these schools were chosen in 2000, the year the study began.

Before starting the research in Los Angeles and Oakland, I remembered that twenty-six years earlier I had conducted research in Boston, Massachusetts, for Professor Ithiel de Sola Pool on the very same topic. In 1974 he had been asked by city officials to conduct a field study of the busing program to racially integrate Boston's schools. The study of two schools involved in the program was initiated to assess the policy's effectiveness in achieving social and educational progress and was designed to complement the survey data being collected by analyzing the factors affecting the daily behaviors of participants in the program. Thus I decided to contact those responsible for holding the research materials of the late Professor Pool to see if they could locate the data for that study. They did find the data and I retrieved them. After completing the three-year study of Oakland and Los Angeles schools, I coded and integrated the Boston data into the data set of the Los Angeles and Oakland schools. Thus the total sample of schools for the present study was eight: three each from Oakland and Los Angeles and two from Boston.

GAINING ACCESS

As with all participant-observation research, gaining access to the subjects for observation is essential. For the 2000–2003 portion of the study, once the schools were identified I contacted school authorities from each district to introduce the study. I requested access to observe and talk to individuals while they were on the various schools' campuses. I told them that my home institution's Institutional Review Board (IRB) protocol required that I inform everyone who might be involved in the study as to the nature of the study and its benefits and risks and that I receive signed waivers from subjects and their parents or guardians before a formal interview could be done. They consented to my request to grant me access. After receiving approval, I requested their assistance in three ways. I asked that they (1) inform everyone on the various campuses of my presence and the nature of the study; (2) provide my contact information to anyone in the community who had questions about who I was and the nature of the study; and (3) assure the community that before any formal interview took place the potential participants would be required to sign a waiver form that I would provide to potential participants or their legal guardians or both. The school principals agreed and used all or a mix of the following procedures: a formal memo, an announcement during two faculty meetings, more than two announcements to students during their homeroom meetings, a letter given to students to take home to their parents, and an advertised discussion at two local parent-teacher meetings.

In addition to school officials, I met with representatives of the police departments in each school area to explain that I would be in the area conducting research and to describe the nature of the research project. In the case of Los Angeles it was the Los Angeles School District Police, the Los Angeles County Sheriff's Office, and the Los Angeles Police Department. In Oakland it was the Oakland Police Department. The notification of these law enforcement representatives proved important because they became familiar with my presence in the area. Further, I specified clearly that I would not share data on specific individuals, as mandated by professional ethics and the University of California at Berkeley's IRB.

RECORDING DATA

Three types of data were collected for the study. The first of these was the direct observation of physical behaviors. The second was the direct observation of verbal behaviors, which included formal interviews, conversations in which I participated, and conversations that I was near enough to hear but was not formally part of. Verbal behaviors were operationalized as not merely what people said but how they said it. This included not only the pronunciation of words but the inflection and any bodily motions intended to convey particular meanings. *It should be noted that I did formal interviews, but data from them are not used in this book. They were collected for a different research question and project.*

Physical behaviors were all those bodily movements that involved preaggression emotions, signals of impending action, aggressive actions, and postaggression actions. They were catalogued using a system that I had developed by making symbolic notations first in my notepad on the type of action being recorded and the context in which it occurred. These notations included Roman numerals to designate major substantive areas and Arabic numerals in conjunction with Latin/English alphabetical letters to designate specialized subareas. Each of the designations was defined and placed in the study's General Code Book.

To observe these behaviors it was necessary to place myself in strategic positions. These positions assumed a variety of locations. Before commencing the research I surveyed the routes that the students would take in walking to and from school. I also did some reconnaissance on where the students congregated while they were at school. After gathering this information I planned my research days. I would arrive at the school by 6:30 a.m., one hour and a half before the official 8:00 a.m. start of instruction, and would assume an out-of-sight position in a garage, in an abandoned building, or on the porch of a house (all of these structures I had received prior permission from the owner to occupy) located along the route taken by the students to the school. While at school I would mingle among the students during the morning nutrition period, lunch, and the change of classes, visit classrooms and male bathrooms, and walk around the halls during class time. Throughout this time I would, where appropriate and "natural"—that is, where my actions did not interrupt and create an artificial setting—attempt to become a part of the normal flow of social life. In addition, during nutrition and lunch periods I would sometimes take a position in one of the vacant classrooms on the second floor and use binoculars and my wristwatch's stopwatch function to observe and record students' interactions. Further, when school was officially over I would mingle with students as they were filing out of school, walk with a group of students as they made their way home, or place myself in one of my out-of-sight locations to observe the students going home from school. Finally, I would visit the small local grocery stores that the students usually frequented on their way home, as well as attend the various schools' athletic events and practices, since these were staging areas for violence or places where violence occurred. This allowed me to position myself to observe what led up to a fight, the fight itself, and the people involved in stopping it.

Four other groups of individuals were also included in the study: school administrators, teachers, school security guards, and law enforcement officials (police officers and probation/parole officers). Each of these individuals knew that I was on site to do research on school violence, so I was able to interact with them freely. None of them ever refused to talk to me or prohibited me from entering their offices, classrooms, checkpoints, and squad cars. Thus I was unhindered in both directly interacting with them and observing them carrying out their formal duties. Further, at no time did they request that I open my notebooks to them for their examination, which was something that I had indicated would not be allowed because of my guarantee to protect every subject's identity. I could not have asked for more cooperation from this entire group of professionals.

I used four tools to record the data. The first was small three-by-five-inch pocket notebooks where I would record my notes using a shorthand technique. This technique would allow me to record the statements of individuals nearly verbatim as well as the behaviors observed in detail. The second tool was a pair of Nikon opera binoculars that I chose because they were powerful and easily carried because of their small size. Since the distances that I would be observing were relatively small, these binoculars proved very effective. The third tool was a small voice recorder that I used, especially while looking through the binoculars, to record behavior and thoughts about what was occurring. The fourth and final tool was a stopwatch (a function of my wristwatch) that I used to track the duration of violent interactions.

The verbal data for the study consisted of statements made directly to me or to other individuals that I was close enough to hear. Some of the statements were made in the context of a group that I was a part of; others, made to other people, I was close enough to hear. There is some misunderstanding about what participant observers do. The method is designed for researchers to be a part of the environment they are studying and to record daily life as it is happening. This means hearing people as part of their natural living experience say whatever they want to and recording it as data. There is no difference between recording physical behavior in which one is not directly involved and recording verbal expressions in a context where one is not directly involved. In each case the researcher is attempting to capture the "meanings" that the subjects are giving for various events in their lives, as well as the substantive significance of their behaviors and thoughts for the sociological life of the community (macro, meso, micro) that they are a part of. This is precisely what makes participant-observation methodology different from research using in-depth interviewing techniques.[1] There might be some difference between observed physical and verbal behaviors at the analytic stage, but there are no differences in the data-gathering process or at the ethical level (i.e., hearing conversations in which one does not participate).[2]

Some scholars seem to misconstrue what participant observation entails. In the present 2000–2003 study of violence in six California high schools, statements made by subjects in conversations that I was close enough to hear but was not directly a part of were recorded as data. This method was important because it raised the level of the data's validity: I was gathering the data completely within subjects' natural interactional environment, so there was little chance that I was in any way influencing what the subjects had to say. Likewise, physical behavior that I directly observed but was not directly participating in was recorded as data. There were very few times (a total of eleven) when I included unobserved behavior in the data—usually when a subject reported in a conversation something about his or her own behavior or that of another person. For these occurrences I sought out three *independent* witnesses of the same event and added the occurrence to the data set only when all three fully agreed with the subject's account. Further, these occasions were given a code to signify that they were unobserved behavior (see tables A.1, A.2, and A.3).

During my fieldwork I made a concerted effort to record the behaviors and statements that subjects repeatedly engaged in each and every time they did so. When one is conducting participant-observation fieldwork, it is tempting to record only new statements or behaviors because they are new and this makes them particularly interesting to the researcher. However, I conscientiously avoided this temptation because only repetitive data can be used to establish patterns in both how people think and act, and only these patterns can allow generalizations to be made with confidence.

Researchers engaged in multiyear field research face the task of organizing hundreds and sometimes thousands of field notes. Ever since they have been available, I have utilized computer-assisted qualitative data programs to organize the data I have gathered. At the time of the 1974–77 Boston research project, no programs were available, so I took notes for this study the old-fashioned way, with three-by-five-inch note cards, and placed them in boxes similar to those found in libraries for index cards. However, in the 2000–2003 study I jotted down in small pocket notebooks the notes that I took shorthand during the day and recorded other notes on a Dictaphone; in the evening I transferred them to the computer-assisted qualitative data program called Folio Views. At the time I was doing the study, this program was fully capable of using a complex coding scheme to categorize and organize field notes. Other programs were also available at the time, but Folio Views was particularly strong and in my judgment was the most strategically effective of all the programs that were on the market.[3] All the data that I did gather was categorized, coded, and entered into the program. The codes were developed to address theoretical positions, as well as hypotheses related to them, and as such were used to designate substantive issues to be addressed. The codes were generated using both deductive and inductive means to assign demographic status to individuals and groups, their behaviors, the subjective meanings individuals gave to thoughts and events, and the meanings of their thoughts and behaviors for the functions of society. The codes were not only essential for organizing the data but indispensable for the analysis stage.

As I mentioned earlier, I also used data from my study conducted in Boston from 1974 to 1977. The Boston data consisted of both physical and verbal behavior, but the recording process was completely different. Observations in the field were taken longhand, as I had not yet taken the course in which I learned the shorthand system that I would use in my subsequent studies (including the 2000 California schools research). The notes in the Boston study were recorded on small three-by-five cards. I reread all of the observations from these cards and coded them using the same coding scheme that was being used in the California study to facilitate cross–time context comparisons. Once that was done, I entered these data into the Folio Views data set that contained the California data. This created a unified data set with observations of ethnic violence in schools some twenty-nine years apart.[4]

DATA ANALYSIS

The analysis focused on factors that influenced or caused violence to occur between students from different ethnic backgrounds, maintained it for a period of time, and contributed to its demise. The Folio Views program contained a very powerful search function that aided me in determining what patterns existed. A pattern was determined to exist when (1) a verbal or physical behavior occurred a substantial number of times; or (2) a verbal or physical behavior occurred only a few times but always in the same situation.

The first part of the analysis was to determine what behaviors occurred and when they occurred. Then the second part was to determine what factors were involved in influencing or causing these behaviors. The third part was to explain how these factors worked to produce the behaviors observed. Finally, the analysis focused on why the factors worked and produced what they did.

Ultimately, the analysis identified the general patterns related to each substantive area of interest and the patterns that were idiosyncratic. When idiosyncrasies were found they were reported as such, and every attempt was made to determine why they occurred. Further, even after I found a general pattern and interpreted it, I consistently tried to deal with potential counterfactuals. I made every effort to consider counterfactuals before rendering a final interpretation of the "what," "when," "how," and "why" in the identified patterns. I did this not simply to increase the confidence level of the interpretation but to build the foundation for specifying under what conditions particular behaviors and outcomes from them occurred. Without this aspect of the analysis it would be difficult to predict future behaviors with any degree of certainty.

ETHICS

The primary purpose of the study was to gain a greater understanding of the dynamics that causes ethnic violence to occur in schools: how it actually starts, keeps going, and declines. This was done so that effective interventions might be developed to prevent such occurrences on other campuses and thus to reduce the number of individual students sustaining bodily injury, the amount of learning time missed, and the amount of property destroyed. The Robert Wood Johnson Foundation funded the project because of a position, shared by the US Center for Disease Control, that violence is a serious public health issue for certain groups in American society and needs to be addressed in an effort to promote a more healthy society.

Effectiveness in developing policies to control this type of violence required firsthand observation, and that is what I provided. Every study involves some degree of ethics, but one that deals with the study of violence is certainly more likely to be scrutinized. My research proposal was initially submitted to the university's IRB and was approved after a number of changes were incorporated to eliminate the potential harm to participating subjects. Next, all of the populations that were potential subjects received mailings and announcements that introduced them to the project and identified me by name as the researcher. That occurred for each school that I studied as well as with various police in the area of the schools. Thus school administrators, deans, teachers, security guards, school police, and city police were made aware of my presence and what I was studying. Students and parents were also informed of my presence on each of the campuses.

I also sought permission from some residents of the school's neighborhood to occupy space on their porches, in their garages, or in their front yards for some small amount of time when the students were going to school or coming home. In each case, the resident was told what I was studying and what the purpose of the study was. Although none of the residents whose property I wished to enter was to be a subject of the study, I provided them with verbal and written details of the study I was conducting. Not one person that I asked permission for access to their property refused, and all said they were happy to do what they could to help.

Formal interviews were conducted with a small number of subjects. Before any formal interview began, each interviewee and his or her legal guardian read the consent form that outlined the study and the pledge to keep the student anonymous and maintain confidentiality; then the interviewee and the guardian signed the form, acknowledging that they gave consent to be a part of the study. However, as previously mentioned, none of the data that emerged from these formal interviews were used in the present book.

The observation of violence among the youth attending these schools presented an ethical dilemma. In most situations in the social world, a researcher who did not try to interfere with the daily life of the subjects he or she was studying would be considered someone who was maintaining high ethical standards. However, when subjects of a study are in danger of or in the process of being hurt, not intervening into their daily life can be considered ethically problematic.

This is the dilemma I faced, and my decision was not to intervene for a number of reasons, not all of which were related to obtaining important data. The fact is that I did not intervene in any situations in which violence was about to occur or was occurring. As I mentioned in the Introduction, I did feel uneasy about that, but I had no formal authority to intervene. Thus, rather than become physically involved myself in an altercation where I had no weapon even though many of the individuals in the fights I was observing had weapons, I chose non-involvement.

Other issues related to the ethics of intervening in fights also present a dilemma. First, direct intervention might involve hurting another individual oneself, and this could be viewed as unethical. Second, informing the police meant that I would have become a formal witness and would be required to provide evidence against another person in a formal court of law. More than compromising my neutrality, this would have put me in the position of having to legally identify the individuals involved and what they did, thereby increasing their risk of being convicted of a crime and punished. This would have violated the formal agreement to keep the subjects of the study anonymous and maintain confidentiality, and in the process I would completely surrender my ethical obligation and IRB directive to protect my subjects from any harm directly associated with the research.

TABLE A.I   VIOLENT EPISODES OVER SCHOOL YEAR I

	Sept.	Oct.	Nov.	Dec.	Jan.	Feb.	March	April	May	June	TOTALS
Los Angeles											
Individual	12	18	15	11	13	5	4	5	4	4	91
Ad hoc	2	5	6	4	5						22
Brawls				3	2	6	7	7	4	3	32
Riot # 1					2						2
Riot # 2					1	1					2
Riot # 3							1 →	2			3
Stampede								1	1	2	4
Oakland											
Individual	9	15	14	15	9	6	3	4	4	4	83
Ad hoc		2	5	6	3	3	1				20
Brawls				1	1	4	6	6	4	1	23
Riot # 1					1 →	1					2
Riot # 2				1	1	2					4
Riot #3							2		2		4
Stampede								1	3	2	6
Boston											
Individual	23	17	16	7	7	4	6	5	7	3	95
Ad hoc	3	4	4	4	3	1					19
Brawls			2	2	4	6	8	3	2	1	28
Riot # 1			2	→	2						
Riot # 2			1	1							2
Riot # 3							1	1	2	1	5
Stampede			1	1		1	3	1	2	2	11

NOTE: These numbers come from my field notes. Obviously I could not be in every place that the events occurred, so the numbers of events tabulated are not the total numbers but only those that I observed and recorded—except in the case of riots and stampedes, where the data from my field notes has been supplemented by reports from school authorities that such events occurred while I was not present. Two administrators, two teachers, two students, and two security guards were given the definitions for a stampede and for each type of riot and then were asked to assign the event to one of the categories. The agreement was between 87.5 percent (seven of eight were in agreement) and 100 percent (eight of eight were in agreement).

I did not inform school or law enforcement officials of the incidents that I observed, and with the exception of one event where I was one of a group of people present when a violent incident occurred and was briefly questioned, none of them asked me about whether I had observed any incidents that they were investigating. They simply went about their jobs of investigating and left me to go about mine. In the overwhelming number of incidents that I observed, I did not know the names of the individuals involved. Luckily I observed no fatalities, although some individuals suffered serious injuries. However, the

TABLE A.2   VIOLENT EPISODES OVER SCHOOL YEAR 2

Location	Sept.	Oct.	Nov.	Dec.	Jan.	Feb.	March	April	May	June	TOTALS
Los Angeles											
Individual	4	4	2	4	2	4	2	3	2	2	29
Ad hoc	1										1
Brawls	1	5	8	5	6	4	5	4	4	2	44
Riot #1					1						1
Riot # 2	1										1
Riot # 3			1	1	1			1			4
Stampede				1		1	1	1			4
Oakland											
Individual	8	5	7	3	2	2	4	4	4	4	43
Ad hoc	1										1
Brawls	4	6	7	6	8	7	9	6	4		57
Riot # 1											0
Riot # 2											0
Riot # 3			1		1		1	1			4
Stampede								1	2		3
Boston											
Individual	10	8	7	6	4	4	4	4	5	2	54
Ad hoc											0
Brawls	7	8	5	6	4	7	7	2	3		49
Riot # 1			1								1
Riot # 2											0
Riot # 3			1	2		1	1				5
Stampede			1	1	1		2				5

NOTE: The data were sourced and categorized as in table A.1.

upshot was that the evidence from the study did provide an increased understanding of the dynamics surrounding this type of school violence.

In sum, the ethnic violence that I observed would have occurred whether I was present or not, and it is important to understand the causes and processes of this phenomenon if we are to have a chance to improve the situation for the students who are confronted with this problem, and by extension to improve the larger community in which we live. Finally, the communities and individuals involved in this research project were not tricked. They were supportive of my effort to better understand the problem. The results of this study have served as a resource for my briefings to school authorities as they develop policies to address this problem in the future.

TABLE A.3   VIOLENT EPISODES OVER SCHOOL YEAR 3

	Sept.	Oct.	Nov.	Dec.	Jan.	Feb.	March	April	May	June	TOTALS
Los Angeles											
Individual	5	4	6	3	2	3					23
Ad hoc											0
Brawls	2	4	3								9
Riot # 1											0
Riot # 2											0
Riot # 3											0
Stampede		1	1								2
Oakland											
Individual	5	5	5	2	3	1	1				22
Ad hoc	1										1
Brawls	4	5	4	1							14
Riot # 1											0
Riot # 2											0
Riot # 3											0
Stampede		1									1

NOTE: The data were sourced and categorized as in table A.1.

Notes

INTRODUCTION

1. Names have been changed to protect the privacy of the individuals quoted. I was at the school's front door observing students when Mrs. Benitez arrived and was greeted by Mr. Talbot; I took down their exchange in shorthand. Mrs. Benitez's son Hector had been in a fight and had been stabbed in the stomach. He was taken to the local hospital, where his injuries were determined to be non–life threatening. However, his injury did require numerous stitches to close the wound. At the time of the meeting between Mrs. Benitez and Mr. Talbot, the extent of the injuries was not known.

2. See Katherine Newman, Cybelle Fox, Wendy Roth, Jal Mehta, and David Harding, *Rampage: The Social Roots of School Shootings* (New York: Basic Books, 2004).

3. Because youth are a societally protected category, there is a great deal of sensitivity toward violence in institutions that are designed to serve them. However, there are also other places where the general public would find violence particularly unacceptable: places used by a broad spectrum of average people and assumed to be safe, like hospitals or malls.

4. To name just a few, there were shootings at Sandy Hook Elementary in Newtown, Connecticut (2012); West Nickel Mines School in Lancaster, Pennsylvania (2006); and Red Lake Reservation School in Red Lake, Minnesota (2005).

5. On June 26, 2012, the *Chicago Tribune* reported that 24 students in the Chicago public school system, all of whom were from inner-city schools, had been killed during the 2012 school year and that the number of students shot during the year was 319, the highest in four years. National statistics do not exist for this type of violence, but on a national scale the Center for Disease Control reported that in 2010 homicide was the leading cause of death among

ten- to twenty-year-old African Americans, the second leading cause of death for Hispanics, and the third for Native Americans. When comparing the statistics, the CDC reported that the rate for African American youth was 55.5 per 100,000, 13.5 per 100,000 for Hispanics, and 2.9 per 100,000 for whites. It is important to note that African American and Hispanics have disproportionately lower incomes and thus that these figures reflect both race and class issues. One of the facts that remains most significant is that more nonwhite individuals under the age of twenty-one die from violence than from any other cause, yet comparatively there has been little national public outrage about this situation as there has been in the cases of mass shootings occurring in Colorado (Columbine High School), Connecticut (Sandy Hook Elementary), and Kentucky (Heath High School). Among the books that focus on youth violence in lower-class neighborhoods, see especially Deborah Prothrow-Stith, *Deadly Consequences: How Violence Is Destroying Our Teenage Population and a Plan to Begin Solving the Problem* (New York: Harper-Collins, 1991); Deborah Prothrow-Stith and Howard A. Spivak, *Murder Is No Accident: Understanding and Preventing Youth Violence in America* (San Francisco: Jossey-Bass, 2001); John Devine, *Maximum Security: The Culture of Violence in Inner-City Schools* (Chicago: University of Chicago Press, 1997); and David Harding, *Living the Drama: Community, Conflict, and Culture among Inner-City Boys* (Chicago: University of Chicago Press, 2010).

6. When ethnic violence occurs in schools it is reported, and this has been the case over time; see, out of the many news stories on the subject, Carla Rivera and Eric Lichtblau, "After-School Fight Blamed on Ethnic Tension," *Los Angeles Times,* September 19, 1991; Hector Becerra, "Schools Beef Up Patrols after Fights," *Los Angeles Times,* December 3, 2004; Jeffrey Gettleman and Lee Condon, "Glendale Shaken by Slaying of Student," *Los Angeles Times,* May 7, 2000; "Racial Tensions Grow Violent at Philly High School," *National Public Radio,* December 16, 2009; Chelsea Jensen, "Kealakehe High Closed Today after Two Days of Fights," *West Hawaii Today,* December 7, 2013; Steve Brandt and Allie Shah, "South High Regroups after Brawl," *Minneapolis Star Tribune,* February 16, 2013.

7. For a social history involving the continuities in some elements of American identity, see Claude S. Fischer, *Made in America: A Social History of American Culture and Character* (Chicago: University of Chicago Press, 2010).

8. See Newman et al., *Rampage,* 3–21; Mark H. Moore, Carol V. Petrie, Anthony A. Baraga, and Brenda L. McLaughlin, eds., *Deadly Lessons: Understanding Lethal School Violence* (Washington, DC: National Academies Press, 2003), chaps. 1–6.

9. Samantha Neiman, Jill F. DeVoe, and Kathryn Chandler, *Crime, Violence, Discipline, and Safety in U.S. Public Schools: Findings from the School Survey on Crime and Safety, 2007–08* (Washington, DC: National Center for Education Statistics, US Department of Education, 2009), 7 nn. 1 and 2; Danice K. Eaton et al., "Youth Risk Behavior Surveillance—United States, 2009," *Surveillance Summaries* 59 (SS05).

10. See Eaton et al., "Youth Risk Behavior Surveillance," 8; Denise L. Haynie, Tonia Nansel, Patricia Eitel, Aria Davis Crump, Keith Saylor, and Kai Yu,

"Bullies, Victims, and Bully/Victim: Distinct Groups of At-Risk Youth," *Journal of Early Adolescence* 21, no. 1 (2001): 29–49; Randal Collins, *Violence: A Micro-sociological Theory* (Princeton, NJ: Princeton University Press, 2008), 165–74; Dan Olweus, *Bullying at School: What We Know and What We Can Do* (Oxford: Oxford University Press, 1993).

11. See Collins, *Violence,* 165–74; Kristin D. Eisenbraun, "Violence in Schools: Prevalence, Prediction, and Prevention," *Aggression and Violent Behavior* 12 (2007): 459–69.

12. H. Xie, D.J. Swift, B.D. Cairns, and R.B. Cairns, "Aggressive Behaviors in Social Interaction and Developmental Adaptation: A Narrative Analysis of Interpersonal Conflicts during Early Adolescence," *Social Development* 11 (2002): 205–24.

13. R. Oliver and J.H. Hoover, "The Perceived Roles of Bullying in Small-Town Midwestern Schools," *Journal of Counseling and Development* 72 (1994): 416–20; Lee A. Beaty and Erick B. Alexeyev, "The Problem of School Bullies: What the Research Tells Us," *Adolescence* 43, no. 169 (2008): 1–11.

14. See Dorothy L. Espelage, Kris Bosworth, and Thomas R. Simon, "Examining the Social Context of Bullying Behaviors in Early Adolescence," *Journal of Counseling and Development* 78 (2000): 326–33; Robert Faris and Dianne Felmlee, "Social Struggles: Network Centrality and Gender Segregation in Same- and Cross-gender Aggression," *American Sociological Review* 76 (2010): 48–73.

15. Wolfgang Retz, Petra Retz-Junginger, Tillman Supprian, and Michael Rösler, "Research Report: Association of Serotonin Transporter Promoter Gene Polymorphism with Violence: Relation with Personality Disorders, Impulsivity, and Childhood ADHD Psychopathology," *Behavioral Science and Law* 22 (2004): 415–25.

16. Even though violence in inner-city schools has been reported by the media (usually the print media) more often than violence in predominantly middle-class schools, the attention to it has been qualitatively different. There appears to be less of an emotional concern among the general public with the violence in inner-city schools than with violence in other school contexts. No doubt, the fact that it is much more common in inner-city areas, and that the vast majority of nation's children do not attend such schools, provides some answer to why the general public seems to expect that it will occur in the schools of those areas and is less anxious about it.

17. Certainly Philippe Bourgois's *In Search of Respect: Selling Crack in El Barrio* (New York: Cambridge University Press, 1995), 174–212, and Elijah Anderson's *Code of the Street: Decency, Violence and the Moral Life of the Inner City* (New York: W.W. Norton, 2000) would apply, as well as John H. Laub and Janet L. Lauritsen's "The Interdependence of School Violence with Neighborhood and Family Conditions," in *Violence in American Schools,* ed. Delbert S. Elliot, Beatrix A. Hamburg, and Kirk R. Williams (Cambridge: Cambridge University Press, 1998), 127–55, and Harding's *Living the Drama.*

18. Much research has reported on this relationship. Three examples include Daisy S. Ng-Mak, Suzanne Salzinger, Richard Feldman, and C. Ann Stueve, "Pathological Adaptation to Community Violence among Inner City Youth,"

American Journal of Orthopsychiatry, Mental Health and Social Justice 74, no. 2 (2004): 196–208; Ashli J. Sheidow, Deborah Gorman-Smith, Patrick H. Tolan, and David B. Henry, "Family and Community Characteristic Risk Factors for Violence Exposure in Inner-City Youth," *Journal of Community Psychology* 29, no. 3 (2001): 345–60; and Deborah Gorman-Smith, Patrick H. Tolan, Rolf Loeber, and David B. Henry, "Relation of Family Problems to Patterns of Delinquency Involvement among Urban Youth," *Journal of Abnormal Child Psychology* 26, no. 5 (1998): 319–33.

19. See Devine, *Maximum Security;* and Jessica Halliday and Karolyn Tyson, "Other People's Racism: Race, Rednecks, and Riots in a Southern Town," *Sociology of Education* 86, no. 1 (2013): 83–102.

20. According to the research provided in Amanda K. Miller and Kathryn Chandler's *Violence in U.S. Public Schools: 2000 School Survey on Crime and Safety,* US Department of Education, National Center for Education Statistics, NCES 2004-314 (Washington, DC: Government Printing Office, 2003), about 6 percent of the violence reported during the recording period was associated with ethnic conflict in schools.

21. See Howard Pinderhughes, *Race in the Hood: Conflict and Violence among Urban Youth* (Minneapolis: University of Minnesota Press, 1997); and Ronald P. Formisano, *Boston against Busing: Race, Class, and Ethnicity in the 1960s and 1970s* (Chapel Hill: University of North Carolina Press, 1991).

22. Rami Benbenishty and Ron Avi Astor, *School Violence in Context: Culture, Neighborhood, Family, School, and Gender* (New York: Oxford University Press, 2005). This study is not about violence between Israelis and Palestinians but about violence among Jewish Israelis and among Arab Israelis (the two groups almost never go to the same schools).

23. There is considerable research on the relationship between psychopathology and violent behavior with an emphasis on the functions of the brain. See a review of this literature in Pamela P. Perez, "The Etiology of Psychopathy: A Neuropsychological Perspective," *Aggression and Violent Behavior* 17, no. 6 (2012): 519–22.

24. Literature that directly addresses the role of structural conditions in promoting ethnic violence does not to any meaningful degree exist. However, some studies employ a Marxist or a non-Marxist conceptual framework that inferentially operates under this premise. I shall just mention a few examples. On the Marxist side, see Stanley B. Greenberg, *Race and State in Capitalist Development: Comparative Perspectives* (New Haven, CT: Yale University Press, 1980). For a non-Marxist approach, see Susan Olzak, *The Dynamics of Ethnic Competition and Conflict* (Stanford, CA: Stanford University Press, 1992); Mathew Lange, *Education and Ethnic Violence* (Cambridge: Cambridge University Press, 2012); and David Cunningham, "Mobilizing Ethnic Competition," *Theory and Society* 41 (2012): 505–25.

25. Toon Kuppens, Thomas V. Pollet, Cátia P. Teixeira, Stéphanie Demoulin, S. Craig Roberts, and Anthony C. Little, "Emotions in Context: Anger Causes Ethnic Bias but Not Gender Bias in Men but Not Women," *European Journal of Social Psychology* 42, no. 4 (2012): 432–41.

26. Collins, *Violence,* 39–133, discusses the importance of initiators in the violence process.

27. The vast majority of the research on school violence, regardless of whether it has had an ethnic content, has relied on "ex post facto" data: that is, on data gathered using survey questionnaires or in-depth interview techniques that ask respondents/subjects if they have engaged in, been the victim of, or witnessed a violent act. Thus respondents are asked to reconstruct what occurred from memory. Since memory is subject to lapses, this presents some worry that errors are, or could be, present in these reenactments.

28. For the ethnic conflict between Armenians and Latino students in the Los Angeles area, see Harry Sahag Bedevian, "Student, Staff, and Parent Perceptions of the Reasons for Ethnic Conflict between Armenian and Latino Students," (EdD diss., University of Southern California, May 2008); for a study on conflicts between Albanian students and Latino or African American students, see Pinderhughes, *Race in the Hood.*

29. Having two sets of schools, one with interethnic violence and the other not, provides leverage for comparisons of what the two have in common and what is different that produces variance in the results. In a sense, the schools that do not have violence, even though they are experiencing ethnic change, act as a "control group"—not in the sense of classic experimental design but more in the sense of the designs found in statistical analyses.

30. See Jack Katz, *How Emotions Work* (Chicago: University of Chicago Press, 1999), 309–15. Katz draws on George Herbert Mead's *Mind, Self and Society* (1934; repr., Chicago: University of Chicago Press, 1967) and Erving Goffman's *The Presentation of Self in Everyday Life* (New York: Doubleday, 1959) to argue that emotions entail both hidden content and internal actions of identity. What Mead, Goffman, and Katz miss is the interplay of the body and culture. That is, they miss the role of culture in generating and expressing emotions by not considering the interaction of physical electrode signals within the brain generated as a response to encounters, whether by actions compliant with or deviant from the existing social norms. The field of cognitive psychology continues to investigate the linkages of emotions and culture. See Jean R. Seguin, Patrick Sylvers, and Scott O. Lilienfeld, "The Neurobiology of Violence," and Kenneth A. Dodge and Michelle Sherrill, "The Interaction of Nature and Nurture in Antisocial Behavior," both in *The Cambridge Handbook on Violence and Aggression,* ed. Daniel J. Flannery, Alexander T. Vazsoni, and Irwin D. Waldman (Cambridge: Cambridge University Press, 2007), 187–214 and 215–44, respectively; Jana L. Bufkin and Vicki R. Luttrell, "Neuroimaging Studies of Aggressive and Violent Behavior," *Trauma, Violence, Abuse* 6, no. 2 (2005): 176–91; and Roy Goodwin D'Andrade, "The Cultural Part of Cognition," *Cognitive Science* 5, no. 3 (1981): 179–95, all of which look at the physical elements and processes of the brain, the bodily responses they call for, and the normative behavioral actions that are produced.

31. For a discussion of the various computer-assisted qualitative programs that were available at the time of this research, see Daniel Dohan and Martín Sánchez-Jankowski, "Using Computers to Analyze Ethnographic Field Data:

Theoretical and Practical Considerations," *Annual Review of Sociology* 24 (1998): 477–98.

32. See Noel Ignatiev, *How the Irish Became White* (New York: Routledge, 1995), and Mathew Frye Jacobson, *Whiteness of a Different Color: European Immigrants and the Alchemy of Race* (Cambridge, MA: Harvard University Press, 1999).

1. TOWARD AN UNDERSTANDING OF ETHNIC VIOLENCE IN SCHOOLS

1. The concept of "life course" in sociology has usually assumed the character of individual characteristics over time within certain circumstances, and consequently other concepts such as "temporal sequencing," and "dynamics" would seem at first glance to be more precise. However, the concept of "life course" best portrays the actual experience of ethnic violence in schools and perhaps even ethnic violence more generally as it proceeds through its different incarnations. Often people will remark that "this type of violence has a life of its own" because it existentially proceeds with a beginning, with an appetite to continue, followed by an end.

2. See Randall Collins, *Violence: A Micro-sociological Theory* (Princeton, NJ: Princeton University Press, 2009); Donald L. Horowitz, *Ethnic Groups in Conflict*, 2nd ed. (Berkeley: University of California Press, 2000), and *The Deadly Ethnic Riot* (Berkeley: University of California Press, 2001).

3. Collins, *Violence*, 115–21, 39–133.

4. See Monica Duffy Toft, *The Geography of Ethnic Violence* (Princeton, NJ: Princeton University Press, 2003); May Lim, Richard Metzler, and Yaneer Bar-Yam, "Global Pattern Formation and Ethnic/Cultural Violence," *Science* 307, no. 5844 (2007): 1540–44.

5. See Horowitz, *Ethnic Groups in Conflict* and *Deadly Ethnic Riot*.

6. Horowitz, *Deadly Ethnic Riot*, 67, 71–123.

7. Nearly every ethnic group that has immigrated to the United States has had to face some adversity associated with bigotry. See the work of Gustavus Meyers, *The History of Bigotry in the United States* (New York: Random House, 1943), as well as the various histories of ethnic groups as they entered. There is a vast literature associated with the difficulties each ethnic group encountered with bigotry and discrimination. I will simply mention a few: Noel Ignatiev, *How The Irish Became White* (New York: Routledge, 1995); Mathew Frye Jacobson, *Whiteness of a Different Color: European Immigrants and the Alchemy of Race* (Cambridge, MA: Harvard University Press, 1999); Stanley Lieberson, *A Piece of the Pie: Blacks and White Immigrants since 1880* (Berkeley: University of California Press, 1981); and Cybelle Fox, *Three Worlds of Relief: Race, Immigration, and the American Welfare State from the Progressive Era to the New Deal* (Princeton, NJ: Princeton University Press, 2012).

8. For recession effects, see David B. Grusky, Bruce Western, and Christopher Wimer, eds., *The Great Recession* (New York: Russell Sage Foundation, 2011), 3–20. The entire deindustrialization thesis has been used to describe this trend in the United States. See Barry Bluestone and Bennett Harrison, *The Dein-*

dustrialization of America: Plant Closings, Community Abandonment, and the Dismantling of Basic Industry (New York: Basic Books, 1984). For its impact on African Americans, see William Julius Wilson, When Jobs Disappear: The New World of the Urban Poor (New York: Knopf, 1996). These recessions, which are generally less extreme than a depression, set the stage for unrest and do not ignite unrest. Like the example of kindling, setting the stage is a prerequisite, but the actual fire, or outburst of ethnic violence, is ignited by subsequent events.

9. See, for example, Ethan Bronner, "U.S. Workers Sue as Big Farms Rely on Immigrants," New York Times, May 7, 2013.

10. In the United States the Irish came to the New England area in large numbers and were given jobs for less money that had previously been held by Anglo-native Protestants; Chinese were given jobs building the transnational railroad that had been held by the Irish; African and Mexican Americans were recruited to take industrial jobs in the Midwest that had been held by white European ethnics: Mexicans have been used to take jobs previously held by African Americans; Somalis have been used to take jobs held by a variety of American workers; and Mexican nationals (without legal status) and Indigenous groups from Mexico have been used to supplant workers who are second- and beyond-generation Mexican Americans. Ethnic competition leading to conflict has been present in other societies as well. For a discussion of ethnic competition and conflict throughout the world, see Horowitz, Ethnic Groups in Conflict.

11. This is a particular problem in the developing world; see United Nations Human Settlements Programme, The Challenge of Slums: A Global Report on Human Settlement (New York: UN-Habitat United Nations, 2003). In the United States the problem of ethnic discrimination in the housing market can cause a shortage for some groups, and although there is a vast literature on this effect an excellent example is Douglas S. Massey and Nancy A. Denton's American Apartheid: Segregation and the Making of the Underclass (Cambridge, MA: Harvard University Press, 1993). For studies on density and behavior, see Ray Forrest, Adrienne La Grange, and Yip Ngai-Ming, "Neighbourhood in a High Rise, High Density City: Some Observations on Contemporary Hong Kong," Sociological Review 50, no. 1 (2002): 215–40; and Robert Edward Mitchell, "Some Social Implications of High Density Housing," American Sociological Review 36, no. 1 (1971): 18–29. I use two studies some thirty years apart to show the consistency in the findings between density and conflict behavior.

12. I take these cultural differences—in worldviews, values, dress, food tastes, interactional styles, and, critically, language—to be real and prior to the conflict, as opposed to those who say they are either absent or unimportant and are merely blown up into importance by the conflict itself.

13. Edna Bonacinch, "A Theory of Ethnic Antagonism: The Split Labor Market," American Sociological Review 37 (October 1972): 549–59.

14. Michael Hout, Asaf Lavanon, and Erin Cumberworth, "Job Loss and Unemployment," in The Great Recession, ed. David Grusky, Bruce Western, and Christopher Wimer (New York: Russell Sage Foundation, 2011), 59–81.

15. Douglas S. Massey, *Categorically Unequal: The American Stratification System* (New York: Russell Sage Foundation, 2007).

16. Timothy M. Smeeding, Jeffrey P. Thompson, Asaf Levanon, and Esra Burak, "Poverty and Income Inequality in the Early Stages of the Great Recession," in Grusky, Western, and Wimer, *Great Recession*, 82–126; and Gary Burtless and Tracy Gordon, "The Federal Stimulus Programs and Their Effects," in Grusky, Western, and Wimer, *Great Recession*, 249–93.

17. See Martín Sánchez-Jankowski, *City Bound: Urban Life and Political Attitudes among Chicano Youth* (Albuquerque: University of New Mexico Press, 1986).

18. This of course happened in the case of New Orleans when Hurricane Katrina hit and caused a great deal of tension between the whites and African Americans who were residing there. See Michael Eric Dyson, *Come Hell or High Water: Hurricane Katrina and the Color of Disaster* (New York: Basic Civitas Books, 2006).

19. There was considerable evidence of an increase in ethnic tensions before and after the Los Angeles riot. See Albert Bergesen and Max Herman, "Immigration, Race, and Riot: The 1992 Los Angeles Uprising," *American Sociological Review* 63, no. 1 (1998): 39–54.

20. See Lyn Lofland, *A World of Strangers: Order and Action in Urban Public Space* (Longview, IL: Waveland Press, 1985); Gerald Suttles, *Social Order of the Slum: Ethnicity and Territory in the Inner City* (Chicago: University of Chicago Press, 1968); William Kornblum, *Blue Collar Community* (Chicago: University of Chicago Press, 1975); and Irving Goffman, *Behavior in Public Places: Notes on the Social Organization of Gatherings* (New York: Free Press, 1963).

21. What underlies this and other tensions leading to sparks is the energy emanating from those emotions, which stimulates actions and reactions. For a discussion of some issues related to the role of emotions in stimulating violence, see Peggy Thoits, "Managing the Emotions of Others," *Symbolic Interaction* 19, no. 2 (1996): 85–109; and Thomas J. Scheff and Suzanne M. Retzinger, *Emotions and Violence: Shame and Rage in Destructive Conflicts* (Lexington, MA: Lexington Books, 1991).

22. While psychopathology and other psychological antecedents may explain some of the variation, they are not sufficient to explain patterns.

23. There is a good deal of literature on this, ranging from psychoanalytic writings, such as Sigmund Freud's work on instincts and the relation between the id and the ego, to Antonio Damasio's work on the biological origins of emotional expressions. Much of Freud's writing is concerned with pathologies, as psychoanalysis developed out of an effort to understand their origins, but for an example of id and ego issues related to emotions and social conditions see Sigmund Freud, *Civilization and Its Discontents* (1930; repr., New York: W. W. Norton, 1962), 14–15; and Antonio Damasio, *The Feeling of What Happens: Body and Emotion in the Making of Consciousness* (Orlando, FL: Harvest Books, 2000).

24. It was Martin Heidegger who argued that a movement from "I" to "we" begins with the emotions associated with social bonds to the group, but for violence to emerge between ethnic groups, the "I" and "we" must be mixed

together. See Martin Heidegger, *Being and Time* (1953; repr., Albany: State University of New York Press, 1993), 118–22.

25. For a penetrating analysis of the role that injustice plays in societies, see Barrington Moore, *Injustice: The Moral Bases of Obedience and Revolt* (White Plains, NY: M.E. Sharpe, 1978).

26. See Randall Collins, *Interaction Ritual Chains* (Princeton, NJ: Princeton University Press, 2004). My conception of a chain reaction has much in common with that advanced by Collins. One difference, however, is that the chain reaction I am proposing has less, if any, association with ritual actions, even if we extend the meaning of "ritual" to include actions beyond the ceremonial that are associated with specific occasions.

27. The deadly ethnic riot and forms of genocide are examples. See Horowitz, *Deadly Ethnic Riot;* and Leo Kuper, *Genocide: Its Political Use in the Twentieth Century* (New Haven, CT: Yale University Press, 1983).

28. See Nicolás C. Baca, *Presumed Alliance: The Unspoken Conflict between Latinos and Blacks and What It Means for America* (New York: HarperCollins, 2004)

29. See Gustave Le Bon, *The Crowd: A Study of the Popular Mind* (1896; repr., New Brunswick, NJ: Transaction Books, 2002); and Herbert Blumer, "Social Movements" in *New Outline of Principles of Sociology,* ed. A.M. Lee (New York: Barnes and Noble, 1946).

30. See Erik H. Erikson, *Identity, Youth, and Crisis* (New York: W.W. Norton, 1968).

31. See Jack Katz, *Seductions of Crime: Moral and Sensual Attractions in Doing Evil* (New York: Free Press, 1988), 52–75, 142–54, who follows in the footsteps of Edward Banfield, *The Unheavenly City Revisited* (Boston: Little-Brown, 1974), 211–33, who found one, if not the main, attraction of aggression within riots to be the desire to experience fun and profit.

32. The term *Thermidor period* invoked by Crane Britton in relation to political or social revolutions is apropos to the situation in schools when brawls, riots, and stampedes related to interethnic conflict have recently ceased, although underlying tensions between the groups remain. See Crane Britton, *The Anatomy of Revolution* (1938; repr., New York: Random House, 1965), 205–38.

33. Ibid., 237–49.

34. The history of neighborhoods in the United States has shown that there is general pattern of demographic change. Thus, even in those neighborhoods where the overwhelming majority of residents are from families that are poor and marginalized, new ethnic groups will come to occupy them. For an analysis of the dynamics of social change in poor neighborhoods, see Martín Sánchez-Jankowski, *Cracks in the Pavement: Social Change and Resilience in Poor Neighborhoods* (Berkeley: University of California Press, 2008); Louis Winnick, *New People in Old Neighborhoods* (New York: Russell Sage Foundation, 1990); Albert Hunter, *Symbolic Communities: Studies of the Persistence and Change of Chicago's Local Communities* (Chicago: University of Chicago Press, 1975); and Robert J. Sampson, *The Great American City: Chicago and the Enduring Neighborhood Effect* (Chicago: University of Chicago Press, 2013).

35. This point was forcefully made by Emile Durkheim in *Suicide: A Study in Sociology* (New York: Free Press, 1979) and *The Division of Labor in Society* (New York: Free Press, 1984), 141–42.

2. KINDLING

1. Randall Collins, *Violence: A Micro-sociological Theory* (Princeton, NJ: Princeton University Press, 2008), 22–23, 11–117.

2. See Stanley Greenberg, *Race and State in Capitalist Development* (New Haven, CT: Yale University Press, 1980); Howard Winant, *The World Is a Ghetto: Race and Democracy since World War II* (New York: Basic Books, 2001).

3. Harold Isaacs, "Basic Group Identity: The Idols of the Tribe," in *Ethnicity: Theory and Experience*, ed. Nathan Glazer and Daniel P. Moynihan (Cambridge, MA: Harvard University Press, 1975), 31–52, first clearly identified the basic elements of ethnic group identity, and subsequent researchers have generally adopted these with little alteration, but in every period since there has been a great deal of research analyzing their impact on identity and behavior. The studies of social psychologists have been particularly important. See Henri Tajfel, *Human Groups and Social Categories* (Cambridge: Cambridge University Press, 1981); John Turner, *Social Influence* (Milton Keynes: Open University Press, 1991); the various readings in W. Peter Robinson, ed., *Social Groups and Identities* (Oxford: Butterworth and Heinemann, 1996); Elizabeth Sabine French, Edward Seidman, LaRue Allen, and J. Lawrence Aber, "The Development of Ethnic Identity during Adolescence," *Developmental Psychology*, 42, no. 1 (2006): 1–10; and Jean S. Phinney, "Ethnic Identity Exploration in Emerging Adulthood," in *Emerging Adults in America: Coming of Age in the 21st Century*, ed. Jeffrey Jensen Arnett and Jennifer Lynn Tanner (Washington, DC: American Psychological Association, 2006), 117–34.

4. I designated "lower-class schools" by using census data on median family income for the area from which the school drew its students; the percentage of families who were at 200 percent or less of the official poverty level; and the percentage of students in the school who qualified for the school lunch program, which provided free lunches for students from families whose incomes were near the poverty level.

5. It should be remembered that De Neve High School in Los Angeles is an ethnically mixed school, with the student body being mostly Mexican and African American. The students come from predominantly middle-class families, and during the time of the study, and for two years afterward, no ethnic violence was reported.

6. I took this quote shorthand as Denise was talking to three friends while they were all waiting to be picked up by the parent of one of the group members. I was standing in the mix of students behind them.

7. I took this quote shorthand as Enrique was talking to five Mexican students while they were waiting for gym class to start. I was standing with a group of students immediately behind them.

8. See Karl Mannheim, *Ideology and Utopia: An Introduction to the Sociology of Knowledge* (New York: Harcourt, Brace, and World, 1936), 138, which

discusses the use of history to create fictitious illusions about one's place in history, including one's place in the present social epoch or social movement. This has relevance for the present study because it was one of the processes occurring in the students in this study.

9. The issue of moral boundaries—that is, the assessment of what is good and bad for those considered the in-group (i.e., "us") and those for the out-group(s) (i.e., "them")—is discussed by Michèle Lamont, *The Dignity of Working Men: Morality and the Boundaries of Race, Class, and Immigration* (New York: Russell Sage Foundation, 2000). The idea of being heroic or a pathetic failure is a persistent underlying conception of minorities who have over an extended period of history suffered physical and psychological harms inflicted by members of majority groups. A significant number of ethnic groups that came to the United States experienced trials and tribulations, but many "non-white" groups like Native, African, Mexican, and Puerto Rican Americans experienced them for hundreds of years. A study that looks at the tendency to depict African Americans as either pathetic victims or villains is Daryl Michael Scott, *Contempt and Pity: Social Policy and the Image of the Damaged Black Psyche, 1880–1996* (Chapel Hill: University of North Carolina Press, 1997).

10. I took this quote shorthand as JaRod was talking to two other African American students in the gym. They were waiting for class to start, and I was with two other African American students who were playing a portable electronic game.

11. I took this quote shorthand while listening to Peter talk to a group of ten students in the cafeteria. I was with a teacher who was assigned to be a monitor during lunch when I overheard the conversation.

12. I took this quote shorthand while listening to Antonia talk to a teacher and two other Mexican American friends before her math class began. I was standing at the locker next to them with three boys who were conversing about sports.

13. The issue of legitimacy for some in an ethnic group concerns the length of time they have suffered oppression vis-à-vis other groups. Some of the identity associated with being Jewish, Gypsy, or African American can be attributed to the idea of continued oppression. The experience of common suffering is an important ingredient of identity formation and maintenance. Also, these groups can use such ideas to define who should be included and who should be excluded. See Donald Horowitz, "Ethnic Identity," in Glazer and Moynihan, *Ethnicity*, 111–40, which discusses issues related to identity expansion and contraction among ethnic groups.

14. I took this quote shorthand as Marco was talking to three of his friends at a high school soccer game. I was sitting behind them.

15. I took this quote longhand as Candace was talking to two friends standing in line to be checked for weapons before school started. I was standing in line immediately in front of them.

16. I took this quote shorthand as Logan was talking to a friend while eating lunch. I was at the table immediately next to his.

17. See Monica McDermott, *Working-Class White: The Making and Unmaking of Race Relations* (Berkeley: University of California Press, 2006),

51; and Brian Dooley, *Black and Green: The Fight for Civil Rights in Northern Ireland and Black America* (London: Pluto Press, 1998), 71.

18. I took this quote while Sidney was talking to a local restaurant worker as he ate some ice cream. I was sitting in a seat immediately next to his at the counter.

19. I took this quote longhand as Jody was talking to three friends at a community center in the area where she lived. I was sitting down and they were standing a few feet from me.

20. Edward was talking to four friends while walking to school. I was in a garage observing students walk to school.

21. Mona was talking to two friends in front of the school, waiting for the doors to open and school to officially begin. I was standing in the crowd of students very close to her.

22. I took this quote shorthand. Diego was talking to a friend while they were buying some snacks at a small store on the way home from school. I was in the store in the aisle immediately on the other side of the food shelves. I could look through the shelves and see them.

23. Laura was talking to five friends as they were sitting waiting for an assembly to begin. I was sitting in the row immediately behind them and to their right about three seats.

24. I counted fifty-nine statements made by Mexican students in low-income schools similar to the ones provided in the text, and only twelve made by the Mexican students attending middle-class schools. I counted sixty-six African American students making comments similar to the ones provided in the text, but only ten made by African American students attending the middle-class schools. Given that I spent nearly the same amount of time in both schools during this period, there was an equal chance of hearing students making these types of statements.

25. Each of the students mentioned here was first observed in schools where no violence was reported to have occurred. These students were first observed making statements about their group's history, and those statements were recorded. There were, of course, many more students than these who made such statements, but these students were representative of those others and not unique in any way.

26. Ethnic identity always involves some sense of history, and this has been consistently found in studies focused on the bases of such an identity for individuals and groups. See in particular Harold Isaacs's *Idols of the Tribe: Group Identity and Political Change* (New York: Harper and Row, 1975), 15–143, for a discussion of the role of history in creating group identity, and fifteen years later Richard D. Alba, *Ethnic Identity: The Transformation of White America* (New Haven, CT: Yale University Press, 1990), 195–96. See as well the more recent study by Benedict Anderson, *Imagined Communities: Reflections on the Origin and Spread of Nationalism* (London: Verso Press, 2006).

27. See Isaacs, "Basic Group Identity."

28. Tajfel, *Human Groups,* 187–206.

29. The issue of moral boundaries is relevant here. See Lamont, *Dignity of Working Men,* 57–60.

30. See Tajfel, *Human Groups,* 117, 143–67; Stanley Lieberson, "Stereotypes: Their Consequences for Race and Ethnic Interaction," in *Social Structure and Behavior: Essays in Honor of William H. Sewell,* ed. Robert H. Hauser, D. Mechanic, A. O. Haller, and T. S. Hauser (New York: Academic Press, 1982), 47–68; Don Operario and Susan T. Fiske, "Stereotypes: Content, Structures, Processes, and Context," in *Blackwell Handbook of Social Psychology: Intergroup Processes,* ed. Rupert Brown and Sam Gaertner (Oxford: Blackwell, 2003), 22–44.

31. See Myron Rothbart, "Category Dynamics and the Modification of Outgroup Stereotypes," in Brown and Gaertner, *Blackwell Handbook,* 60.

32. I took this quote shorthand as Andrea was talking to two friends at a local grocery store on her way home from school. I was in the store pretending to be part of a conversation with three boys.

33. I took this quote shorthand as Lane was talking to four friends during school lunch hour. I was at the table next to theirs eating my lunch.

34. Henri Tajfel, "Social Stereotypes and Social Groups," in *Intergroup Behavior,* ed. John C. Turner and Howard Giles (Oxford: Basil Blackwell, 1981).

35. I took this quote shorthand as Keysha was talking to five people while waiting in line to get into a basketball game. I was standing on the other side of the door inside the gymnasium, and neither she nor her friends knew I was there.

36. I took this quote shorthand while Susana was talking to two friends at her locker. I was standing at the door of a classroom about six feet away. They were focused on each other and were not aware that anyone was paying attention to them.

37. I took this quote longhand while Ted was talking to three people watching a hockey game at a local ice rink. I was there to interview one of the school's coaches about future plans for having African Americans join his team.

38. I took this quote longhand as Ronald was talking with five other students, four male and one female, after a general meeting of school officials and family members informing parents and the students who were in attendance about the program to bus students to Paul Revere High School in a week. I was in the audience and following Ronald and the five other students as they walked out of large room where the presentation occurred.

39. By *identity,* I am referring to the distinguishing character or personality of an individual, or those character traits composing people's unique sense of who they think they are.

40. Alan S. Waterman, "Developmental Perspectives on Identity Formation: From Adolescence to Adulthood," in *Ego Identity: A Handbook for Psychosocial Research,* ed. J. E. Marcia, A. S. Waterman, D. R. Matteson, S. L. Archer, and J. L. Orlofsky (New York: Springer-Verlag, 1993), 42–68. The establishment of "who I am as a person" often includes the development of a singular internal and private identity that has various facets capable of being socially displayed in varying forms and depth.

41. See Susan Olzak, *The Dynamics of Ethnic Competition and Conflict* (Stanford, CA: Stanford University Press, 1992); William Julius Wilson and

Richard P. Taub, *There Goes the Neighborhood: Racial, Ethnic, and Class Tensions in Four Chicago Neighborhoods and Their Meaning for America* (New York: Knopf, 2006).

42. An individual often thinks of him- or herself as a person with certain characteristics. One of these characteristics has to do with ethnicity, either in the form of ancestral symbolic legacy (i.e., my forefathers were members of this particular ethnic group) or in the transmission of cultural practices associated with a particular ethnic group as part of the everyday habitus of the individual. To establish this identity the individual needs to compare him- or herself to others, and this involves cognitively discriminating who is in the group and who is not, and prejudging both groups as a tool for determining how to get along with others.

43. The use of prejudice would run counter to that predicated on the content of the social interaction that is so important to researchers operating under a symbolic interaction or ethnomethodological method. Both would argue that the content of an interaction's meaning is determined by the actions and reactions of the individuals while in it. See Harold Garfinkel, *Studies in Ethnomethodolgy* (Englewood Cliffs, NJ: Prentice-Hall, 1967), and Herbert Blumer, *Symbolic Interaction: Perspective and Method* (Berkeley: University of California Press, 1969).

44. An emerging literature in cognitive science and cultural sociology shows that "practical consciousness" and everyday behaviors do not operate by conscious, discursive processes. See Stephen Vaisey, "Motivation and Justification: A Dual-Processing Model of Culture in Action," *American Journal of Sociology* 114, no. 6 (2009): 1675–1715; Lisa Feldman Barrett, Michele M. Tugade, and Randall W. Engle, "Individual Differences in Working Memory Capacity and Dual Process Theories of the Mind," *Psychological Bulletin* 130, no. 4 (2004): 553–73; and Jonathan St. B. T. Evans, "Dual-Processing Accounts of Reasoning, Judgement, and Social Cognition," *Annual Review of Psychology* 59 (2008): 255–78. The psychology literature on unconscious bias is also relevant. See John F. Dovidio, Samuel E. Gaertner, Kerry Kawakami, and Gordon Hudson, "Why Can't We Just Get Along? Interpersonal Biases and Interracial Distrust," *Cultural Diversity and Ethnic Minority Psychology* 8, no. 2 (May 2002): 82–102; Susan T. Fiske, "What We Know about Bias and Intergroup Conflict: The Problem of the Century," *Current Directions in Psychological Science* 11, no. 4 (2002): 123–28; and Lincoln Quillian, "Does Unconscious Racism Exist?," *Social Psychology Quarterly* 71, no. 1 (2008): 6–11.

45. See Samuel Roundfield Lucas, *Theorizing Discrimination in an Era of Contested Prejudice* (Philadelphia: Temple University Press, 2009), 18–21.

46. For a discussion of the use of various information sources to establish stereotypes, see Gordon Allport, *The Nature of Prejudice* (Cambridge, MA: Addison-Wesley, 1954), and Rupert Brown, *Prejudice: The Social Psychology* (Oxford: Blackwell, 1995), 82–92.

47. Ethnic pride is an important ingredient in the establishment of a positive self-identity as well as a resource to encourage young people to continue the legacy of their forefathers. This can also be seen in efforts to have youth take advantage of the opportunities that their ancestors did not enjoy and the sacri-

fices they made to have subsequent generations succeed. See Alejandro Portes and Rubén G. Rumbaut, *Legacies: The Story of the Immigrant Second Generation* (Berkeley: University of California Press, 2001), 107–11. This was in part the impetus to rewrite the history books of the United States so that all youth, but especially those in ethnic minorities, could have an appreciation of the contributions that members of their group had made to the development of contemporary US society. See, for example, Lerone Bennett, Jr., *Before the Mayflower: History of the Negro American* (New York: Penguin Books, 1966), and John Hope Franklin's *From Slavery to Freedom: A History of the Negro American*, 3rd ed. (New York: Alfred Knopf, 1967), as well as the various Afrocentric studies like Martin Bernal, *Black Athena: Afroasiatic Roots of Classical Civilization*, vol. 1 (New Brunswick, NJ: Rutgers University Press, 1987).

48. I took this quote shorthand as Tom was talking to three of his classmates before a school hockey game. I was in the stands immediately behind them while they were talking.

49. I took this quote shorthand as Erica was talking to three friends at a small grocery store on the way to school. I was in the store talking to the owner. It should be noted that the school Erica was attending had no reported physical altercations between Mexican Americans and African Americans at the time.

50. I took this quote shorthand while John was having a conversation with five other young African Americans as they waited in the hallway to start class. I was standing next to them as they talked. They were totally uninhibited by my standing next to them, whether because I looked Latino to them and they felt a Latino would share these beliefs about the Irish or whether the situation had reached a point where they really did not care what others believed.

51. I took this quote longhand while Sheila was talking to two friends as they waited for the school bus to take them back to their section of town. I was in the crowd of students who were waiting for the bus when the conversation was occurring.

52. I took this quote shorthand as Hector was talking to five other students on the way to school. I was in a garage observing the students as they were walking by and could hear all their conversations as they slowly passed. The students were not aware that I was in the garage, as I purposely was concealing myself so that I could observe any violent behavior if it occurred.

53. I took this quote using a tape recorder as I interviewed various youth after school.

54. I took this quote shorthand as Carlos was having a discussion with six other students in the cafeteria. I was sitting at the table next to them having lunch.

55. I took this quote shorthand as Ida was talking to three of her friends at the bus stop. I was also there waiting for the bus to take us back to where the students lived.

56. Clearly within any group there will be variation as to how much people believe the prevailing cultural tropes, and the fact that many will not openly resist them indicates a certain decision is being made to follow the existing line. However, in following the dominant line to avoid negative sanctions or access to resources, individuals often begin to internalize some part of it.

57. I took this quote shorthand while Patricia was talking to two other friends in the cafeteria line. I was standing in line separated by two other students. One of the students that she was warning became an active leader of the girls who would attack Mexican American girls as they walked home. Clearly the girl that Patricia was talking to had internalized some of the dominant prejudices that existed among the African American students.

58. I took this quote from an interview I had with Richard after school was out and he was walking home. Richard would become one of the leaders of vigilante groups seeking out African American students to attack in retaliation for some aggression toward one of the Irish American students. This is another example of a student gradually internalizing some of the dominant prejudices that were present among the Irish Americans in the school and community.

59. There is much literature on this point, but one of the classic statements is made in Erik H. Erikson, *Identity, Youth, and Crisis* (New York: W. W. Norton, 1968).

60. I took this quote shorthand while Jenna was talking to two friends in between classes at her locker. I was standing three lockers to their left and was watching and listening to the conversation.

61. I took this quote shorthand as Yale was talking to four friends while watching the high school football team practice after school. They were sitting in the stands watching, and I was four rows in back of them.

62. I took this quote shorthand as Gabriella was talking to two girls during lunch hour. I was sitting on a bench that was on the side of where they were sitting and talking.

63. I took this quote shorthand as Mark was talking to four friends during gym class. I was standing talking to the teacher's aide about five feet behind them as they stood in line waiting to start playing basketball.

64. See Donald L. Horowitz, *Ethnic Groups in Conflict* (Berkeley: University of California Press, 1985), 141–43.

65. See Herbert Gans, "Symbolic Ethnicity: The Future of Ethnic Groups and Culture in America," *Ethnic and Racial Studies* 2 (January 1979): 1–20; and Mary Waters, *Ethnic Options: Choosing Identities in America* (Berkeley: University of California Press, 1990).

66. I took this quote shorthand as Neal was talking to other students at his locker before the next class was to begin. I was in the crowded corridor standing behind them.

67. I took this quote shorthand as Tina was talking to the other students during the morning homeroom period when the principal made announcements to all the students. I was in the homeroom standing in back of where the students were talking.

68. I took this quote shorthand as I was listening to a conversation that Julon and three other students were having during the second week of school. They were all attending a mandatory assembly for students, and I was seated behind them and to their right.

69. I took this quote shorthand as Claudia was talking to four other students during lunch period. I was at the table immediately behind them.

70. Ethnicity has been one of the most salient aspects of identity in America and has a long history of dividing people for varying periods of time and social contexts.

3. CLIMATE AND WEATHER

1. Much of the work on the role of prejudice and discrimination in instigating violence is found in the political science and psychology literature. There is a large volume of research in this tradition, so I will simply cite a few representative examples. For psychology, see Rupert Brown, *Prejudice: Its Social Psychology* (Oxford: Blackwell, 1995). For political psychology, see David O. Sears and John B. McConahay, *The Politics of Violence: The New Urban Blacks and the Watts Riot* (Boston: Houghton-Mifflin, 1973); Robert Ted Gurr, *Why Men Rebel* (Princeton, NJ: Princeton University Press, 1970); Paul Sniderman and Thomas Piazza, *Black Prejudice and Black Pride* (Princeton, NJ: Princeton University Press, 2002); and Paul Sniderman and Louk Hagendoorn, *When Cultures Collide: Multi-culturalism and Its Discontents* (Princeton, NJ: Princeton University Press, 2007). The general problems associated with this approach can be seen in the work of Sniderman and Hagendoorn when they try to make an analytic separation between self-interest and non-self-interest bigotry (i.e., a dislike with no articulated self-interest expressed) toward out-groups. Yet both of these lines of bigotry express self-interest: one is tied primarily to the person as an individual and secondarily to the person as a citizen of a nation, while the other is tied primarily to the person as a citizen of a nation and secondarily to the person as an individual. Both lead to the same point and are measuring the same attitude, which is founded on the belief that members of the out-group are a negative presence for both the society and the individual.

2. For examples of this approach, see Tanja Wranik and Klaus R. Scherer, "Why Do I Get Angry? A Componential Appraisal Approach," in *International Handbook of Anger* (New York: Springer, 2010), 243–66; Klaus R. Scherer, Ronald P. Abeles, and Claude S. Fischer, *Human Aggression and Conflict: Inter-disciplinary Perspectives* (Englewood Cliffs, NJ: Prentice-Hall, 1975), 257–95; and Randall Collins, *Violence: A Micro-sociological Theory* (Princeton, NJ: Princeton University Press, 2008), 1–133.

3. See John Dollard, Leonard Doob, N. Miller, O.H. Mowrer, and R.R. Sears, *Frustration and Aggression* (New Haven, CT: Yale University Press, 1937); Robert A. Baron, *Human Aggression* (New York: Plenum, 1977); Jack Katz, *The Seductions of Crime: Moral and Sensual Attractions in Doing Evil* (New York: Basic Books, 1988); and Collins, *Violence*.

4. A good deal of theoretical and empirical literature suggests that structural economic conditions are critical in producing interethnic conflict. See Ewa Morawska, "Immigrant-Black Dissension in American Cities: An Argument for Multiple Explanations," in *Problem of the Century: Racial Stratification in the United States,* ed. Elijah Anderson and Douglas Massey (New York: Russell Sage Foundation, 2001), 47–50.

5. This concern with the decline in housing values was first experienced in the early nineteenth century when a variety of new ethnic groups began to

immigrate to America and occupy areas that had been the primary residence for a different ethnic group. Most often the new group was considered economically poorer and socially of lower status. This stimulated the current residents to find housing in another section of the city, and as they left the value of the housing continued to decline. There was a constant influx of new groups (the Irish, Italians, various Eastern European groups, African Americans) that were poorer and considered threats to economic interests of the incumbent groups. This is documented in many books, so I shall mention just a few: Olivier Zunz, *The Changing Face of Inequality: Urbanization, Industrial Development, and Immigrants in Detroit, 1880–1920* (Chicago: University of Chicago Press, 1982); Harvey Warren Zorbaugh, *The Slum and the Gold Coast* (Chicago: University of Chicago Press, 1929); Noel Ignatiev, *How the Irish Became White* (New York: Routledge, 1995); Tomás Almaguer, *Racial Fault Lines: The Historical Origins of White Supremacy in California* (Berkeley: University of California Press, 1994). In the twentieth century African Americans' moving into previously exclusively white areas was followed by a large and quick exodus of whites from their residential areas. The most acute cases involved Detroit and Gary, Indiana, but the pattern was the same in every large city. See, for example, Thomas Sugrue, *The Origins of the Urban Crisis: Race and Inequality in Postwar Detroit* (Princeton, NJ: Princeton University Press, 1996); Yona Ginsberg, *Jews in a Changing Neighborhood* (New York: Macmillan, 1975); and Hillel Levine and Lawrence Harmon, *The Death of an American Jewish Community: The Tragedy of Good Intentions* (New York: Free Press, 1991).

6. Many studies document racial discrimination from realtors and lending agencies for African and Latino American residents. Some of the more influential are Douglas Massey and Nancy Denton, *American Apartheid: Segregation and the Making of the Underclass* (Cambridge, MA: Harvard University Press, 1993); Nancy Denton and Douglas Massey, "Residential Segregation of Blacks, Hispanics, and Asians by Socioeconomic Status and Generation," *Social Science Quarterly* 69 (1988): 797–818; and George Galaster, "Racial Steering in Urban Housing Markets," *Review of Black Political Economy* 18 (1990): 105–29.

7. See Melvin L. Oliver and Thomas M. Shapiro, *Black Wealth/White Wealth: A New Perspective on Racial Inequality* (New York: Routledge, 1995).

8. For two representative studies that influenced the relatively recent historical concern with mortgage-lending discrimination, see Robert Shafer and Helen F. Ladd, *Discrimination in Mortgage Lending* (Cambridge, MA: MIT Press, 1981); and Mary Austin Turner and Felicity Skidmore, eds., *Mortgage Lending Discrimination: Review of Existing Evidence* (Washington, DC: Urban Institute, 1999).

9. I took this quote shorthand while Royce was talking to a group of two other students and one of the school deans. I was in the dean's office when the conversation occurred.

10. I took this quote shorthand as Claudia was talking with a teacher and two other students between classes. I was standing next to the teacher.

11. I took this quote longhand as Cindy was talking to one of the adult boxing coaches at the local community center. I was with the group of five people having the conversation.

12. This is vividly documented in Jonathan Rieder, *Canarsie: Jews and Italians of Brooklyn against Liberalism* (Cambridge, MA: Harvard University Press, 1985); and J. Anthony Lukas, *Common Ground: A Turbulent Decade in the Lives of Three American Families* (New York: Random House, 1985).

13. I took this quote longhand while I was with Jenny and three of her girlfriends waiting in line to get a pizza slice from a pizzeria on their way home.

14. I took this quote shorthand while Damien was talking to four other students at a small store where they went to get soft drinks on their way home. I was in the store on another aisle buying some bottled water.

15. I took this quote longhand as Aldo was talking to one of the teachers during lunchtime. I was sitting with the teacher and two other students as he was talking.

16. I took this quote shorthand as Germina was talking in a group of two students and two adults. I was one of the adults of this conversation, and the students were outside waiting to get picked up by the brother of Germina's friend Lupe.

17. I took this quote longhand as Shawna was talking to two adult aides that were assigned to protect them as they rode the bus from Roxbury into South Boston High School. They were talking in the morning before boarding the bus for the day. I was standing with the entire group as they were waiting for the bus to arrive.

18. I took this quote shorthand while Felix was talking to another friend as he was arriving at school. I was talking to his friend when he came up to share his morning experience.

19. I took this quote shorthand while Alina was with seven other students talking as they were walking home. I was walking behind them.

20. I took this quote shorthand while Cristiano was talking to two friends as he stood outside a small store that he had stopped in front of to talk to other students. I was standing in front of the store drinking a Pepsi and sitting immediately to the right of the conversation.

21. Nobel laureate Thomas Shelling reports this occurring in the numerous experimental studies he conducted. See Thomas Shelling, *Choice and Consequence: Perspectives of an Errant Economist* (Cambridge, MA: Harvard University Press, 1985).

22. I took this quote longhand as Wilson was talking to one of the teachers escorting the African American students to the bus that would take them back to Roxbury. I was walking with a group of students immediately in back of Wilson and the teacher.

23. I took this quote shorthand as Amelia was talking to two girls and a boy in the hall waiting for the next class to start. I was standing with another group of students but could easily hear the conversation, since I was immediately next to Amelia's group.

24. The concept of relative deprivation was utilized by Robert Ted Gurr in his exploration of the causes for individual and collective action. See his *Why Men Rebel*, 22–57.

25. There is evidence that both African Americans and Mexican Americans in Los Angeles have stereotypes about the other (and Asians) and that competition

is one of the key elements. See Lawrence Bobo and Devon Johnson, "Racial Attitudes in a Prismatic Metropolis: Mapping Identity, Stereotypes, Competition, and Views on Affirmative Action," in *Prismatic Metropolis: Inequality in Los Angeles,* ed. Lawrence D. Bobo, Melvin L. Oliver, James H. Johnson Jr., and Abel Valenzuela (New York: Russell Sage Foundation, 2000), 81–163.

26. African Americans' feelings of being denied the same chances as other groups to achieve economic success have been reported in previous research. Many studies have argued that African Americans have faced more structural impediments to economic success than other minority groups in the United States. See in particular Stanley Lieberson, *A Piece of the Pie: Blacks and White Immigrants since 1880* (Berkeley: University of California Press, 1981), and Loïc Wacquant, *Urban Outcasts: A Comparative Sociology of Advanced Marginality* (Cambridge: Polity Press, 2008). The same point that African Americans faced more structural difficulties in America than other ethnic groups was made after the Los Angeles riots following the Rodney King episode; see Melvin Oliver, James H. Johnson, Jr., and Walter C. Farrell Jr., "Anatomy of a Rebellion: A Political-Economic Analysis," in *Reading Rodney King/Reading Urban Uprising,* ed. Robert Gooding-Williams (New York: Routledge, 1993), 117–41.

27. I took this quote shorthand as DeShaun was talking to his friend while sitting on a bench and watching the high school football team practice. I was also in the stands watching practice three rows below them. After I recorded the quote, I stood up and casually looked to see who was talking as I pretended to stretch.

28. I took this quote shorthand while Courtney was talking to two fellow students as she was eating lunch. I was eating at the table immediately behind her.

29. I took this quote shorthand as Facundo was talking to a friend at a high school soccer game. I was in the stands immediately in front of him.

30. I took this quote shorthand while Renata was talking to two friends as she was eating lunch. I was sitting at the table next to hers.

31. I took this quote longhand as Connor was talking to three friends and a counselor at the local community center after school. I was with the group listening to the conversation.

32. I took this quote longhand as Deirdre was talking to friends at a small local restaurant where they were buying hamburgers to eat after school. I was walking with a large group of students and talking with them about the day's activities.

33. A subculture is defined as a set of values, norms, and customs that originate in larger societies but over time and circumstances have assumed among a subgroup of a particular society a character that is marked by differences in the form and degree of emphasis they assume within that population as well as their accepted meanings and the behaviors ascribed to those meanings. In this regard, I am using the term as described by Claude S. Fischer, "Toward a Sub-culture Theory of Urbanism," *American Journal of Sociology* 80, no. 20 (1975): 1319–41, and "Toward a Sub-culture Theory of Urbanism: Twentieth-Year Assessment," *American Journal of Sociology* 101 (November 1995): 543–77.

34. I have analyzed this situation in a previous study. See Martín Sánchez-Jankowski, *Cracks in the Pavement: Social Change and Resilience in Poor*

Neighborhoods (Berkeley: University of California Press, 2008), 30–31, 44–51, 105–6, 174, 184–85, 262–64, 218–26, 314–15, 321–23.

35. I took this quote shorthand while Shawana was talking to six other students at the bus stop. I followed the group to the bus stop and was standing only a few feet from them.

36. I took this quote longhand while Brandon was talking to a group of people as they were eating during school lunchtime. I was part of the group.

37. See Gerald D. Suttles, *The Social Order of the Slum: Ethnicity and Territoriality in the Inner City* (Chicago: University of Chicago Press, 1968); William Kornblum, *Blue Collar Community* (Chicago: University of Chicago Press, 1975); Albert Hunter, *Symbolic Communities: The Persistence and Change of Chicago's Local Communities* (1974; repr., Chicago: University of Chicago Press, 1982); William Julius Wilson and Richard P. Taub, *There Goes the Neighborhood: Racial, Ethnic, and Class Tensions in Four Chicago Neighborhoods and Their Meaning for America* (New York: Knopf, 2006); and more recently Robert J. Sampson, *Great American City: Chicago and the Enduring Neighborhood Effect* (Chicago: University of Chicago Press, 2012).

38. I took this quote shorthand while Bartin was talking to three friends and a teacher outside the classroom before the start of the next teaching period. I had been there with the teacher before the conversation started and stayed as it was proceeding.

39. I took this quote longhand while Clare was talking to one of the woodshop teachers during class. I was in the class observing the students and standing at a machine just a few feet away.

40. See John Devine, *Maximum Security: The Culture of Violence in Inner-City Schools* (Chicago: University of Chicago Press, 1996), 18–45.

41. David Eitle and Tamela Eitle, "Segregation and School Violence," *Social Forces* 82 (2003): 589–616.

42. For a discussion of a variety of educational problems associated with tracking, as well as some generalized social problems, though none directly related to violence per se, see Samuel Roundfield Lucas, *Tracking Inequality: Stratification and Mobility in American High Schools* (New York: Columbia Teachers College Press, 1999).

43. Lissa J. Yogan, "School Tracking and Student Violence," *Annals of the American Academy of Political and Social Science* 567, no. 1 (2000): 108–22.

44. I recorded this event using shorthand as it was happening. I was observing inside the classroom when this incident occurred. I also was present in the latter tracked class when the students began to fight.

45. The major distinctions within schools are the separate categories of special education, even though the arrangement is to integrate these students within "regular courses" as much as possible; general education; and enhanced education (honors and advanced placement).

46. Of course, the prevailing (2014) legal interpretation of the US Constitution would not allow for segregating schools by race, although there is no current prohibition when it comes to ethnicities. This is important because one the implications of this finding is that if the schools were ethnically segregated this type of violence could be reduced until the community undergoing ethnic

change had become more socially integrated. These communities do become more integrated, and the conflict between the groups does dissipate over time. For evidence supporting the eventual social integration of poor neighborhoods experiencing ethnic change, see Sanchez-Jankowski, *Cracks in the Pavement*.

47. I took this quote shorthand while Miranda was talking to three friends and waiting for her brother to pick all of them up from school. They were standing next to a mobile cart vendor who was selling flavored shaved ices. I was standing in the line to buy a shaved ice.

48. I took this quote shorthand as Caleb was talking to an African American janitor, a security guard, and one of his friends. I walked into the conversation before the recorded statement, and my presence seems to have had no inhibiting effect even though I am ethnically Mexican looking. It is most likely that they viewed me as being from outside Los Angeles and thus not a part of the competing group.

49. I took this quote shorthand as Delfina was talking to her cousin and her cousin's friend at a Chumash High School girls' soccer game. I was in back of them watching the game.

50. I took this quote shorthand as Justin was talking to three other boys, one of whom was a leader in the violence against Mexican students at the school. The conversation was occurring on a playing field before the start of a gym class. I was there waiting for the gym class to begin.

51. This finding is due to individuals' recognition that their segregated position gives them increased advantages to make successful transitions to the colleges of their choice.

52. See Eitle and Eitle, "Segregation and School Violence," who find that desegregation produced more violence rather than less. Of course, one of the flaws in the literature is that it has focused rather heavily on desegregation between African Americans and whites rather than between African Americans and a host of other nonwhite ethnic groups.

53. I took this quote longhand while Jerry and two other teachers were talking after school as they walked to their cars to go home. I was walking with them because Jerry was going to give me a ride to the subway station for my trip home.

54. I took this quote shorthand as two teachers were conversing in the school's teachers' lounge. I was sitting with them as they talked.

55. I took this quote longhand as Fiona was talking to two adults at the local community center. I was the third adult present while she was talking.

56. I took this quote longhand as Rudy was talking to an adult social worker at a local community center in the section of town that was predominantly African American. I was standing with the social worker listening to him.

57. I took this quote shorthand as Damario was talking to two adults at a local taqueria. I was sitting at the bar of the small restaurant when he came in to pick up a takeout order. As he was waiting he was talking to the owner and his wife.

58. I took this quote shorthand while Alyssa was talking to two adults as she watched her boyfriend warm up for a high school basketball game. The two adults were cousins of another African American player on the high school team. I was sitting in the stands immediately behind them and to their right.

59. Feeling trapped in the school is something that was reported by Ione Malloy, *Southie Won't Go: A Teacher's Diary of the Desegregation of South Boston High School* (Urbana: University of Illinois Press, 1986).

60. See Zunz, *Changing Face of Inequality;* Hunter, *Symbolic Communities;* Louis Winnick, *New People in Old Neighborhoods* (New York: Russell Sage Foundation, 1990); Wilson and Taub, *There Goes the Neighborhood;* and Jeremy F. Pais, Scott J. South, and Kyle Crowder, "White Flight Revisited: Multiethnic Perspectives on Neighborhood Out-Migration," *Population Research and Policy Review* 28, no. 3 (June 2009): 321–41.

61. Although residents from these neighborhoods moved to various places, in the Los Angeles case many African Americans moved east to places like Pomona and other smaller cities in the San Bernardino Valley. In Oakland, African American residents continue to move to the southern tip of Oakland city limits and occasionally to San Leandro and Hayward. In Boston, some of the Irish were able to move to towns like Everett, Revere, and Lynn.

62. The "defended neighborhood" was a concept first used by Gerald Suttles in *The Social Construction of Communities* (Chicago: University of Chicago Press, 1972), 21–43. Later research has found similar conflict dynamics as described by Suttles. See Emmett H. Buell Jr., "Busing and the Defended Neighborhood: South Boston, 1974–1977," *Urban Affairs Review* 16, no. 2 (1980):161–88; Donald P. Green, Dara Z. Strovitch, and Janelle S. Wong, "Defended Neighborhood, Integration, and Racially Motivated Crime," *American Journal of Sociology* 104, no. 2 (1998): 379–403; and Christopher J. Lyons, "Defending Turf: Racial Demographics and Hate Crime against Blacks and Whites," *Social Forces* 87, no. 1 (September 2008): 357–85.

63. I took this quote longhand as Delores was talking to two friends and a teacher that she said she was very close to. I was with the group at one of the school's orientations as they were conversing.

64. I took this quote shorthand as Logan was talking to five friends while standing in the lunch line. I was behind them with one of the janitors as they were talking.

65. I took this quote shorthand as Dalia was talking to two friends while they waited to buy some shaved ice from a Mexican vendor. I was standing in line behind them waiting to buy some shaved ice.

66. My note included twenty-two of these students from California schools, twelve in Los Angeles and ten in Oakland; and fifteen in Boston schools. I did not follow each of these students, as in a longitudinal type of study; rather, I noted their friendships before the violence started, and as violence proceeded I noted when and how these students participated.

4. SPARKS AND SMOKE

1. Randall Collins, *Violence: A Micro-sociological Theory* (Princeton, NJ: Princeton University Press, 2008), 40–133.

2. On frustration-aggression, see John Dollard, Leonard Doob, N. E. Miller, O. H. Mowrer, and Robert R. Sears, *Frustration and Aggression* (New Haven, CT: Yale University Press, 1939). The theory of innate drives to dominate was

provided by Thomas Hobbes in *Leviathan or the Matter, Forme, and Power of a Commonwealth Ecclesiastical and Civil,* ed. Michael Oakeshott (1651; repr., Oxford: Blackwell, 1965), and was then extended in Sigmund Freud, *Civilization and Its Discontents* (New York: W.W. Norton, 2005); Albert Einstein, Sigmund Freud, and Stuart Gilbert, *Why War?* (Paris: International Institute of Intellectual Cooperation, League of Nations, 1933); and ethnologist Konrad Lorenz, *On Aggression* (New York: Bantam Books, 1966). On ethnic conflicts as struggles over group status, see Herbert Blumer, "Race Prejudice as a Sense of Group Position," *Pacific Sociological Review* 1, no. 1 (1958): 3–7.On violence over material possessions, see Karl Marx, *Civil War in Paris* (Peking: Foreign Language Press, 1970).

3. I took this quote shorthand as Alphonso was talking to a group of Mexican American students while they were leaving school for the day. I was following the whole group as they were leaving.

4. I took this quote longhand as Rosalyn was talking to two relatives at the bus stop and waiting to be picked up for transport to Paul Revere High School. I was with the group of people she was talking to.

5. See Beverly Daniel Tatum, *Why Are All the Black Kids Sitting Together in the Cafeteria?* (New York: Basic Books, 2003).

6. I recorded this interaction shorthand as I was standing about four to five feet from where Alejandro and the two African Americans were interacting. I was standing in this area observing group interactions during school free periods.

7. I took this quote shorthand as Jordan was talking to two other African Americans while riding in a bus on his way home after school. I was in the bus one seat back on the other side of where he and his two companions were sitting.

8. Kioka was talking to five friends and one of the counselors at the school. I was in the next room waiting for another counselor to arrive.

9. Caitlin was talking to five other girls at a small grocery store on the way home from school. I followed them and went into the grocery store to buy some gum and was within five feet of them as they talked.

10. This situation could easily be associated with the general category of "anomie" that Durkheim utilized in his analysis of problems of in-group solidarity and that Sewell later used in his analysis of French revolutionary events. See Emile Durkheim, *Suicide* (New York: Free Press, 1997); and William Sewell Jr., "Historical Events as Transformations of Structure: Inventing Revolution at Bastille," *Theory and Society* 25 (1996): 841–81.

11. See John Dollard, *Caste and Class in a Southern Town* (1937; repr., Madison: University of Wisconsin Press, 1989). This work discusses the type of aggression that is related to loathing. Further, there is evidence that the loathing of African Americans by southern whites provided some of the emotional predispositions for lynching. See Amy Kate Bailey, Stewart E. Tolnay, E.M. Beck, and Jennifer D. Laird, "Targeting Lynch Victims: Social Marginality or Status Transgressions?," *American Sociological Review* 76, no. 3 (2011): 412–36.

12. See Erik H. Erikson, *Identity, Youth, and Crisis* (New York: W. W. Norton, 1968. The nature of the adolescent period is conducive to violence, and

because it is a time when individuals tend to categorize and separate for the purpose of identity formation, making friends and enemies is a natural outcome of the process.

13. I recorded this conversation shorthand. Damien was talking to five other male friends in the bathroom at the high school. I came in while they were standing at the urinals and went to one of the stalls and closed the door so that they did not know what my ethnicity was. The tone and content of their conversation did not indicate that they cared who was in the bathroom.

14. When observing violent incidents I would use a stopwatch to determine their duration.

15. Recording the amount of time for each event was important to establish because of the policy implication of how rapidly authorities would have to respond to effectively limit physical injuries.

16. I was in front of the building observing and was able to hear the words spoken and actions taken that constituted the entire event. As with all of my observation positions, I tried to conceal my presence, and I did carry a stopwatch to record the length of each violent episode in order to better understand the duration of different types of incidents.

17. I recorded this incident shorthand. I was standing outside the building as the students were leaving to return to their homes, and I observed the entire incident.

18. Humberto was talking to three girls and a boy just after they had been robbed. I was in the garage of a house with a camouflaged opening to observe. I was about twenty feet from where they were standing and had just been confronted.

19. The ethnic conflict that occurs in school is generally an extension of the conflict experienced in the neighborhoods that feed the school its students. For an examination of this, see Martín Sánchez-Jankowski, *Cracks in the Pavement: Social Change and Resilience in Poor Neighborhoods* (Berkeley: University of California Press, 2008), 44–53.

20. This was observed in the bigoted words, facial expressions, and tones of voice used to express loathing, the frequency of its expression, and the disregard for the social context in which it was expressed.

21. See Michael Patrick MacDonald, *All Souls: A Family Story from Southie* (Boston: Beacon Press, 1999), 79–80.

22. I took this quote shorthand as Bartolo was talking to six friends (two boys and four girls) at the high school's women's soccer game. I was to their left in the row in back of them as they were talking.

23. See J. Anthony Lukas, *Common Ground: A Turbulent Decade in the Lives of Three American Families* (New York: Random House, 1985), which discusses each of these and the impact they had on the behavioral events that occurred. Also see MacDonald, *All Souls*, 78, 83–84.

24. I took this quote shorthand as the group was conversing during lunch hour. Jason was talking to two other boys and two girls. I was at the next table cleaning off debris that was left behind. I was assuming the role of school janitor.

25. I was at the sporting event and recorded the entire interaction.

26. The behavior of Tim and his associates has some aspects that appear to fit the description of a "forward panic" in Collins, *Violence*, 83–133, but some other aspects of the interaction would indicate that it was not a "forward panic." For example, there was no observable buildup of fear on the part of Tim and his associates before the attack, no specific trigger to produce the outbreak of violence, and no obvious evidence of the "entrainment" of emotions that Collins associates with a "forward panic"; rather, there was aggression with some type of internal calculus as to what constituted enough, and then it stopped.

27. I recorded this incident shorthand as I was observing it from the upper porch of a house I used for that purpose. Devon and his friends did not know that I was there.

28. Joaquin was talking to six students during lunch hour as they were discussing when to meet to go home. I was at the table next to them.

29. I recorded this shorthand. Marcy was talking to her friends (three girls and two boys) as she waited in line to enter the school. I was also in line but three people behind them.

30. I recorded this shorthand. Juana was talking to three other Mexican students, two female and one male, while standing in the lunch line. I was standing in front of her, with one person in between us.

31. I recorded this shorthand. Adrian was talking to five other people as they waited for the door to be opened for their history class. I was standing in the hall next to the group of people waiting to get into the class as well.

32. The data on the average of five to thirteen minutes were obtained from my recording of each incident's duration using the timer function on my wristwatch.

33. Resentment involving some sense of injustice has not been overly researched as a cause for violence, but it was found to be particularly present in the current study. For supporting findings concerning resentment as an instigator of violence, see Kellina M. Craig, "Examining Hate-Motivated Aggression: A Review of the Social Psychological Literature on Hate Crimes as a Distinct Form of Aggression," *Aggression and Violent Behavior* 7, no. 1 (2002): 85–101; and Roger D. Petersen, *Understanding Ethnic Violence: Fear, Hatred, and Resentment in Twentieth Century Eastern Europe* (Cambridge: Cambridge University Press, 2002).

34. I took this quote shorthand as Símon was talking to four other students after the fight he engaged in was broken up by security personnel at the school. He and the other four students who had been in the fight were sitting in the assistant principal's office waiting for him to arrive and interview them as to what had happened and tell them what the penalty would be for fighting. I was waiting in the assistant principal's office for him to arrive and was listening to Símon's conversation with the other students.

35. This aggression to alleviate resentments about perceived slights or injustices also supported positive feelings toward a person's own ethnic group much as social identity theory postulates. See Henri Tajfel and John C. Turner, "The Social Identity Theory of Intergroup Behavior," in *Psychology of Intergroup Relations,* 2nd ed., ed. Stephen Worchel and William G. Austin (Chicago: Nelson-Hall, 1986).

36. I took this quote shorthand as Jeremy was talking to a friend while being led by the assistant principal to the office after having been in a fight with a group of Mexican Americans. The fight started in the hall as classes were in the process of change. I observed the fight and its breakup and walked behind the assistant principal, Jeremy, and his friend on their way to the office.

37. I took this quote shorthand as Nicolas was being handcuffed by school police after a fight he was in with a group of African American students. Two African Americans along with another Mexican American were in police custody, and Nicolas was talking to the school dean awaiting the police to take all of them to the station for processing. I observed the start of the fight that began during the lunch period. I was standing listening to the conversation next to the dining table where the school police were handcuffing the four students before taking them to their office for processing.

38. I recorded the conversation when all four were in the restaurant eating hamburgers and I was also there eating in a booth behind them. Either they did not see me sit down in the booth behind them, or because they had seen me at school and around the neighborhood with no apparent connection to either the police or the African Americans whom they viewed as their adversaries, they did not seem to mind.

39. I assumed they were all meeting on Troy's porch just as they had discussed, but I did not know for sure if it was Troy's house or one of the others.

40. I accumulated the data for this example in two phases and ways. First, I was at a sporting event where Horace and his friends were in the stands talking about school situations. I was sitting with an African American spectator for the entire game, and because there were so many people packed into the stadium my identity as a Mexican American was concealed from Horace and his friends while they talked. What was more striking was their apparent lack of inhibition in talking about what they were going to do. Second, I made observations as I positioned myself in a concealed room with binoculars focused on the school's hallways to record violence that occurred there. I was not following Horace and his group, just generally observing if any violence would occur when Horace and his affiliated group attacked their victims.

41. See Howard Pinderhughes, *Race in the Hood: Conflict and Violence among Urban Youth* (Minneapolis: University of Minnesota Press, 1997), 131–33.

42. I recorded this shorthand. Dante was talking to four other male students in front of a small grocery store on the way home from school. I was at the store observing students as they traveled home from school.

43. Rory was talking to nine other male students at a community center after school. I was at the community center interacting with a number of youth who had come to play sports when I recorded this conversation.

44. After listening to Dante, I decided to follow him after school and see what route he took home in order to see if he and his friends would do anything. The event that is presented occurred on the way home from school. I was in one of my "makeshift blinds" (i.e., concealed areas) observing students without their knowing I was there. The various weapons used in the fight were placed in a large nylon bag and planted behind the store's dumpster.

45. Students were constantly trying to bring weapons into the school, and authorities were constantly vigilant against students attempting to do this. The availability of guns made them the preferred weapon, but it was extremely difficult to get these weapons through security. So the students would use objects that were designed for other purposes as weapons because these objects were more available and less recognized as weapons than guns. Thus bats used in gym classes or by the boys' baseball and girls' softball teams were taken and used as weapons. So too were chains that could be found in the various workshop classrooms.

I did not personally observe this event. It was reported by the police, and then I talked to two other people who had witnessed it, the one a sister of one of the combatants who was walking home at the time and the other a taxi driver; both corroborated the police report as to what had occurred.

46. This participation in violence as "fun" is identical to the phenomenon that occurred in England during the 1980s known as "Paki bashing," where white English youth would ride around and randomly attack individuals who appeared to be Pakistanis or Indians, or the phenomenon found throughout the world referred to as "gay bashing," where individuals ride around and find a person they believe to be gay and then proceed to beat him or her severely. See Neil Duncan, *School Bullying: Gender Conflict and Pupil Culture in Secondary Schools* (London: Routledge, 2001).

47. I recorded this shorthand. Frank, Lem, Dion, and three other young men were having this conversation at one of the local barbershops on a Saturday. I was in the barbershop getting a shave with a hot towel over my face concealing that I was Mexican and providing them with the belief that they could freely express themselves before I looked up and saw the barber indicate to them that I was in the chair. They left shortly after that.

48. I took this quote longhand as Paul was talking to two female friends at a recreation center after school. I was sitting at the same table they were.

49. I took this quote shorthand as Silas was talking to a female student while they were sitting eating during lunch hour. I was with the janitor trying to rake up debris that the students had left on the ground while eating. Silas was never caught engaging in violence, although I did observe him in a later incident kicking at three Mexican students who had been knocked down on the ground during a fight.

50. Silas was about five foot, five inches tall and weighed around 140 pounds, and Paul was about five foot, six inches tall and weighed about 150 pounds. Paul would go on to participate in two other attacks and be apprehended by police. He went to court, was found guilty, and was given probation with the additional provision that he perform three months of community service. The penalty was not more severe because there was no evidence that he had actively hit someone. He was therefore considered an accomplice.

51. This idea that the school belonged to the incumbent ethnic students was also reported by Pinderhughes in his study of the ethnic conflict between Albanians and Puerto Ricans and between Albanians and African Americans in a Bronx High School. Pinderhughes also reported that prior to this conflict there had been ethnic conflict between the incumbent Italian students of the time and the newly arrived Albanian students. See Pinderhughes, *Race in the Hood*, 144–46.

52. For a sociological and psychological examination of humiliation, see Gopal Guru, ed., *Humiliation: Claims and Contexts* (Delhi: Oxford India, 2011).

53. See James Gilligan, *Violence: Reflections on a National Epidemic* (New York: Vintage, 1996), 103–38. Gilligan finds shame to be a particularly important emotion in the process of stimulating violence and finds that, as in the present study, shame originates in feelings of violation. In an early work on Mexican American youth, anthropologist Celia Heller suggested that the intense aggression engaged in by Mexican American boys was best understood as a cultural response to violations of the "honor code" endemic in Latino culture that involved issues of shame from being humiliated. See Celia Heller, *Mexican American Youth: Forgotten Youth at the Crossroads* (New York: Random House, 1966), 36–38.

54. I recorded this longhand. Brian was with a group of thirteen African American students in the back of the bus that transported them to and from school. I was sitting three seats from them on the bus while they were talking. My presence was neither a distraction nor a deterrent from their speaking what they were thinking because I was a member of an ethnic group that was not involved in the conflict.

55. I recorded this shorthand. I observed both of the attacks as they took place. I also was able to record Raphael's talk with the students at school because I was understood by the group to be part of the custodial staff.

56. See the work of Barrington Moore Jr., *Injustice: The Social Bases of Obedience and Revolt* (White Plains, NY: M.E. Sharpe, 1978); and David O. Sears and John B. McConahay, *The Politics of Violence: The New Urban Blacks and the Watts Riot* (Boston: Houghton-Mifflin, 1973).

57. I recorded this longhand. Julius was talking to two other African American students (one male, the other female) while they were waiting for the bus to take them to Paul Revere High School. I was also in line conversing with a number of students, but I was not directly participating in Julius's conversation.

58. Tomás was talking to another student while they were waiting for a counselor. I was in the counselor's office waiting for him to return while listening to their conversation, which I recorded using shorthand.

59. It is difficult to state emphatically that this violent incident involved what Collins, *Violence*, 83–133, has referred to as the primary dynamic in violent confrontations, that is, "forward panic," because it is impossible to be inside a person's mind to observe what exactly is going on. However, on the basis of the different kinds of movements by the participants it is likely that some, if not all, of the elements described by Collins for a "forward panic" were present with some of the individuals involved. However, others involved appeared to be using some strategy (i.e., rational calculus) as to how to thwart an attack and how to gain the advantage. Therefore, I am a little less confident that elements of the "forward panic" were operative in all, or even most, of those engaging in this violent incident.

60. This incident occurred about an hour after school had been let out. I was in one of my observational posts along the main route that students used to return to their homes when I observed and recorded this incident using shorthand.

61. Nothing has been more destructive to cities than suburbanization, and nothing has accelerated it more than "white flight" fueled by racial fears. The most extreme case of this occurred in Detroit and is documented in Thomas J. Sugrue, *The Origins of the Urban Crisis: Race and Inequality in Postwar Detroit* (Princeton, NJ: Princeton University Press, 1996).

62. One of the reasons why residents felt they had to defend their neighborhood from the "invasion" of elements that would reduce the equity of their homes and bring other social ills to their area was that they could not sell their home and buy another in a different place that would improve or maintain their home's equity and thus their total assets. Usually the inability to buy in another area was caused either by an inadequate amount of total wealth to purchase a home in a higher-valued area or by realtors' and lenders' discrimination in the housing market on the basis of the race/ethnicity of individuals attempting to secure a loan or be shown available homes. For an analysis of the issues related to wealth accumulation and housing discrimination, see Melvin L. Oliver and Thomas M. Shapiro, *Black Wealth/White Wealth: A New Perspective on Racial Inequality* (New York: Routledge, 1995); Dalton Conley, *Being Black, Living in the Red* (Berkeley: University of California Press, 1999); and Douglas Massey and Nancy A. Denton, *American Apartheid: Segregation and the Making of the Underclass* (Cambridge, MA: Harvard University Press, 1993).

63. I took this quote using shorthand. Oscar and Rob were talking to a friend while they were attending a girls' basketball game at Los Angeles's De Neve High School. I was part of the conversation, as I had come to know all three fathers as a result of attending the various sporting events at the school. Both Oscar and Rob were employed in upper-middle-class occupations. Oscar was as a financial analyst for a medical research company, and Rob was an attorney.

64. I took this quote shorthand as Connie was talking to two friends, one male and the other female, as they were waiting to enter a school general assembly with a guest speaker. The speaker was a member of the state assembly and was talking to students about the efforts of government to increase spending for public education and reduce the costs of going to college. I was standing in line waiting to enter the auditorium with them.

65. Individual interests varied and could be associated with participating in sports, government, academic clubs, language clubs, the arts, etc.

66. It is difficult to assess whether this finding would be repeated outside California. I would predict that in middle-class schools throughout the United States where there are significant numbers of racial minority students who are also from middle-class families we would find similar results. However, in regions like the South and the Southwest where there is a history of rigid caste-like racial differentiation, the situation *could* be different. Clearly more research is necessary to determine whether middle-class schools in general use primarily, though not exclusively, nonethnic criteria to create an internal stratification system.

67. On the suicide of Jamey Rodemeyer due to bullying, see Anahad O'Connor, "Suicide Draws Attention to Gay Bullying," *New York Times,* September 21, 2011; on that of Amanda Todd, see Ryan Grenoble, "Amanda Todd: Bullied Canadian Teen Commits Suicide after Prolonged Battle Online and in

School,"*Huffington Post,* October 11, 2012; and on that of Jadin Bell, see "Jadin Bell Dead: Gay Oregon Teen Who Hanged Himself Dies after Being Taken Off Life Support," *Huffington Post,* February 4, 2013.

68. I took this quote shorthand as Noah was talking to a male friend while both were helping to place posters for the school play on the hallway walls. I was standing in the hall as they were working and talking.

69. I took this quote shorthand as Ricardo was talking to two other male students while they were eating their lunch. I was eating lunch at the table next to them.

70. It is important to emphasize that both the incumbent and new students in a school experience the "other" as being "new."

71. See Collins, *Violence,* 19–133.

72. See ibid., 93–94.

73. For a good introduction to group dynamics, see Donelson R. Forsyth, *Group Dynamics,* 5th ed. (Belmont, CA: Wadsworth Cengage, 2010).

5. FIRE

1. See Erving Goffman, *The Presentation of Self in Everyday Life* (Garden City, NY; Doubleday, 1959), 77–105, which discusses the impact of teams in the formation of identity and the execution of tasks.

2. Examples would include India-China, India-Pakistan, and Israel-Syria. The strategy of deterrence is quite standard in the field of international relations. See Alexander George and Richard Smoke, *Deterrence in American Foreign Policy: Theory and Practice* (New York: Columbia University Press, 1974); and Robert Jervis, "Deterrence Theory Revisited," *World Politics* 31, no. 2 (1979): 289–324.

3. I took this quote longhand without a tape recorder while talking to Tara, who was waiting for her mother to pick her up from school.

4. I took this quote shorthand as Wilma was talking to three of her friends during lunchtime. I was next to the table where they were eating.

5. I took this quote shorthand as Sonia was talking to a friend at a local taco stand where they were buying food on the way home. I was in line with them as they were talking.

6. I recorded this longhand as I was in the cafeteria of the school observing student interaction. This incident occurred about ten feet from where I was sitting.

7. I recorded this event shorthand as I was in the school gym observing physical education classes to see if these types of classes produced more or less conflict than regular academic courses. I was with a teacher's aide within about twenty feet of the incident.

8. I recorded this event shorthand. I was standing about ten feet from the line observing students in the commons area when I focused on the line and the events that evolved.

9. I recorded this event shorthand. I was standing next to the line waiting for one of the teachers that I had gone to the game with to finish his purchase and observed the interaction. I was about five feet from these students.

10. On the importance of moral outrage, see Hein F. M. Lodewijdx, Gaby L. E. Kersten, and Martijn van Zomeren, "Dual Pathways to Engage in 'Silent Marches' against Violence: Moral Outrage, Moral Cleansing and Modes of Identification," *Journal of Community and Applied Psychology* 18, no. 3 (2008): 153–67; and Jean-Pierre Reed, "Emotions in Context: Revolutionary Accelerators, Hope, Moral Outrage, and Other Emotions in the Making of Nicaragua's Revolution," *Theory and Society* 33 (2004): 653–703.

11. Randall Collins discusses the impact of audiences on a violent incident's level of intensity. He also discusses the entertainment aspect of fights, but his discussion appears to be different from my finding of the audience's desire to be entertained by the fighting through the masquerade of support for one side of the encounter. See Randall Collins, *Violence: A Micro-sociological Theory* (Princeton, NJ: Princeton University Press, 2008), 236–37, 242–81.

12. John Devine, *Maximum Security: The Culture of Violence in Inner-City Schools* (Chicago: University of Chicago Press, 1997), 40, also reports that audiences are important for the continuance of fights.

13. I took this quote shorthand as Matías was talking to two friends waiting for the school dean to arrive and interview them about the fight they were in. I was in the office sitting at a desk by the dean's office as they were conversing.

14. This is also reported in Ione Malloy's *Southie Won't Go: A Teacher's Diary of the Desegregation of South Boston High School* (Urbana: University of Illinois Press, 1986), 37, 76–77.

15. See Tanja Wranik and Klaus R. Scherer, "Why Do I Get Angry? A Componential Appraisal Approach," in *International Handbook of Anger*, ed. Michael Portegal, Gerhard Stemmler, and Charles Spielberger (New York: Springer, 2010), 243–66.

16. For a discussion of the underlying motives for jokes, see Sigmund Freud, *Jokes and Their Relationship to the Subconscious* (New York: W. W. Norton, 1960). However, their social impact in situations where antagonism exists between members of different ethnic groups is to create hostilities. For a theoretical discussion of the impact of stigma on the behaviors of individuals, see Erving Goffman, *Stigma: Notes on the Management of Spoiled Identity* (New York: Simon and Schuster, 1963). The findings of both these studies provide insights into the dynamic of "stimulus and response" that forms the basis for initiating fights.

17. I recorded this incident shorthand as I was observing student behavior at the close of instruction for the day. I was standing about five feet back of the bus stop as the interaction occurred.

18. Certain ethnic groups that operate under "honor systems" as opposed to "respect systems" are particularly prone to engage in violence to avenge a slight to their honor. Because honor systems usually involve the entire family or those closely associated with the object of a disparaging comment or action, the act of dishonoring an individual will include everyone associated with that individual. For a discussion of this difference, see J. G. Peristiany, ed., *Honor and Shame: The Values of Mediterranean Society* (London: Weidenfeld and Nicholson, 1965); and Martín Sánchez-Jankowski, *Cracks in the Pavement: Social Change and Resilience in Poor Neighborhoods* (Berkeley: University of California Press, 2008), 140–41.

19. The general trend for the vast majority of individuals is as I reported. Of course, in the schools studied some individuals had sociopathic tendencies, and for these individuals the process was different. They simply needed to see an opportunity to act out their desires to inflict pain and suffering as a means of satisfying both emotional and/or identity needs. However, because these individuals constituted such a small proportion of the student population, their influence on the general sociological trend I describe for most of the students involved in the ethnic violence dynamics was negligible.

20. The use of *bean* as a derogatory term to refer to Mexicans may have its origins in the fact that (1) Mexicans are generally, though not uniformly, brown in color like cooked pinto beans; or (2) beans are one of the staples of the Mexican diet. Whatever the origin, it is generally understood to refer to Mexicans in a derogatory manner.

21. I recorded this event shorthand as I observed it from a house porch that I used for the primary purpose of viewing the comings and goings of students to school. I was about thirty feet away.

22. On identifying a member of another ethnic group as the source of one's discontent, see Mathew Mayer and Peter Leone, "School Violence and Disruption Revisited: Equity and Safety in the School House," *Focus on Exceptional Children* 40, no. 1 (2007): 1–28; Christopher J. Ferguson, Claudia San Miguel, and Richard D. Hartley, "A Multivariate Analysis of Youth Violence and Aggression: The Influence of Family, Peers, Depression, and Media Violence," *Journal of Pediatrics* 166, no. 6 (2009): 904–8; Jayne A. Fulkerson, Mary Story, Alison Mellin, Nancy Leffert, Dianne Neumark-Sztainer, and Simone A. French, "Family Dinner Meal Frequency and Adolescent Development: Relationships with Developmental Assets and High-Risk Behaviors," *Journal of Adolescent Health* 39, no. 3 (2006): 337–45; P. R. Smokowski and K. H. Kopasz, "Bullying in School: An Overview of Types, Effects, Family Characteristics, and Intervention Strategies," *Children and Schools* 27, no. 2 (2005): 101–10.

23. On displacing internal feelings of discontent onto political conflict, see Harold Laswell, *Psychopathology and Politics* (1930; repr., Chicago: University of Chicago Press, 1977). On scapegoating marginal and vulnerable members of the other ethnic group, see Amy Kate Baily, Stewart E. Tolnay, E. M. Beck, and Jenifer D. Laird, "Targeting Lynching Victims: Social Marginality or Status Transgressions?," *American Sociological Review* 76 (June 2011): 412–36, a study of lynching in the South that found violence toward members of competing/conflicting ethnic groups was related to whether the victim was a marginal member of the community in which he or she was currently living.

24. I recorded this conversation shorthand before the students entered the class for instruction to begin. I was just on the inside of the door to the room, and they were on the outside next to the door.

25. I observed the incident in which Anthony used the rock to hit the other student and was not identified. I did not observe the brawl incident but arrived after the school police were already on the scene and saw them handcuff and detain all the students who had been involved. I observed Anthony as being one of them and saw the police marking the steel rod as having been used by him in the fight. I did not follow what happened to Anthony after he was dismissed from school.

26. A significant part of the impetus to engage in violence is predicated on being frustrated with one's present living situation and blaming the other group for this. Perceptions of past injustices feed into blaming the other group for current frustrations, and this in turn leads to the use of violence, as discussed in relation to nonwhites against white colonizers in Franz Fanon's *The Wretched of the Earth* (1961; repr., New York: Grove Press, 2004). Interestingly, whites who have been poor but who are members of the power group by virtue of their white skin color experience both the frustration of being downtrodden because of discrimination by whites in the upper classes and the fear that the white upper class is using nonwhite groups to reduce the socioeconomic conditions of one's own group. This leads to further violence against the nonwhite group, both because it is not possible to attack the white upper class without additional risk and because the white upper class will tolerate violence toward the nonwhite group(s). This is clearly brought out in the classic study by John Dollard, *Caste and Class in a Southern Town* (1937; repr., Madison: University of Wisconsin Press, 1989), 315–63.

27. I took this quote shorthand while watching a fight between Henry and an African American that occurred after a heated exchange in the bathroom. I was in the bathroom washing my hands when the argument began and then went out to observe the fight.

28. I took this quote shorthand as Aaron was fighting with a Mexican American student during lunch hour. I was watching various students during the lunch period and focused on these two as they engaged in an exchange of words that erupted into a fight.

29. There is evidence that second-generation and beyond Mexican-origin citizens are frustrated with their misfortune and do have antagonistic attitudes toward and physical conflict with more recent Mexican immigrants to the United States. For the documentation on the problems that some, not all, Mexican Americans in the second and beyond generation are having with socioeconomic mobility, see Edward Telles and Vilma Ortiz, *Generations of Exclusion: Mexican Americans, Assimilation, and Race* (New York: Russell Sage Foundation, 2008). For discussions of the conflict that is often seen among different generations of Mexican-origin populations, see David Gutiérrez, *Walls and Mirrors: Mexican Americans, Mexican Immigrants, and the Politics of Ethnicity* (Berkeley: University of California Press, 1995); Jason L. Morin, Gabriel R. Sanchez, and Matt A. Barreto, "Perception of Competition," in *Just Neighbors? Research on African American and Latino Relations in the United States*, ed. Edward Telles, Mark Q. Sawyer, and Gaspar Rivera-Salgado (New York: Russell Sage, 2011), 106–13.

30. See Martín Sánchez-Jankowski, *Islands in the Street: Gangs and American Urban Society* (Berkeley: University of California Press, 1991), 156, which reported that individuals who had experienced feelings of personal weakness and vulnerability hated to see this in others because it reminded them of their own fears and weaknesses and would exhibit intense aggression toward them.

31. I recorded this incident shorthand as I observed it occurring from start to finish. I was observing from a garage immediately across the street from the incident and could easily see and hear the full extent of the interaction.

32. Ted Robert Gurr, *Minorities at Risk: A Global View of Ethnopolitical Conflicts* (Washington, DC: United States Institute of Peace Press, 1993), 34–132; Donald L. Horowitz, *Ethnic Groups in Conflict* (Berkeley: University of California Press, 1985), 72–74, 266–67.

33. Of course, the impact of the group on individual behavior was a major contribution of Emile Durkheim. See his *The Division of Labor in Society* (New York: Free Press, 1984).

34. See Donald L. Horowitz, *The Deadly Ethnic Riot* (Berkeley: University of California Press, 2001), 74–94, which also found that rumors were important in initiating riots.

35. I took this quote shorthand as Lorenzo and two of his friends were talking to a school security guard during the lunch break. I was talking to a janitor who was next to the security guard.

36. See Charles Tilly, *The Politics of Collective Violence* (New York: Cambridge University Press, 2003), 151–70.

37. I recorded this incident shorthand as I followed the students who had heard the rumor to where the reputed fight was occurring, and I continued to record the behavior of the students before, during, and after the fight.

38. I took this quote shorthand while Reginio was in the school dean's office. Reginio was an honor student, and the dean was surprised that he was involved, so he called Reginio to his office to gather information about what had started the fight and how he had gotten involved. I was just outside the dean's office talking to two security guards.

39. I took this quote shorthand while Bartley was in the dean's office telling him about the fight and how he had gotten involved. Bartley was an honor student, and the dean was surprised that he was involved, so he called Bartley to his office to gather information about what had started the fight and how Bartley had come to be involved. I was in the dean's office while he was talking to Bartley.

40. I took this quote longhand after Orton returned to school. I was part of a large group of students talking to him about his involvement and suspension.

41. I took this quote shorthand as Lucas was talking to the school counselor and waiting for the assistant principal to arrive. I was also in the office while he and the counselor talked, and I observed the brawl that Lucas was described as participating in.

42. I took this quote shorthand while the student was being interviewed about the fight by the dean. I was in the office while the dean was talking to the student and waiting for the parents of the students to arrive and take them home because they were being suspended.

43. Vigilante groups exist throughout the world, and they have been a part of the social environment in the United States for much of its history. See Richard Maxwell Brown, "The American Vigilante Tradition," in *The History of Violence in America: A Report to the National Commission on the Causes and Prevention of Violence,* ed. Hugh Davis Graham and Ted Robert Gurr (New York: Bantam, 1969), 154–226; for specific urban contexts, see Gerald D. Suttles, *The Social Construction of Communities* (Chicago: University of Chicago Press, 1972), 189–232, and Gary T. Marx and Dane Archer, "The Urban Vigilante," *Psychology Today,* January 1973, 45–51.

44. For a discussion of the different forms of illegal associations that become involved in "ganging behavior," see Martín Sánchez-Jankowski, "Gangs and Social Change," *Theoretical Criminology* 7, no. 2 (2003): 191–216.

45. I took this quote shorthand as Felipe was talking to some other Mexican students that had been involved in an incident at Oakland's Kaiser High School. All of the students were in a holding room with the school's assistant principal. I accompanied the assistant principal to the room where all the individuals were being held and were waiting for the police to decide whether to take all them to the station for formal processing.

46. A sense of injustice has been the cornerstone of both individual and group action in the social and political realm. On the political front, see Barrington Moore, *Injustice: The Social Bases of Obedience and Revolt* (White Plains, NY: M. E. Sharpe, 1978); and David O. Sears and John B. MacConahay, *The Politics of Violence: The New Urban Blacks and the Watts Riot* (Boston: Houghton-Mifflin, 1973).

47. I took this quote longhand as Katy was talking to a group of students who were with their parents at a rally against school busing to Shawmut High School. I was in the group as she and others talked.

48. I took this quote shorthand as Jade was talking to one of the security guards who was a friend of his. I was standing only a few feet from their conversation.

49. See Robert Fogelson, *Violence as Protest: A Study of Riots and Ghettos* (Garden City, NY: Anchor Books, 1971), which argues that the race riots during the 1960s were driven by the rioters' sense of frustration with society's lack of effort to address the injustices toward specific minorities. His description of the causes of these riots is similar to those I am calling "Type 1 Riots."

50. I recorded these comments longhand as Cooper was talking to a student friend of his as they were taking part in the riot. I was in the hall observing the activity.

51. Observations like this on the part of law enforcement, members of the general public, and some analysts have led them to conclude that individuals enter riots merely for fun or profit. This line of argument was advanced by Edward Banfield in *The Unheavenly City Revisited* (Boston: Little-Brown, 1970), 211–33; and Jack Katz, in *Seduction of Crime: Moral and Sensual Attractions in Doing Evil* (New York: Basic Books, 1988), 312–13, who adapted it to claim that the motive was one of emotional satisfaction.

52. See Horowitz, *Deadly Ethnic Riot*, 124–50. For Horowitz, this type of riot consists of individuals from rival ethnic groups targeting individuals for killing and maiming before the riot even begins, but to my knowledge this has not been reported for the rioting that has occurred in any of the high schools in the United States. If it has occurred, at the time of this book's writing it was not a dominant occurrence.

53. See ibid., 60–61.

54. See the work of Stanley Tambiah, *Leveling Crowds: Ethnonational Conflict and Collective Violence in South Asia* (Berkeley: University of California Press, 1997), 213–95.

55. The idea of self-protection has both a physical component (protecting one's body from injury) and a psychological one (protecting one's sense of self and one's public identity). The protection of the identity that one has developed and nurtured, especially during adolescence, when identity formation is in process, is critical in understanding the ability of adolescent youth to overcompensate for challenges to this presentation of self. Not to defend this presentation of self would be seen by one's peer group as an admission that this identity was fake and would make the peer group feel that they had been lied to, a reaction that could lead to peer group shunning (i.e., stigmatizing). Thus individuals are more likely to engage in violence during adolescence to protect themselves from having their identities spoiled. Two of Erving Goffman's books that bear directly on the establishment and maintenance of identity are *The Presentation of Self In Everyday Life* and *Stigma: Notes on the Management of Spoiled Identity* (New York: Simon and Schuster, 1963).

56. I was aware of the rumor circulating among the students concerning this incident and recorded it on seven different occasions involving different groups of students.

57. On the issue of moral righteousness in the use of violence, see William T. Vollman, *Rising Up and Rising Down: Some Thoughts on Violence, Freedom and Urgent Means* (San Francisco: McSweeny, 2003), vols. 2 and 3.

58. I took this quote shorthand while Trey was talking to two of his friends at a school basketball game. I was in the same line to use the lavatory as they were. I had also previously observed the behavior of Trey while the riot was occurring.

59. I took this quote shorthand while Max was talking to the dean after being picked up by school police for fighting with African Americans during the riot. He was waiting for the police to decide on whether to formally charge him with a crime. I was in the dean's office as Max was talking. I observed the behavior of Max while the riot was occurring as well.

60. The statements by Litia were recorded shorthand as she was talking to two of her friends and a counselor who was trying to gather information as to what had happened during the riot. Litia was considered such a good student that school authorities counted on students like her to provide accurate information on what had occurred so they could work toward stopping this type of violence from occurring again. I was in the larger office where the conversation was occurring.

61. The school counselor was surprised that Litia had acted as she did, since she was a straight "A" student who had never been in any trouble prior to this, but this did inform them that when riot-type events occur everyone becomes a potential participant in antisocial behavior.

62. I took this quote shorthand as Alfredo was talking to a mail delivery person whom he seemed to know in a small grocery store one afternoon on his way home from school. I was in the store observing whether there would be any violence taking place at the store or just outside it.

63. I took this quote shorthand as Ivan was talking to a local clergyman who was visiting a sick parishioner that lived across the street from the school and

who came to see if he could provide aid in calming the students after they exited the building. I was part of the group of students that he first interacted with.

64. I took this quote longhand as Denise was explaining to a school aide worker right after exiting the school what she had experienced once the students attempted to rush out of the building. I was there taking notes on the violence while she was talking to the aide.

65. I took this quote shorthand as Omar was talking to two friends in the parking lot of the school. They had just rushed out of school after there was a fight between two groups of African American and Mexican American students during lunch hour. I was next to him, having also left the building with the students.

66. See Gustav Le Bon's classic *The Crowd: A Study in the Popular Mind* (1896; repr., Kitchener, Ontario: Batoche Books, 2006), 13–47.

67. One might imagine that weather would be a factor in that in eastern cities like Boston the cold weather might suppress riot behavior. However, in the present study, weather had no impact: students were perfectly willing to riot and stampede in the cold months of December, January, and February. See the aggregate data in table A.1 in the Methodological Appendix.

68. Collins, *Violence,* 19–20.

6. DOUSING AND SUFFOCATING THE FLAMES

1. See the work of Stanley Lieberson, *Making It Count: The Improvement of Social Research and Theory* (Berkeley: University of California Press, 1985), who warned that one cannot simply reverse the "cause" and assume that the "effect" will go away.

2. See Klaus R. Scherer, Ronald P. Abeles, and Claude S. Fischer, *Human Aggression and Conflict: Interdisciplinary Perspectives* (Englewood Cliffs, NJ: Prentice-Hall, 1975), 9–152; Nancy G. Guerra, L. Rowell Huesmann, and Anja Spindler, "Community Violence Exposure, Social Cognition, and Aggression among Urban Elementary School Children," *Child Development* 74, no. 5 (2003): 1561–76; Catherine P. Bradshaw and James Garbarino, "Social Cognitions as a Mediator of Influence of Family and Community Violence on Adolescent Development: Implications for Intervention," *Annals of the New York Academy of Sciences* 103 (December 2004): 85–105.

3. See Frantz Fanon, *Wretched of the Earth* (1961; repr., New York: Grove Press, 2004); and Philippe Bourgois, *In Search of Respect: Selling Crack in El Barrio* (New York: Cambridge University Press, 1996), 165–67 (these pages provide just an example, as Bourgois's entire book is permeated with this argument).

4. The entire body of social control theory would argue this. On this theory, see Ruth Rosner Kornhauser, *Social Sources of Delinquency: An Appraisal of Analytic Models* (Chicago: University of Chicago Press, 1978), 51–138. Some representative examples can be seen in Travis Hirschi, *Causes of Delinquency* (New Brunswick, NJ: Transaction Press, 2001); Robert J. Sampson and John A. Laub, *Crime in the Making: Pathways and Turning Points through Life* (Cambridge, MA: Harvard University Press, 1993).

5. Examples would be Ruth Horowitz and Gary Schwartz, "Honor, Normative Ambiguity and Gang Violence," *American Sociological Review* 39, no. 2 (1974): 238–51; and Randall Collins, *Violence: A Micro-sociological Theory* (Princeton, NJ: Princeton University Press, 2008).

6. See Martín Sánchez-Jankowski, *Islands in the Street: Gangs and American Urban Society* (Berkeley: University Press, 1991), 142.

7. This behavior of victorious combatants posturing to "their intended public" can be seen in both animals and people after a physical contest. It is especially seen in sports when one of the contestants beats another and physically gestures to the audience that he or she has prevailed over the competitor. In American football this is referred to as "flaunting." There is much literature on this, but see the classic work on aggression by Konrad Lorenz, *On Aggression* (Boston: Mariner Books, 1974). For sports teams, see Collins, *Violence*, 302–34, 413–62, as it applies to receiving attention.

8. I recorded this episode longhand as I was walking down the hallway on my way to a teacher's meeting. The African American student appeared to sustain some severe injuries and rushed to a local Boston hospital. I was not able to find out the exact severity of the injuries he sustained, but I was able to confirm that the blows with the clubs were being delivered with such force that they caused some fractures.

9. I recorded the first episode shorthand as I was observing from the vantage of a stair landing above that occupied by the African Americans who started the incident. As the African Americans proceeded down the stairs to confront the victim I followed to the next landing. I could hear the conversation because they were shouting at each other. I recorded the second episode shorthand as I was observing with binoculars from the vantage of a rooftop on one of the school buildings.

10. I recorded this event shorthand as I watched from the site of an abandoned garage that was about thirty yards from where the fight was occurring. I had a stopwatch and also recorded the length of the various intervals of the fight.

11. Obviously, some form of calculus was occurring for both to recognize that there was a high enough probability that continuing the fight would produce diminishing returns in the form of injury and/or status in the event that they were not capable of physically defending themselves and they lost the fight. There has not been a great deal of research on whether, and how, individuals engaged in a fight use some form of risk assessment that informs their future behavior, and this is one area that needs attention. Some evidence, however, suggests that contrary to the idea of the body having a life of its own with the capability of continuing to act even though the mind has determined it cannot go on, there is an end point where the body will not function even if the mind says it should. A fight is one of those situations, where danger of being hurt is present but the body is so fatigued that it cannot go on and injury is imminent if one's opponent is less fatigued and is capable of continuing the battle. For an excellent theoretical statement concerning the autonomy of the body, see Loïc Wacquant, *Body and Soul: Notebooks of an Apprentice Boxer* (New York: Oxford University Press, 2004), 58–78, 97–98.

12. I recorded this event verbally into a Dictaphone while it was occurring and later in the evening coded and then transferred the account to the computer program Folio Views. I observed the event from the front porch of a house that was located on the primary street that students used to return from school to their homes.

13. Of course, this is a classic example of a Durkheimian ritual reifying group membership and cohesion. See Emile Durkheim, *Elementary Forms of Religious Life* (1915; repr., New York: Free Press, 1995); and John Devine, *Maximum Security: The Culture of Violence in Inner-City Schools* (Chicago: University of Chicago Press, 1997), 48.

14. See Karen D. Randolph, "Implicit Theories of Peer Relations," *Social Development* 19, no. 1 (2010): 113–29.

15. See Corey Abramson and Darren Modzelewski, "Caged Morality: Moral Worlds, Subculture, and Stratification among Middle-Class Cage Fighters," *Qualitative Sociology* 34 (March 2011): 143–75.

16. See Erik H. Erikson, *Identity, Youth, and Crisis*, (New York: W. W. Norton, 1968), 253; and Lawrence S. Friedman, "Adolescence," in *The Child: An Encyclopedic Companion*, ed. Richard A. Shweder (Chicago: University of Chicago Press, 2009), 18–20.

17. See A. D. Farrell, S. May, A. Bettencourt, and E. H. Erwin, "Environmental Influences on Fighting Versus Nonviolent Behavior in Peer Situations," *American Journal of Community Psychology* 46, nos. 1–2 (2010): 19–35.

18. I recorded the encounter shorthand as I observed it from the porch of a house on a popular route used by students to return to their homes after school. After recording the fight, I followed the students to a small grocery store where they bought snacks. I was standing in an aisle listening to the conversation between Calinda and the other African American student as I waited in line to pay the cashier.

19. I recorded the fight and quote shorthand as I stood in the school commons area watching the students who were on their scheduled afternoon break.

20. There are times that students think that cruelty is appropriate. These occasions are usually when their coethnic is in the act of revenging some aggression that the person being attacked perpetrated against one of their group.

21. I recorded the quotes shorthand as Evan, David, and Victor were conversing before they entered their first-period class. I was in the hall immediately to their right with two other students as both groups were conversing before school started.

22. The students in this study used all of these statements, but they were not the only ones used to indicate the desire for a fight to stop.

23. This occurred as the students were just leaving school to go home. I was there among a group of fifteen students watching the fight. I recorded this event shorthand.

24. Communication through the use of language and physical symbols is analyzed by Erving Goffman, *Encounters: Two Studies in the Sociology of Interaction* (Indianapolis, IN: Bobbs-Merrill, 1961), 97–105.

25. These are a sample of the actual comments used and recorded at the time the fight was being observed. I recorded them shorthand and in every case

exactly as were expressed; later I entered them into the computer-assisted qualitative data program Folio Views.

26. I recorded these phrases in my field notes either at the time they were made or within minutes of their having been expressed. There were many statements used to convey the same warning; I have simply randomly selected these as examples from the notes recorded in the computer-assisted qualitative program Folio Views.

27. Alan Mazur, "A Hormonal Interpretation of Collin's Micro-sociological Theory of Social Behavior," *Journal for the Theory of Social Behavior* 38, no. 4 (2009): 434–47.

28. The linkages connecting these events are very similar to those theorized by Randall Collins in *Interaction Ritual Chains* (Princeton, NJ: Princeton University Press, 2004).

29. I was in the hall when the fight broke out and recorded what happened longhand in a notebook immediately after the event.

30. I recorded the fighting part of the event from my observation point on the roof of the main building on campus; then after the warning sounded I ran down to mingle among the students as the police and school authorities tried to determine what had occurred. I recorded shorthand Jessica's and the other students' statements to the police who were questioning them about the disturbance.

31. It should be noted that regardless of the accuracy of the warning from the "lookouts" the effect was to stop the fighting.

32. I recorded this event shorthand as I observed it. I was in a location immediately in front of where it was occurring.

33. See Ione Malloy, *Southie Won't Go: A Teacher's Diary of the Desegregation of South Boston High School* (Urbana: University of Illinois Press, 1986), 51–55.

34. This is a problem associated with maintaining group solidarity and discipline. See Michael Hechter, *Principles of Group Solidarity* (Berkeley: University of California Press, 1972),40–73, and Scherer, Abeles, and Fischer, *Human Aggression and Conflict*, 153–84, where there is a discussion concerning the factors influencing cooperation for group behavior and the rational calculus of "prisoner's dilemma" when confronting varying outcomes in high-risk situations.

35. See Anthony R. Mawson, *Mass Panic and Social Attachment* (Burlington, VT: Ashgate, 2007), 113–18.

36. See Malloy, *Southie Won't Go*, 611, 141. Also one can see the same strategy used by authorities in the large urban riots that have occurred throughout the world. On riots in general, see Donald Horowitz, *The Deadly Ethnic Riot* (Berkeley: University of California Press, 2001), 489–90, which finds that when police have the capability and determination they can stop the violence more quickly and that when they do not they often revert to policies that aid in maintaining a riot. On this, see Sidney Fine, *Violence in the Model City: The Cavanagh Administration, Race Relations, and the Detroit Riot of 1967* (Ann Arbor: University of Michigan Press, 1990), 172–82.

37. I recorded this event shorthand. I was roaming the lunch area when the fight started and got caught up with the group of African Americans who exited

the front of the building; then, after ducking into a classroom, I went to the second floor of the building, where I could observe both groups of students as they exited the building.

38. I recorded this event shorthand as the events associated with this riot were occurring.

39. The removal of leadership can have an important impact on social movement effectiveness. See Jenna Jordan, "When Heads Roll: Assessing the Effectiveness of Leadership Decapitation," *Security Studies* 18 (2009): 719–55.

40. I recorded this event longhand as I was in the community center while the meeting was going on. I was with three other individuals listening to the conversation between these leaders.

41. Fear of making things worse for individuals or group goals is something that affects the internal operations within social movements more generally. See Jeffrey Goodwin and Steven Pfaff, "Emotion Work in High-Risk Social Movements: Managing Fear in the U.S. and East German Civil Rights Movements," in *Passionate Politics: Emotions and Social Movements,* ed. Jeff Goodwin, James M. Jasper, and Francesca Polletta (Chicago: University of Chicago Press, 2001), 282–302.

42. See, for example, Malloy, *Southie Won't Go,* 83.

43. See Hans H. Toch, *Violent Men: An Inquiry into the Psychology of Violence* (Chicago: Aldine Press, 1969), 160–63, 137–153.

44. It should be remembered that leadership was strategically important in organizing individual fights, brawls, walkouts, riots, and stampedes. Further, the role of "troublemakers" was particularly critical in initiating and maintaining both the violent incident and the number of incidents. On the importance of leaders, see Kathleen M. Carley, Ju-Sung Lee, and David Krackhardt, "Destabilizing Networks," *Connections* 24, no. 3 (2001): 79–92; and Edgar Schein, *Organizational Culture and Leadership* (San Francisco: Jossey-Bass, 1985).

45. I took this quote shorthand while Gilberto was talking to a friend as they walked to their next class. I was walking in the same direction immediately behind them.

46. I took this quote shorthand as Dixon was talking with one of the school aides. I was with the aide and Dixon when the conversation was occurring.

47. I took this quote shorthand as Danica was talking to three of her friends in the school cafeteria during lunch. I was at the table next to them.

48. I took this quote shorthand as Cameron was talking to four other male friends at a school basketball game. I was in the stands immediately in back of them.

49. I took this quote shorthand as Matías was talking to five other students (three boys and two girls) during lunch. I was at the table behind the one he was using.

50. I took this quote longhand of a conversation Doris was having with two of her girlfriends and two male friends at the local community center. I was sitting at the table immediately next to theirs having cookies and tea that were provided by the community center during one of the "social breaks."

51. Rebecca E. Klatch, "The Underside of Social Movements: The Effects of Destructive Affective Ties," *Qualitative Sociology* 27, no. 4 (2004): 487–509.

52. For the impact of rational choice in promoting group solidarity, see Hechter, *Principles of Group Solidarity.*

53. See Abigail Halcli, "AIDS, Anger, and Activism: Act Up as a Social Movement Organization," in *Waves of Protest: Social Movements since the Sixties,* ed. Jo Freman and Victoria Johnson (Lanham, MD: Rowman and Littlefield, 1999), 135–50; and Kimberly Dugan and Jo Roger, "Voice and Agency in Social Movement Outcomes," *Qualitative Sociology* 29 (2006): 467–89.

54. I took this quote longhand as Brandon was talking to two of his friends at a local community center. I was next to them watching two other youth play a ping-pong game.

55. I took this quote shorthand as Malik was talking to five of his friends during halftime of a school basketball game. They were talking in the stands and I was seated two rows above them.

7. MONITORING THE EMBERS

1. I took this quote longhand while Janet was talking with a group of students at a small grocery store as they walked home. I was with the group of students walking to my car.

2. I took this quote shorthand while Taylor was talking to four friends at a school basketball game. I was in line to buy refreshments behind him.

3. I took this quote longhand as Kim was talking to two friends at a community center in Roxbury where she lived and from where she was bused. I was at the center as a guest of the director and had just talked to one of the students that Kim was talking to.

4. I took this quote shorthand as Julián was talking to a counselor and two other friends during a school recess. I was standing to the left of the counselor and Julián while they were talking.

5. I took this quote longhand as I was with Darcy and one of his friends at a local high school hockey game.

6. I took this quote shorthand as Isaiah was making these comments to two friends while they were at a small grocery store on the way home from school. I was in the store standing near the owner and a few feet from where Isaiah was talking to his friends.

7. I took this quote shorthand as Nora was talking to one of her friends and waiting for the gym teacher to begin class. I was standing on the outside of the line waiting for the class to start. Nora was in the outside lane, so I was very close to her and her friends.

8. I took this quote longhand as Tad was talking to another student and a community liaison person working in the school. Tad was standing at the door to the front office waiting to see a vice principal with some papers that a teacher had asked him to take to the office. I was standing immediately next to them waiting to get into the front office to renew my general pass to the school.

9. Although the exact saying "Hurt me once, shame on you, hurt me twice, shame on me" was never used, students' cautiousness was predicated on the principles entailed in this phrase.

10. I took this quote longhand of a conversation between Tammy and five friends at the school cafeteria where they were sitting talking about it being nice that there had been no violence for the last two and half months. They and I were all sitting at one long table; I was eating lunch immediately next to one of the five students.

11. I took this quote shorthand as I listened to the conversation between Ricardo and two other Mexican American students while they were talking on their way home from school. I was following in the crowd of students as they began their passage home.

12. The attitude associated with "guardedness" in accepting the gestures of friendship offered by members of the rival group featured elements of alienation from the entire social environment in which students found themselves and made healthy social interaction problematic. See Barbara M. Newman and Phillip R. Newman, "Group Identity and Alienation: Giving the We Its Due," *Journal of Youth and Adolescence* 30, no. 5 (2001): 515–38.

13. I took this quote longhand while Andy was talking to another friend as they were waiting to get on the bus to take them back to their neighborhood. I was standing a couple of feet away as they were talking.

14. I took this quote shorthand as Inez was talking to four friends while standing in line to buy some snacks at the school store. I was in line to buy a soda immediately behind her and the four other students.

15. One example happened in the Boston situation. In *Southie Won't Go: A Teacher's Diary of the Desegregation of South Boston High School* (Urbana: University of Illinois Press, 1986), 20–21, Ione Malloy also reports their use in the Boston school in which she taught.

16. During earlier periods of violence, students often snuck up behind someone and struck him or her in the back or side of the head with a cup that had a jagged end along the rim.

17. Zip guns are makeshift guns put together from whatever material is available. They are usually constructed with metal pipe strong enough to withstand the firing mechanism. They will use buckshot (small pellets) or .22 caliber bullets. The technology is crude, but information on how to construct such a weapon has been around for more than seventy years. Currently there are pages on the Web that provide a blueprint for making these types of guns. See, for example, J. David Trub, *Zips, Pipes, and Pens: Arsenal of Improvised Weapons* (Boulder, CO: Paladin Press, 1993), a book that would certainly be controversial among those who favor gun control. Paladin Press, the publisher of this book, was started by Robert K. Brown, who also started the magazine *Soldier of Fortune*, catering to readers who fancy paramilitary activity. This press was subsequently purchased by Peder Lund, and it remains in the business of publishing material on paramilitary activities.

18. See David Montejano, *Quijote's Soldiers: A Local History of the Chicano Movement, 1966–1981* (Austin: University of Texas Press, 2010), 55–79, and *Sancho's Journal: Exploring the Political Edge with the Brown Berets* (Austin: University of Texas Press, 2012), 20–42. Although the latter book is full of references to ex-gang members becoming Brown Berets and protecting community residents from various societal elements trying to take advantage of them,

it was the Brown Berets' gang affiliation that enabled them to call on members they knew for continued help in organizing political action.

19. See Martín Sánchez-Jankowski, *Islands in the Street: Gangs and American Urban Society* (Berkeley: University of California Press, 1991), 178–211, and *Cracks in the Pavement: Social Change and Resilience in Poor Neighborhoods* (Berkeley: University of California Press, 2008), 268–69. This idea of obligation to a particular group is part of the identity process discussed in an earlier work on violence by Hans Toch, *Violent Men: An Inquiry into the Psychology of Violence* (Chicago: Aldine Press, 1969), 148–53.

20. I took this quote shorthand as Nestor and two other students were talking with a security guard and a teacher after school. I was sitting with the security guard as the students approached to talk to him. The teacher joined the conversation a few minutes after the students and the security guard began talking.

21. I took this quote shorthand as Tito was talking to three other students at a school assembly. I was seated in the row behind and immediately to their left.

22. See Sánchez-Jankowski, *Islands in the Street*, 44–47, 51–59.

23. See Montejano, *Quijote's Soldiers*, 55–79, 99–116, 260–62, and *Sancho's Journal*, 174–97; Sánchez-Jankowski, *Cracks in the Pavement*, 340–41; and Douglas E. Thompkins, "School Violence: Gangs and the Culture of Fear," *Annals of the American Academy of Political and Social Science* 567, no. 1 (2000): 54–71.

24. See Gerald D. Suttles, *The Social Construction of Communities* (Chicago: University of Chicago Press, 1972), 189–229; Howard Pinderhughes, *Race in the Hood: Conflict and Violence among Urban Youth* (Minneapolis: University of Minnesota Press, 1997), 50–84; Jonathan Rieder, *Cannarsie: Jews and Italians of Brooklyn Against Liberalism* (Cambridge, MA: Harvard University Press, 1985), 23–24.

25. Usually the leadership structure was founded on charismatic characteristics of individual students. See Max Weber, *Economy and Society* (1956; repr., Berkeley: University of California Press, 1978), 241–71; and for gang structures Sánchez-Jankowski, *Islands in the Street,* 75–78.

26. Malloy, *Southie Won't Go,* 256.

27. I took this quote shorthand as Junior was talking with a group of nine people in front of a small grocery store on the way home from school. I was following a large number of students as they went home and was standing outside observing when Junior came out and started to converse with the nine other students in the front of the store.

28. I took this quote longhand as Sybil was talking to four people during homeroom period. I was in the room observing the teacher passing out information to the students about upcoming events.

29. In most cases the students who had been in legal trouble were on probation and not parole. A few had been sent to prison for felonies and were on parole, but most were on probation. Thus, in addition to the police the primary agent of the judicial system present on the campuses was the probation officer.

30. I took this quote shorthand as Dorisha was talking to one of her friends at the school basketball game. I was sitting one row in back of them and immediately to their right.

31. I took this quote shorthand as Mateo was talking to his cousin and his cousin's girlfriend at one of the school's general assemblies. I was standing just off to his left as he waited in line to get into the auditorium.

32. Earlier in this book I noted that many of the security guards who had been hired were reluctant to become directly involved and either looked the other way or intervened purposely late in an effort to have the participants stop the violence on their own, a situation that was also observed by John Devine (*Maximum Security: The Culture of Violence in Inner-City Schools* [Chicago: University of Chicago Press, 1996], 42–43) and that helps to show how in-school violence is related to the tensions existing in the local community. Security guards acted this way because they had to return to their neighborhoods and face their respective ethnic communities, and they did not want to be shunned because members of their group considered them "traitors to their people" for having stopped a fight, helped an "enemy student" in the process, and gotten one of their own group in trouble with the police.

33. I was at the gym class when Ricky was injured and was with Arland when the student talked about wanting his friends to retaliate against Lester. Arland did not say anything when it was mentioned, and I did not say anything either, as these types of comments were quite normal in the everyday activities of students both during the violent period and in this new time of calm. On the day that the attack was supposed to occur, I made my way over to where the woodshop was located. I placed myself in a custodial room immediately next to the entrance of the woodshop where there was tinted glass so that I could see Arland and the others. I could also hear their conversation without their noticing me. I recorded the situation and conversation shorthand.

34. I took this quote longhand as Gerry was talking to one of the assistants at the local community center. I was in the community center when Gerry was talking to the assistant and stood with two other male students listening to the conversation.

35. I took this quote shorthand as Eugenio was talking to one of the janitors fixing a cafeteria table. I was with another student who was seated at the next table over from the one where Eugenio and the janitor were conversing.

36. For this position in the Boston schools during the turbulent forced busing period, see Malloy, *Southie Won't Go*, 127. Most teachers are provided this perspective while engaged in professional training at the various universities' professional education schools. Generally, they are also reminded of these issues during mandatory professional workshops provided by the school districts that employ them.

37. I took this quote shorthand as Jared was talking to two teachers in the teachers' lounge. I had been invited into the lounge by another teacher and was sitting immediately next to the table where Jared and the other teachers were talking.

38. I took this quote shorthand as Cynthia was talking to five other teachers in the teachers' cafeteria. I was in the cafeteria sitting with these teachers while they were discussing the morning's faculty meeting.

39. The issue of deciding first what is news and second how it should be represented, followed by where and when it should be represented, are dis-

cussed in Herbert Gans, *Deciding What's News: A Study of CBS Evening News, NBC Nightly News, Newsweek, and Time* (New York: Random House, 1980).

40. See Karen A. Cerulo, *Deciphering Violence: : The Cognitive Structure of Right and Wrong* (New York: Routledge, 1998), 1–110.

41. I took this quote longhand as Kerry was talking to two friends and me while walking to a neighborhood community center after school.

42. I took this quote shorthand as Carla was talking to a friend at the bus stop. I was standing behind them while they were talking.

43. I took this quote shorthand as the reporter talked to me over the phone. I had asked him if I could quote him, and he said I could without attribution.

44. I talked to a number of reporters, and they seemed quite sensitive to their obligation to report the news and not create it. There is some additional evidence that the media are sensitive to their potential role of promoting contagious violent behavior. An example of this is mentioned in Katherine Newman, Cybelle Fox, Wendy Roth, Jal Mehta, and David Harding, *Rampage: The Social Roots of School Shootings* (New York: Basic Books, 2004), 72; and there is a discussion of journalist ethics from the Society of Professional Journalist Ethics Committee in *Journalism Ethics: Casebook of Professional Conduct for News Media* (Portland, OR: Marion Street Press, 2011), 79, especially points 4 and 5 as they might relate to the issues of school violence and the behavior of the media in schools such as those under study in this book.

45. I took this quote shorthand as Nigel was talking to four friends and one of the security guards while eating his lunch. I was sitting at a table immediately behind them. It should be noted that he never was detained for being involved in a violent act and that he graduated the next year. During the height of the violence he had been detained four times, but only on suspicion that he aided those who were involved in fights.

46. I took this quote shorthand as Sergio was talking to two female students at a corner bus stop while they were waiting to be picked up. I was at the bus stop a couple of feet from them. Sergio was not detained for being in a violent incident, and he graduated a year and a half later. At the height of the violence Sergio had been detained two times on suspicion of aiding other students who were directly involved in fights.

47. I took this quote shorthand as Shirley was talking to four friends at a football game. I was sitting immediately in back of her and to her left.

48. I took this quote shorthand as Cameron was talking to two friends while they were standing in line waiting to get into a school basketball game. I was standing in a parallel line immediately to their left.

49. I took this quote shorthand as Dana was talking to seven other students outside the room for their next class. I was standing behind the group waiting to enter the classroom as well.

50. I took this quote shorthand as Omar was talking to a group of students consisting of one African American boy, two African American girls, and a Mexican American girl. They were talking in class while the teacher was out of the room getting some chalk for the blackboard. I was sitting in the back of the room trying to fix one of the video machines that had trapped some of the tape.

51. See Sánchez-Jankowski, *Cracks in the Pavement,* 42, 179, 258–59.

52. See Devine, *Maximum Security,* 75–78; Pedro Noguera, *City Schools and the American Dream* (New York: Teachers College Press, 2003), 103–41; and David Harding, *Living the Drama: Community, Conflict, and Culture among Inner-City Boys* (Chicago: University of Chicago Press, 2010), 27–106.

53. See Elijah Anderson, *Code of the Street: Decency, Violence and the Moral Life of the Inner City* (New York: W. W. Norton, 2000), and Sánchez-Jankowski, *Cracks in the Pavement,* 42, 179, 258–59.

CONCLUSION

1. This aspect of the study rectifies one of the weaknesses that Michael Burawoy states is inherent in participant-observation studies using a positivist approach, namely that they do not adequately capture how things change over time. See Michael Burawoy, *The Extended Case Method: Four Countries, Four Decades, Four Great Transformations and One Theoretical Tradition* (Berkeley: University of California Press, 2009), 285–86.

2. For the conflict in Hawaiian Garden and Cypress Park, see Heidi Beirich, "California Latino Gang Is Accused of Targeting Blacks," *Hate Watch* (Southern Poverty Law Center), June 8, 2011; Don Terry, "Latino Gang Leader Convicted in LA Ethnic Cleansing Campaign," Hate Watch, Southern Poverty Law Center, January 15, 2013.

3. This does not mean that students in middle-class schools never use violence, because on some occasions they will. However, these occasions are few, and compared to the times when other nonphysically violent forms of aggression are used, they are deviant cases.

4. On socioeconomic differences in resources to aid one's children in educational achievement, see Annette Lareau, *Unequal Childhoods: Class, Race and Family Life* (Berkeley: University of California Press, 2003).

5. See Paul Willis, *Learning to Labor: How Working Class Kids Get Working Class Jobs* (New York: Columbia University Press, 1981), 11–52, 89–116; Martín Sánchez-Jankowski, *Cracks in the Pavement: Social Change and Resilience in Poor Neighborhoods* (Berkeley: University of California Press, 2008), 178–79, 199, 257, 259, 266–67.

6. See Michael Patrick MacDonald, *All Souls: A Family Story from Southie* (Boston: Beacon Press, 1999), 223–53, who talks about corruptness of the police as it related to his brother's case, but there is reference to the police being adversarial to the local residents throughout the book. Also see Alice Goffman, *On the Run: Fugitive Life in an American City* (Chicago: University of Chicago Press, 2014).

7. See David Harding, *Living the Drama: Community, Conflict, and Culture among Inner-City Boys* (Chicago: University of Chicago Press, 2010), which discusses the strategies used by lower-class kids to avoid the violence in their neighborhoods and schools.

8. The shootings at Columbine High School in Colorado and Sandy Hook in Connecticut are examples, but there are more. There are many examples of

middle-class students getting bullied and committing suicide without the authorities doing any prior interventions.

9. On frustration-aggression, see John Dollard, Leonard Doob, N.E. Miller, O.H. Mowrer, and Robert R. Sears, *Frustration and Aggression* (New Haven, CT: Yale University Press, 1939). On violence and psychopathology, see Eric Hoffer, *The True Believer* (New York: Harper and Row, 1951); Lewis Yablonsky, *The Violent Gang* (New York: Macmillan, 1962); Klaus R. Scherer, Ronald P. Abeles, and Claude S. Fischer, *Human Aggression and Conflict: Interdisciplinary Perspectives* (Englewood Cliffs, NJ: Prentice-Hall, 1975), 1–38. On social learning of violence, see Albert Bandura, *Aggression: A Social Learning Analysis* (Englewood Cliffs, NJ: Prentice-Hall, 1973). On relative deprivation, see Ted Robert Gurr, *Why Men Rebel* (Princeton, NJ: Princeton University Press, 1970; and Hans Toch, *Violent Men: An Enquiry into the Psychology of Violence* (New York: Aldine Press, 1969), 133–48. On group dynamics and violence, see Scherer, Abeles, and Fischer, *Human Aggression and Conflict*, 153–84, who reviews the earlier work of group dynamics; and Randall Collins, *Violence: A Micro-sociological Theory* (Princeton, NJ: Princeton University Press, 2008), who also reviews a great deal of literature in arriving at his "interactional chain of events" theory.

10. See Sánchez-Jankowski, *Cracks in the Pavement.*

11. This is consistent with what Elijah Anderson reports in *Code of the Street: Decency, Violence and the Moral Life of the Inner City* (New York: W.W. Norton, 2000) among what he labels "decent folk," but it would also be true among those he calls "street." Even among the "street" folk there are codes of conduct related to violence that consist of behaviors normatively approved and disapproved of. Thus there are both general codes of conduct and normative subsets within them.

12. See Donald Horowitz, *The Deadly Ethnic Riot* (Berkeley: University of California Press, 2001), 263–64, who also found that individuals from lower-status groups were more inclined to participate in ethnic-oriented riots than those from higher-status groups. He also found that migrants and new settlers do participate in the killings. He does not say why this is the case, but I have argued that it is a combination of lower-class cultural factors that encourage or allow individuals to take physical action to resolve conflict and structural factors that pressure and confine families within their neighborhood and prevent them from ameliorating their distress by moving to a new neighborhood.

13. This point is certainly implied in John Devine, *Maximum Security: The Culture of Violence in Inner-City Schools* (Chicago: University of Chicago Press, 1996), 75–100, and is more directly addressed in Pedro Noguera, *City Schools and the American Dream* (New York: Teachers College Press, 2003), 103–41.

14. See Jeffrey Pressman and Aaron Wildavsky, *Implementation: Or How The Good Intentions in Washington Are Dashed in Oakland; or Why It's Amazing That Federal Programs Work at All, This Being a Saga of the Economic Development Administration as Told by Two Sympathetic Observers Who Seek to Build Morals on a Foundation of Ruined Hopes* (Berkeley: University of California Press, 1973). Clearly the title of the book spells out the argument presented, but why and how this housing policy became ineffectual requires a reading of the book.

15. Some conservatives and many libertarians hold this position. This can be seen in the work of N. Gregory Mankiw, "Defending the One Percent," *Journal of Economic Perspectives* 27, no. 3 (2013): 21–34; Charles Murray, *Losing Ground: American Social Policy, 1950–1980* (New York: Basic Books, 1984); Charles Murray and Richard Hernnstein, *The Bell Curve: Intelligence and Class Structure in American Life* (New York: Free Press, 1994). For a critique of that position, with special focus on the genetic explanation of rewards, see Claude S. Fischer et al., *Inequality by Design: Challenging the Bell Curve Myth* (Princeton, NJ: Princeton University Press, 1996).

16. America has a long history of being punitive toward those who seem to violate the social codes of providing for their economic well-being or the legal codes of conduct. It has been particularly stingy in its assistance to the poor and particularly severe in its punishment of those who are found guilty of felonies. See James Patterson's *America's Struggle against Poverty in the Twentieth Century* (Cambridge, MA: Harvard University Press, 2000); Robert A. Ferguson, *Inferno: An Anatomy of American Punishment* (Cambridge, MA: Harvard University Press, 2014); Bruce Western, *Punishment and Inequality in America* (New York: Russell Sage Foundation, 2007); and Loïc Wacquant, *Punishing the Poor: The Neoliberal Government of Social Insecurity* (Durham, NC: Duke University Press, 2009).

17. For some evaluations of the Weed and Seed Program, see Terrence Dunworth and Gregory Mills, *National Evaluation of Weed and Seed* (Washington, DC: National Institute of Justice, Office of Justice Programs, US Department of Justice, 1999); and Blaine Bridenball and Paul Jesilow, "Weeding Criminals or Planting Fear: An Evaluation of a Weed and Seed Project," *Criminal Justice Review* 30, no. 1 (2005): 64–89.

18. On ethnic conflict in the community, see Mark Baldassare, *The Los Angeles Riots: Lessons for the Urban Future* (Boulder, CO: Westview Press, 1994); and Jonathan Reider, *Canarsie: The Jews and Italians of Brooklyn against Liberalism* (Cambridge, MA: Harvard University Press, 1987). For that reported in schools, see Howard Pinderhughes, *Race in the Hood: Conflict and Violence among Urban Youth* (Minneapolis: University of Minnesota Press, 1997), for New York; and Harry Sahag Bedevian, "Student, Staff, and Parent Perceptions of the Reasons for Ethnic Conflict between Armenian and Latino Students" (EdD diss., University of Southern California, 2008), for Los Angeles. Each of these schools is no longer experiencing this type of intense violence, and student relations are generally cordial.

19. Michael Patrick MacDonald is a perfect example of using the experience of ethnic violence to develop a more tolerant and cooperative approach to interethnic relations. See his book *All Souls*.

METHODOLOGICAL APPENDIX

1. See Michèle Lamont and Ann Swidler, "Methodological Pluralism and the Possibilities and Limits of Interviewing," *Qualitative Sociology* 37, no. 2 (2014): 153–71.

2. Jack Katz's review of my book *Cracks in the Pavement: Social Change and Resilience in Poor Neighborhoods* in the *American Journal of Sociology* 115 (May 2010): 1950–52, stated that my use of data from conversations in which I was not directly a part was "eavesdropping," a label carrying the insinuation that this was ethically suspect. This is a clear misunderstanding of the participant-observation methodology. Researchers using this methodology place themselves within the environment that their subjects experience and in so doing integrate themselves into their subjects' general routines, but they also try to minimize interfering in their everyday lives because they want to analyze the subjects' behaviors within their "normal" lives and not some "deviant" or "idiosyncratic" condition that they as researchers created. So recording statements made by subjects who were not aware that the researcher was present and recording them creates a higher probability of validity than recording statements made when the subjects are conscious of the researcher being present and taking notes.

3. See the review of these programs in Daniel Dohan and Martín Sánchez-Jankowski, "Using Computers to Analyze Ethnographic Field Data: Theoretical and Practical Considerations," *Annual Review of Sociology* 24 (1998): 477–98.

4. Study in Boston began in September of 1974 and ended in 1977. The study in California began in 2000 and ended in 2003. So the total time span of my observations was from 1974 to 2003, or twenty-nine years.

Bibliography

Abramson, Corey, and Darren Modzelewski. "Caged Morality: Moral Worlds, Subculture, and Stratification among Middle-Class Cage Fighters." *Qualitative Sociology* 34 (2011): 143–75.

Alba, Richard D. *Ethnic Identity: The Transformation of White America*. New Haven, CT: Yale University Press, 1990.

Allport, Gordon. *The Nature of Prejudice*. Cambridge, MA: Addison-Wesley, 1954.

Almaguer, Tomás. *Racial Fault Lines: The Historical Origins of White Supremacy in California*. Berkeley: University of California Press, 1994.

Anderson, Benedict. *Imagined Communities: Reflections on the Origin and Spread of Nationalism*. London: Verso Press, 2006.

Anderson, Elijah. *Code of the Streets: Decency, Violence and the Moral Life of the Inner City*. New York: W. W. Norton, 2000.

Baca, Nicolás C. *Presumed Alliance: The Unspoken Conflict between Latinos and Blacks and What It Means for America*. New York: Harper-Collins, 2004.

Bailey, Amy Kate, Stewart E. Tolnay, E. M. Beck, and Jennifer D. Laird. "Targeting Lynch Victims: Social Marginality or Status Transgressions?" *American Sociological Review* 76, no. 3, (2011): 412–36.

Baldassare, Mark. *The Los Angeles Riots: Lessons for the Urban Future*. Boulder, CO: Westview Press, 1994.

Bandura, Albert. *Aggression: A Social Learning Analysis*. Englewood Cliffs, NJ: Prentice-Hall, 1973.

Banfield, Edward. *The Unheavenly City Revisited*. Boston: Little-Brown, 1974.

Baron, Robert A. *Human Aggression*. New York: Plenum, 1977.

Barrett, Lisa Feldman, Michele M. Tugade, and Randall W. Engle. "Individual Differences in Working Memory Capacity and Dual Process Theories of the Mind." *Psychological Bulletin* 130, no. 4 (2004): 553–73.

Beaty, Lee A., and Erick B. Alexeyev. "The Problem of School Bullies: What the Research Tells Us." *Adolescence* 43, no. 169 (2008): 1–11.

Becerra, Hector. "Schools Beef Up Patrols after Fights Disrupt School Day." *Los Angeles Times*. December 3, 2004.

Bedevian, Harry Sahag. "Student, Staff, and Parent Perceptions of the Reasons for Ethnic Conflict between Armenian and Latino Students." EdD diss., University of Southern California, May 2008.

Beirich, Heidi. "California Latino Gang Is Accused of Targeting Blacks." *Hate Watch*, Southern Poverty Law Center, June 8, 2011.

Benbenisihty, Rami, and Ron Avi Astor. *School Violence in Context: Culture, Neighborhood, Family, School, and Gender.* New York: Oxford University Press, 2005.

Bennett, Lerone Jr. *Before the Mayflower: History of the Negro American.* New York: Penguin Books, 1966.

Bergesen, Albert, and Max Herman. "Immigration, Race, and Riot: The 1992 Los Angeles Uprising." *American Sociological Review* 63, no. 1 (1998): 39–54.

Bernal, Martin. *Black Athena: Afroasiatic Roots of Classical Civilization,* vol. 1. New Brunswick, NJ: Rutgers University Press, 1987.

Bluestone, Barry, and Bennett Harrison. *The Deindustrialization of America: Plant Closings, Community Abandonment, and the Dismantling of Basic Industry.* New York: Basic Books, 1984.

Blumer, Herbert. "Social Movements." In *New Outline of Principles of Sociology,* edited by A. M. Lee. New York: Barnes and Noble, 1946.

———. "Race Prejudice as a Sense of Group Position." *Pacific Sociological Review* 1, no. 1 (1958): 3–7.

———. *Symbolic Interaction: Perspective and Method.* Berkeley: University of California Press, 1969.

Bobo, Lawrence, and Devon Johnson. "Racial Attitudes in a Prismatic Metropolis: Mapping Identity, Stereotypes, Competition, and Views on Affirmative Action." In *Prismatic Metropolis: Inequality in Los Angeles,* edited by Lawrence D. Bobo, Melvin L. Oliver, James H. Johnson, Jr., and Abel Valenzuela. New York: Russell Sage Foundation, 2000.

Bonacinch, Edna. "A Theory of Ethnic Antagonism: The Split Labor Market." *American Sociological Review* 37 (1972): 549–59.

Bourgeois, Philippe. *In Search of Respect: Selling Crack in El Barrio.* New York: Cambridge University Press, 1996.

Bradshaw, Catherine P., and James Garbarino. "Social Cognition as a Mediator of Influence of Family and Community Violence on Adolescent Development: Implications for Intervention." *Annals of the New York Academy of Sciences* 103 (2004): 85–105.

Brandt, Steve, and Allie Shah. "South High Regroups after Brawl." *Minneapolis Star Tribune.* February 16, 2013

Bridenball, Blaine, and Paul Jesilow. "Weeding Criminals or Planting Fear: An Evaluation of a Weed and Seed Project." *Criminal Justice Review* 30, no. 1 (2005): 64–89.

Britton, Crane. *The Anatomy of Revolution.* New York: Random House, [1938] 1965.

Bronner, Ethan. "U.S. Workers Sue as Big Farms Rely on Immigrants." *New York Times.* May 7, 2013.

Brown, Richard Maxwell. "The American Vigilante Tradition." In *The History of Violence in America: A Report to the National Commission on the Causes and Prevention of Violence,* edited by Hugh Davis Graham and Ted Robert Gurr. New York: Bantam, 1969.

Brown, Rupert. *Prejudice: Its Social Psychology.* Oxford: Blackwell, 1995.

Buell, Emmett H. Jr. "Busing and the Defended Neighborhood: South Boston, 1974–1977." *Urban Affairs Review* 16, no. 2 (1980): 161–188.

Bufkin, Jana L., and Vicki R. Luttrell. "Neuroimaging Studies of Aggressive and Violent Behavior." *Trauma, Violence, Abuse* 6, no. 2 (2005) : 176–91.

Burawoy, Michael. *The Extended Case Method: Four Countries, Four Decades, Four Great Transformations, and One Theoretical Tradition.* Berkeley: University of California Press, 2009.

Burtless, Gary, and Tracy Gordon. "The Federal Stimulus Programs and Their Effects." In *The Great Recession,* edited by David Grusky, Bruce Western, and Christopher Wimer. New York: Russell Sage Foundation, 2011.

Carley, Kathleen M., Ju-Sung Lee, and David Krackhardt. "Destabilizing Networks." *Connections* 24, No. 3 (2001): 79–92.

Cerulo, Karen A. *Deciphering Violence: The Cognitive Structure of Right and Wrong.* New York: Routledge, 1998.

Chicago Tribune. June 26, 2012.

Collins, Randall. *Interaction Ritual Chains.* Princeton, NJ: Princeton University Press, 2004.

———. *Violence: A Micro-sociological Theory.* Princeton, NJ: Princeton University Press, 2008.

Conley, Dalton. *Being Black, Living in the Red.* Berkeley: University of California Press, 1999.

Craig, Kellina M. "Examining Hate-Motivated Aggression: A Review of the Social Psychological Literature on Hate Crimes as a Distinct Form of Aggression." *Aggression and Violent Behavior* 7, no. 1 (2002): 85–101.

Cunningham, David. "Mobilizing Ethnic Competition." *Theory and Society* 41 (2012): 505–25.

Damasio, Antonio. *The Feeling of What Happens: Body and Emotion in the Making of Consciousness.* Orlando, Fl.: Harvest Books, 2000.

D'Andrade, Roy Goodwin. "The Cultural Part of Cognition." *Cognitive Science* 5, no. 3 (1981): 179–95.

Denton, Nancy, and Douglas Massey. "Residential Segregation of Blacks, Hispanics, and Asians by Socioeconomic Status and Generation." *Social Science Quarterly,* 69 (1988): 797–818.

Devine, John. *Maximum Security: The Culture of Violence in Inner-City Schools.* Chicago: University of Chicago Press, 1996.

Dodge, Kenneth A., and Michelle Sherrill. "The Interaction of Nature and Nurture in Antisocial Behavior." In *The Cambridge Handbook on Violence and Aggression,* edited by Daniel J. Flannery, Alexander T. Vazsoni, and Irwin D. Waldman. Cambridge: Cambridge University Press, 2007.

Dohan, Daniel, and Martín Sánchez-Jankowski. "Using Computers to Analyze Ethnographic Field Data: Theoretical and Practical Considerations." *Annual Review of Sociology* 24 (1998): 477–98.

Dollard, John, Leonard Doob, N. Miller, O. H. Mowrer, and R. R. Sears. *Frustration and Aggression.* New Haven, CT: Yale University Press, 1937.

———. *Caste and Class in a Southern Town.* Madison: University of Wisconsin Press [1937], 1989.

Dooley, Brian. *Black and Green: The Fight for Civil Rights in Northern Ireland and Black America.* London: Pluto Press, 1998.

Dovidio, John F., Samuel E. Gaertner, Kerry Kawakami, and Gordon Hudson. "Why Can't We Just Get Along? Interpersonal Biases and Interracial Distrust." *Cultural Diversity and Ethnic Minority Psychology* 8, no. 2 (2002).

Dugan, Kimberly, and Jo Roger. "Voice and Agency in Social Movement Outcomes." *Qualitative Sociology* 29 (2006): 467–89.

Duncan, Neil. *School Bullying: Gender Conflict and Pupil Culture in Secondary Schools.* London: Routledge, 2001.

Dunworth, Terrence, and Gregory Mills. "National Evaluation of Weed and Seed." Washington, DC: National Institute of Justice, Office of Justice Programs, US Department of Justice, 1999.

Durkheim, Emile. *Suicide: A Study in Sociology.* New York: Free Press, 1979.

———. *The Division of Labor in Society.* New York: Free Press, 1984.

———. *Elementary Forms of Religious Life.* New York: Free Press, [1915] 1995.

Dyson, Michael Eric. *Come Hell or High Water: Hurricane Katrina and the Color of Disaster.* New York: Basic Civitas Books, 2006.

Eaton, Danice K., et. al., "Youth Risk Behavior Surveillance—United States, 2009." *Surveillance Summaries* 59 (SS-5).

Einstein, Albert, Sigmund Freud, and Stuart Gilbert. "*Why War?*" Paris: International Institute of Intellectual Cooperation, League of Nations, 1933.

Eisenbraun, Kristin D. "Violence in Schools: Prevalence, Prediction, and Prevention." *Aggression and Violent Behavior* 12 (2007): 459–69.

Eitle, David, and Tamela Eitle. "Segregation and School Violence." *Social Forces* 82 (2003): 589–616.

Erikson, Erik H. *Identity, Youth, and Crisis.* New York: W. W. Norton, 1968.

Espelage, Dorothy L., Kris Bosworth, and Thomas R. Simon. "Examining the Social Context of Bullying Behaviors in Early Adolescence." *Journal of Counseling and Development* 78 (2000): 326–33.

Evans, Jonathan St. B. T. "Dual-Processing Accounts of Reasoning, Judgement, and Social Cognition." *Annual Review of Psychology* 59 (2008): 255–78.

Fanon, Franz. *The Wretched of the Earth.* New York: Grove Press, [1961] 2004.

Faris, Robert, and Dianne Felmler. "Social Struggles: Network Centrality and Gender Segregation in Same- and Cross-Gender Aggression." *American Sociological Review* 76 (2010): 48–73.

Farrell, A. D., S. May, A. Bettencourt, and E. H. Erwin. "Environmental Influences on Fighting versus Nonviolent Behavior in Peer Situations." *American Journal of Community Psychology* 46, nos. 1–2 (2010): 19–35.

Ferguson, Christopher J., Claudia San Miguel, and Richard D. Hartley. "A Multivariate Analysis of Youth Violence and Aggression: The Influence of Family, Peers, Depression, and Media Violence." *Journal of Pediatrics* 166, no. 6 (2009): 904–8.

Ferguson, Robert A. *Inferno: An Anatomy of American Punishment*. Cambridge, MA: Harvard University Press, 2014.

Fine, Sidney. *Violence in the Model City: The Cavanagh Administration, Race Relations, and the Detroit Riot of 1967*. Ann Arbor: University of Michigan Press, 1990.

Fischer, Claude S. "Toward a Sub-culture Theory of Urbanism." *American Journal of Sociology* 80, no. 20 (1975): 1319–41.

———. "Toward a Sub-culture Theory of Urbanism: Twentieth-Year Assessment," *American Journal of Sociology* 101 (November 1995): 543–77.

———. *Made in America: A Social History of American Culture and Character*. Chicago: University of Chicago Press, 2010.

Fischer, Claude S., et. al. *Inequality by Design: Challenging the Bell Curve Myth*. Princeton, NJ: Princeton University Press, 1996.

Fiske, Susan T. "What We Know about Bias and Intergroup Conflict: The Problem of the Century." *Current Directions in Psychological Science* 11, no. 4 (2002).

Fogelson, Robert. *Violence as Protest: A Study of Riots and Ghettos*. Garden City, NY: Anchor Books, 1971.

Formisano, Ronald P. *Boston against Busing: Race, Class, and Ethnicity in the 1960s and 1970s*. Chapel Hill, NC: University of North Carolina Press, 1991.

Forrest, Ray, Adrienne La Grange, and Yip Ngai-Ming. "Neighbourhood in a High Rise, High Density City: Some Observations on Contemporary Hong Kong." *Sociological Review* 50, no. 1 (2002): 215–40.

Forsyth, Donelson R. *Group Dynamics*. Belmont, CA: Wadsworth Cengage, 5th ed., 2010.

Fox, Cybelle. *Three Worlds of Relief: Race, Immigration, and the American Welfare State from the Progressive Era to the New Deal*. Princeton, NJ: Princeton University Press, 2012.

Franklin, John Hope. *From Slavery to Freedom: A History of the Negro American*. New York: Alfred Knopf, 3rd ed., 1967.

French, Elizabeth Sabine, Edward Seidman, LaRue Allen, and J. Lawrence Aber. "The Development of Ethnic Identity during Adolescence." *Developmental Psychology* 42, no. 1 (2006): 1–10.

Freud, Sigmund. *Jokes and Their Relationship to the Subconscious*. New York: Norton, 1960.

———. *Civilization and Its Discontents*. New York: W. W. Norton & Company, [1930] 1962.

Friedman, Lawrence S. "Adolescence." In *The Child: An Encyclopedic Companion*, edited by Richard A. Shweder. Chicago: University of Chicago Press, 2009.

Fulkerson, Jayne A., Mary Story, Alison Mellin, Nancy Leffert, Dianne Neumark-Sztainer, and Simone A. French. "Family Dinner Meal Frequency and

Adolescent Development : Relationships with Developmental Assets and High-Risk Behaviors." *Journal of Adolescent Health* 39, no. 3 (2006): 337–45.

Galaster, George. "Racial Steering in Urban Housing Markets." *Review of Black Political Economy* 18 (1990): 105–29.

Gans, Herbert. "Symbolic Ethnicity: The Future of Ethnic Groups and Culture in America." *Ethnic and Racial Studies* 2 (January 1979): 1–20.

———. *Deciding What's News: A Study of CBS Evening News, NBC Nightly News, Newsweek, and Time.* New York: Random House, 1980.

Garfinkel, Harold. *Studies in Ethnomethodology.* Englewood Cliffs, NJ: Prentice-Hall, 1967.

George, Alexander, and Richard Smoke. *Deterrence in American Foreign Policy: Theory and Practice.* New York: Columbia University Press, 1974.

Gettleman, Jeffrey, and Lee Condon,. "Glendale Shaken by Slaying of Student." *Los Angeles Times.* May 7, 2000.

Gilligan, James. *Violence: Reflections on a National Epidemic.* New York: Vintage, 1996.

Ginsberg, Yona. *Jews in a Changing Neighborhood.* New York: Macmillian, 1975.

Goffman, Erving. *The Presentation of Self in Everyday Life.* Garden City, NY: Doubleday, 1959.

———. *Encounters: Two Studies in the Sociology of Interaction.* Indianapolis, IN: Bobbs-Merrill, 1961.

———. *Behavior in Public Places: Notes on the Social Organization of Gatherings.* New York: Free Press, 1963.

———. *Stigma: Notes on the Management of Spoiled Identity.* New York: Simon and Schuster, 1963.

Goodwin, Jeffrey, and Steven Pfaff. "Emotion Work in High-Risk Social Movements: Managing Fear in the U.S., and East German Civil Rights Movements." In *Passionate Politics: Emotions and Social Movements,* edited by Jeff Goodwin, James M. Jasper, and Francesca Polletta. Chicago: University of Chicago Press, 2001: 282–302.

Gorman-Smith, Deborah, Patrick H. Tolan, Rolf Loeber, and David B. Henry. "Relation of Family Problems to Patterns of Delinquency Involvement among Urban Youth." *Journal of Abnormal Child Psychology* 26, no. 5 (1998): 319–33.

Green, Donald P., Dara Z. Strovitch, and Janelle S. Wong. "Defended Neighborhood, Integration, and Racially Motivated Crime." *American Journal of Sociology* 104 , no. 2 (1998): 379–403.

Greenberg, Stanley B. *Race and State in Capitalist Development: Comparative Perspectives.* New Haven: Yale University Press, 1980.

Grusky, David B., Bruce Western, and Christopher Wimer, eds. *The Great Recession.* New York: The Russell Sage Foundation, 2011.

Guerra, Nancy G., L. Rowell Huesmann, Anja Spindler. "Community Violence Exposure, Social Cognition, and Aggression among Urban Elementary School Children." *Child Development* 74, no. 5 (2003): 1561–76.

Gurr, Ted Robert. *Why Men Rebel.* Princeton, NJ: Princeton University Press, 1970.

———. *Minorities at Risk: A Global View of Ethnopolitical Conflicts.* Washington, DC: United States Institute of Peace Press, 1993.

Gutiérrez, David. *Walls and Mirrors: Mexican Americans, Mexican Immigrants, and the Politics of Ethnicity.* Berkeley: University of California Press, 1995.

Halcli, Abigail. "AIDs, Anger, and Activism: Act Up as a Social Movement Organization." In *Waves of Protest: Social Movements since the Sixties,* edited by Jo Freman and Victoria Johnson. Lanham, MD: Rowman and Littlefield, 1999.

Halliday, Jessica and Karolyn Tyson. "Other People's Racism: Race, Rednecks, and Riots in a Southern Town." *Sociology of Education* 86, no. 1 (2013): 83–102.

Harding, David. *Living the Drama: Community, Conflict, and Culture among Inner-City Boys.* Chicago: University of Chicago Press, 2010.

Haynie, Denise L., Tonia Nansel, Patricia Eitel, Aria Davis Crump, Keith Saylor and Kai Yu. "Bullies, Victims, and Bully/Victim: Distinct Groups of At-Risk Youth." *Journal of Early Adolescence* 21, no. 1 (2001): 29–49.

Hechter, Michael. *Principles of Group Solidarity.* Berkeley: University of California Press, 1972.

Heidegger, Martin. *Being and Time.* Albany: State University of New York Press, [1953] 1993.

Heller, Celia. *Mexican American Youth: Forgotten Youth at the Crossroads.* New York: Random House, 1966.

Hirschi, Travis. *Causes of Delinquency.* New Brunswick, NJ: Transaction Press, 2001.

Hobbes, Thomas. *Leviathan or the Matter, Forme, and Power of a Commonwealth Ecclesiastical and Civil,* edited by Michael Oakeshott. Oxford: Blackwell, [1651] 1965.

Hoffer, Eric. *The True Believer: Thoughts on the Nature of Mass Movements.* New York: Harper and Row, 1951.

Horowitz, Donald L. "Ethnic Identity." In *Ethnicity: Theory and Experience,* edited by Nathan Glazer and Daniel P. Moynihan. Cambridge, MA: Harvard University Press, 1975.

———. *Ethnic Groups in Conflict.* Berkeley: University of California Press, 1985.

———. *The Deadly Ethnic Riot.* Berkeley: University of California Press, 2001.

Horowitz, Ruth, and Gary Schwartz. "Honor, Normative Ambiguity and Gang Violence." *American Sociological Review* 39, no. 2 (1974): 238–51.

Hout, Michael, Asaf Lavanon, and Erin Cumberworth. "Job Loss and Unemployment." In *The Great Recession,* edited by David Grusky, Bruce Western, and Christopher Wimer. New York: Russell Sage Foundation, 2011.

Hunter, Albert. *Symbolic Communities: The Persistence and Change of Chicago's Local Communities.* Chicago: University of Chicago Press, 1982.

Ignatiev, Noel. *How the Irish Became White.* New York: Routledge, 1995.

Isaacs, Harold. "Basic Group Identity: The Idols of the Tribe." In *Ethnicity: Theory and Experience,* edited by Nathan Glazer and Daniel P. Moynihan. Cambridge: Harvard University Press, 1975.

———. *Idols of the Tribe: Identity and Political Change.* New York: Harper and Row, 1975.

Jacobson, Mathew Frye. *Whiteness of a Different Color: European Immigrants and the Alchemy of Race.* Cambridge, MA: Harvard University Press, 1999.

Jensen, Chelsea, "Kealakehe High Closed Today after Two Days of Fights," *West Hawaii Today,* December 7, 2013.

Jervis, Robert. "Deterrence Theory Revisited." *World Politics* 31, no. 2 (1979): 289–324.

Jordan, Jenna. "When Heads Roll: Assessing the Effectiveness of Leadership Decapitation." *Security Studies* 18 (2009): 719–55.

Katz, Jack. *Seductions of Crime: Moral and Sensual Attractions in Doing Evil.* New York: Free Press, 1988.

———. *How Emotions Work.* Chicago: University of Chicago Press, 1999.

———. Review of *Cracks in the Pavement: Social Change and Resilience in Poor Neighborhood. American Journal of Sociology* 115 (May 2010): 1950–52.

Klatch, Rebecca E. "The Underside of Social Movements: The Effects of Destructive Affective Ties." *Qualitative Sociology* 27, no. 4 (2004): 487–509.

Kornblum, William. *Blue Collar Community.* Chicago: University of Chicago Press, 1975.

Kornhauser, Ruth Rosner. *Social Sources of Delinquency: An Appraisal of Analytic Models.* Chicago: University of Chicago Press, 1978.

Kuper, Leo. *Genocide: Its Political Use in the Twentieth Century.* New Haven: Yale University Press, 1983.

Kuppens, Toon, Thomas V. Pollet, Cátia P. Teixeira, Stéphanie Demoulin, S. Craig Roberts, and Anthony C. Little. "Emotions in Context: Anger Causes Ethnic Bias but Not Gender Bias in Men but Not Women." *European Journal of Social Psychology* 42, no. 4 (2012): 432–41.

Lamont, Michèle. *The Dignity of Working Men: Morality and the Boundaries of Race, Class, and Immigration.* New York: Russell Sage Foundation, 2000.

Lamont, Michèle, and Ann Swidler. "Methodological Pluralism and the Possibilities and Limits of Interviewing." *Qualitative Sociology* 37, no. 2 (2014): 153–71.

Lange, Mathew. *Education and Ethnic Violence.* Cambridge: Cambridge University Press, 2012.

Lareau, Annette. *Unequal Childhoods: Class, Race, and Family Life.* Berkeley: University of California Press, 2003.

Laswell, Harold. *Psychopathology and Politics.* Chicago: University of Chicago Press, [1930] 1977.

Laub, John H., and Janet L. Lauritsen. "The Interdependence of School Violence with Neighborhood and Family Conditions." In *Violence in American Schools,* edited by Delbert S. Elliot, Beatrix A. Hamburg, and Kirk R. Williams. Cambridge: Cambridge University Press, 1998.

Le Bon, Gustave. *The Crowd: A Study of the Popular Mind.* New Brunswick, NJ: Transaction Books, [1896] 2002.

Levine, Hillel and Lawrence Harmon. *The Death of an American Jewish Community: The Tragedy of Good Intentions.* New York: The Free Press, 1991.

Lieberson, Stanley. *A Piece of the Pie: Blacks and White Immigrants since 1880.* Berkeley: University of California Press, 1981.

———. "Stereotypes: Their Consequences for Race and Ethnic Interaction." In *Social Structure and Behavior: Essays in Honor of William H. Sewell,* edited by Robert H. Hauser, D. Mechanic, A.O. Haller, and T.S. Hauser. New York: Academic Press, 1982.

———. *Making It Count: The Improvement of Social Research and Theory.* Berkeley: University of California Press, 1985.

Lim, May, Richard Metzler, and Yaneer Bar-Yam. "Global Pattern Formation and Ethnic/Cultural Violence." *Science* 307, no. 5844: 1540–44.

Lodewijdx, Hein F.M., Gaby L.E. Kersten, and Martijn van Zomeren. "Dual Pathways to Engage in 'Silent Marches' against Violence: Moral Outrage, Moral Cleansing and Modes of Identification." *Journal of Community and Applied Psychology* 18, no. 3 (2008): 153–67.

Lofland, Lyn. *A World of Strangers: Order and Action in Urban Public Space.* Longview, IL: Waveland Press, 1985.

Lorenz, Konrad. *On Aggression.* New York: Bantam Books, 1966.

Lucas, Samuel Roundfield. *Tracking Inequality: Stratification and Mobility in American High Schools.* New York: Columbia Teachers College Press, 1999.

———. *Theorizing Discrimination in an Era of Contested Prejudice.* Philadelphia: Temple University Press, 2009.

Lukas, J. Anthony. *Common Ground: A Turbulent Decade in the Lives of Three American Families.* New York: Random House, 1985.

Lyons, Christopher J. "Defending Turf: Racial Demographics and Hate Crime against Blacks and Whites." *Social Forces* 87, no. 1 (September 2008): 357–85

MacDonald, Michael Patrick. *All Souls: A Family Story from Southie.* Boston: Beacon Press, 1999.

Malloy, Ione. *Southie Won't Go: A Teacher's Diary of the Desegregation of South Boston High School.* Urbana: University of Illinois Press, 1986.

Mankiw, N. Gregory. "Defending the One Percent." *Journal of Economic Perspectives* 27, no. 3 (2013): 21–34.

Mannheim, Karl. *Ideology and Utopia: An Introduction to the Sociology of Knowledge.* New York: Harcourt, Brace, and World, 1936.

Marx, Gary T., and Dane Archer. "The Urban Vigilante." *Psychology Today,* January 1973, 45–51.

Marx, Karl. *Civil War in Paris.* Peking: Foreign Language Press, 1970.

Massey, Douglas S. *Categorically Unequal: The American Stratification System.* New York: Russell Sage Foundation, 2007.

Massey, Douglas S., and Nancy A. Denton. *American Apartheid: Segregation and the Making of the Underclass.* Cambridge, MA: Harvard University Press, 1993.

Mawson, Anthony R. *Mass Panic and Social Attachment.* Burlington, VT: Ashgate, 2007.

Mayer, Mathew, and Peter Leone. "School Violence and Disruption Revisited: Equity and Safety in the School House." *Focus on Exceptional Children* 40, no. 1 (2007): 1–28.

Mazur, Alan. "A Hormonal Interpretation of Collin's Micro-sociological Theory of Social Behavior." *Journal for the Theory of Social Behavior* 38, no. 4
(2009): 434–47.

Mead, George Herbert. *Mind, Self and Society.* Chicago: University of Chicago
Press, [1934] 1967.

Meyers, Gustavus. *The History of Bigotry in the United States.* New York:
Random House, 1943.

Miller, Amanda K., and Kathryn Chandler. *Violence in U.S. Public Schools:
2000 School Survey on Crime and Safety.* US Department of Education,
National Center for Education Statistics, NCES 2004-314. Washington,
DC: Government Printing Office, 2003.

Mitchell, Robert Edward. "Some Social Implications of High Density Housing." *American Sociological Review* 36, no. 1 (1971): 18–29.

Montejano, David. *Quijote's Soldiers: A Local History of the Chicano Movement, 1966–1981.* Austin: University of Texas Press, 2010.

———. *Sancho's Journal: Exploring the Political Edge with the Brown Berets.*
Austin: University of Texas Press, 2012.

Moore, Barrington. *Injustice: The Social Bases of Obedience and Revolt.* White
Plains, NY: M. E. Sharpe, Inc., 1978.

Moore, Mark H., Carol V. Petrie, Anthony A. Baraga, and Brenda L. McLaughlin, eds. *Deadly Lessons: Understanding Lethal School Violence.* Washington, DC: National Academies Press, 2003.

Morawska, Ewa. "Immigrant-Black Dissension in American Cities: An Argument for Multiple Explanations." In *Problem of the Century: Racial Stratification in the United States,* edited by Elijah Anderson and Douglas Massey.
New York: Russell Sage Foundation, 2001.

Morin, Jason L., Gabriel R. Sanchez, and Matt A. Barreto. "Perception of Competition." In *Just Neighbors? Research on African American and Latino
Relations in the United States,* edited by Edward Telles, Mark Q. Sawyer,
and Gaspar Rivera-Salgado. New York: Russell Sage Foundation, 2011.

Murray, Charles. *Losing Ground: American Social Policy, 1950–1980.* New
York: Basic Books, 1984.

Murray, Charles, and Richard Hernnstein. *The Bell Curve: Intelligence and
Class Structure in American Life.* New York: Free Press, 1994.

Neiman, Samantha, Jill F. DeVoe, and Kathryn Chandler. *Crime, Violence, Discipline, and Safety in U.S. Public Schools: Findings from the School Survey
on Crime and Safety, 2007–08.* Washington, DC: National Center for Education Statistics, US Department of Education, 2009.

Newman, Barbara M., and Phillip R. Newman. "Group Identity and Alienation: Giving the We Its Due." *Journal of Youth and Adolescence* 30, no. 5
(2001): 515–38.

Newman, Katherine, Cybelle Fox, Wendy Roth, Jal Mehta, and David Harding.
Rampage: The Social Roots of School Shootings. New York: Basic Books, 2004.

Ng-Mak, Daisy S., Suzanne Salzinger, Richard Feldman, and C. Ann Stueve.
"Pathological Adaptation to Community Violence among Inner City Youth."
American Journal of Orthopsychiatry, Mental Health and Social Justice 74,
no. 2 (2004): 196–208.

Noguera, Pedro. *City Schools and the American Dream: Reclaiming the Promise of Public Education.* New York: Teachers College Press, 2003.

Oliver, Melvin, James H. Johnson Jr., and Walter C. Farrell Jr. "Anatomy of a Rebellion: A Political-Economic Analysis." In *Reading Rodney King/Reading Urban Uprising,* edited by Robert Gooding-Williams. New York: Routledge, 1993.

Oliver, Melvin L., and Thomas M. Shapiro. *Black Wealth/White Wealth: A New Perspective on Racial Inequality.* New York: Routledge, 1995.

Oliver, R., and J. H. Hoover. "The Perceived Roles of Bullying in Small-Town Midwestern Schools." *Journal of Counseling and Development* 72 (1994): 416–20.

Olweus, Dan. *Bullying at School: What We Know and What We Can Do.* Oxford: Oxford University Press, 1993.

Olzak, Susan. *The Dynamics of Ethnic Competition and Conflict.* Stanford, CA: Stanford University Press, 1992.

Operario, Don, and Susan T. Fiske. "Stereotypes: Content, Structures, Processes, and Context." In *Blackwell Handbook of Social Psychology: Intergroup Processes,* edited by Rupert Brown and Sam Gaertner. Oxford: Blackwell, 2003.

Pais, Jeremy F., Scott J. South, and Kyle Crowder. "White Flight Revisited: Multiethnic Perspectives on Neighborhood Out-Migration." *Population Research and Policy Review* 28, no. 3 (June 2009): 321–41.

Patterson, James. *America's Struggle against Poverty in the Twentieth Century.* Cambridge, MA: Harvard University Press, 2000.

Perez, Pamela P. "The Etiology of Psychopathy: A Neruopsychological Perspective." *Aggression and Violent Behavior* 17, no. 6 (2012): 519–22.

Peristiany, J. G. *Honor and Shame: The Values of Mediterranean Society.* London: Weidenfeld and Nicholson, 1965.

Petersen, Roger D. *Understanding Ethnic Violence: Fear, Hatred, and Resentment in Twentieth Century Eastern Europe.* Cambridge: Cambridge University Press, 2002.

Phinney, Jean S. "Ethnic Identity Exploration in Emerging Adulthood." In *Emerging Adults in America: Coming of Age in the 21st Century,* edited by Jeffrey Jensen Arnett and Jennifer Lynn Tanner. Washington, DC: American Psychological Association, 2006.

Pinderhughes, Howard. *Race in the Hood: Conflict and Violence among Urban Youth.* Minneapolis: University of Minnesota Press, 1997.

Portes, Alejandro, and Rubén G. Rumbaut. *Legacies: The Story of the Immigrant Second Generation.* Berkeley: University of California Press, 2001.

Pressman, Jeffrey and Aaron Wildavsky. *Implementation: Or How the Good Intentions in Washington Are Dashed in Oakland; or Why It's Amazing That Federal Programs Work at All, This Being a Saga of the Economic Development Administration as Told By Two Sympathetic Observers Who Seek to Build Morals on a Foundation of Ruined Hopes.* Berkeley: University of California Press, 1973.

Prothrow-Stith, Deborah. *Deadly Consequences: How Violence Is Destroying Our Teenage Population and a Plan to Begin Solving the Problem.* New York: Harper-Collins, 1991.

Prothrow-Stith, Deborah, and Howard A. Spivak. *Murder Is No Accident: Understanding and Preventing Youth Violence in America.* San Francisco: Jossey-Bass, 2001.

Quillian, Lincoln. "Does Unconscious Racism Exist?" *Social Psychology Quarterly* 71, no. 1 (2008): 6–11.

"Racial Tensions Grow Violent at Philly High School." *National Public Radio,* December 16, 2009.

Randolph, Karen D. "Implicit Theories of Peer Relations." *Social Development* 19, no. 1 (2010): 113–29.

Reed, Jean-Pierre. "Emotions in Context: Revolutionary Accelerators, Hope, Moral Outrage, and Other Emotions in the Making of Nicaragua's Revolution." *Theory and Society* 33 (2004): 653–703.

Retz, Wolfgang, Petra Retz-Junginger, Tillman Supprian and Michael Rösler. "Research Report: Association of Serotonin Transporter Promoter Gene Polymorphism with Violence: Relation with Personality Disorders, Impulsivity, and Childhood ADHD Psychopathology." *Behavioral Science and Law* 22 (2004): 415–25.

Rieder, Jonathan. *Canarsie: Jews and Italians of Brooklyn against Liberalism.* Cambridge, MA: Harvard University Press, 1985.

Rivera, Carla, and Eric Lichtblau. "After-School Fight Blamed on Ethnic Tension." *Los Angeles Times.* September 19, 1991.

Robinson, W. Peter. *Social Groups and Identities.* Oxford: Butterworth and Heinemann, 1996.

Rothbart, Myron. "Category Dynamics and the Modification of Outgroup Stereotypes." In *Blackwell Handbook of Social Psychology: Intergroup Processes,* edited by Rupert Brown and Sam Gaertner. Oxford: Blackwell, 2003.

Sampson, Robert J. *Great American City: Chicago and the Enduring Neighborhood Effect.* Chicago: University of Chicago Press, 2012.

Sampson, Robert J., and John A. Laub. *Crime in the Making: Pathways and Turning Points Through Life.* Cambridge: Harvard University Press, 1993.

Sánchez-Jankowski, Martín. *City Bound: Urban Life and Political Attitudes Among Chicano Youth.* Albuquerque: University of New Mexico Press, 1986.

———. *Islands in the Street: Gangs and American Urban Society.* Berkeley: University of California Press, 1991.

———. "Gangs and Social Change." *Theoretical Criminology* 7, no. 2 (2003): 191–216.

———. *Cracks in the Pavement: Social Change and Resilience in Poor Neighborhoods.* Berkeley: University of California Press, 2008.

Scheff, Thomas J., and Suzanne M. Retzinger. *Emotions and Violence: Shame and Rage in Destructive Conflicts.* Lexington, MA: Lexington Books, 1991.

Schein, Edgar. *Organizational Culture and Leadership.* San Francisco: Jossey-Bass, 1985.

Scherer, Klaus R., Ronald P. Abeles, and Claude S. Fischer. *Human Aggression and Conflict: Interdisciplinary Perspectives.* Englewood Cliffs, NJ: Prentice-Hall, 1975.

Scott, Daryl Michael. *Contempt and Pity: Social Policy and the Image of the Damaged Black Psyche, 1880–1996.* Chapel Hill: University of North Carolina Press, 1997.

Sears, David O., and John B. McConahay. *The Politics of Violence: The New Urban Blacks and the Watts Riot.* Boston: Houghton-Mifflin, 1973.

Seguin, Jean R., Patrick Sylvers, and Scott O. Lilienfeld. "The Neurobiology of Violence." In *The Cambridge Handbook on Violence and Aggression,* edited by Daniel J. Flannery, Alexander T. Vazsoni, and Irwin D. Waldman. Cambridge: Cambridge University Press, 2007.

Sewell, William Jr. "Historical Events as Transformations of Structure: Inventing Revolution at the Bastille." *Theory and Society,* 25 (1996): 841–81.

Shafer, Robert, and Helen F. Ladd. *Discrimination in Mortgage Lending.* Cambridge, MA: MIT Press, 1981.

Sheidow, Ashli J., Deborah Gorman-Smith, Patrick H. Tolan, and David B. Henry. "Family and Community Characteristic Risk Factors for Violence Exposure in Inner-City Youth." *Journal of Community Psychology* 29, no. 3 (2001): 345–60.

Shelling, Thomas. *Choice and Consequence: Perspectives of an Errant Economist.* Cambridge, MA: Harvard University Press, 1985.

Smeeding, Timothy M., Jeffrey P. Thompson, Asaf Levanon, and Esra Burak. "Poverty and Income Inequality in the Early Stages of the Great Recession." In *The Great Recession,* edited by David Grusky, Bruce Western, and Christopher Wimer. New York: Russell Sage Foundation, 2011.

Smokowski, P.R., and K.H. Kopasz. "Bullying in School: An Overview of Types, Effects, Family Characteristics, and Intervention Strategies." *Children and Schools* 27, no. 2 (2005): 101–10.

Sniderman, Paul, and Louk Hagendoorn. *When Cultures Collide: Multiculturalism and Its Discontents.* Princeton: Princeton University Press, 2007.

Sniderman, Paul, and Thomas Piazza. *Black Prejudice and Black Pride.* Princeton, NJ: Princeton University Press, 2002.

Society of Professional Journalist Ethics Committee. *Journalism Ethics: Casebook of Professional Conduct for News Media.* Portland, OR: Marion Street Press, 2011.

Sugrue, Thomas. *The Origins of the Urban Crisis: Race and Inequality in Postwar Detroit.* Princeton: Princeton University Press, 1996.

Suttles, Gerald D. *The Social Order of the Slum: Ethnicity and Territoriality in the Inner City.* Chicago: University of Chicago Press, 1968.

———. *The Social Construction of Communities.* Chicago: University of Chicago Press, 1972.

Tajfel, Henri. *Human Groups and Social Categories.* Cambridge: Cambridge University Press, 1981.

———. "Social Stereotypes and Social Groups." In *Intergroup Behavior,* edited by John C. Turner and Howard Giles. Oxford: Basil Blackwell, 1981.

Tajfel, Henri, and John C. Turner, "The Social Identity Theory of Intergroup Behavior." In *Psychology of Intergroup Relations,* 2nd ed., edited by Stephen Worchel and William G. Austin. Chicago: Nelson-Hall, 1986.

Tambiah, Stanley. *Leveling Crowds: Ethnonational Conflict and Collective Violence in South Asia*. Berkeley: University of California Press, 1997.

Tatum, Beverly Daniel. *Why Are All the Black Kids Sitting Together in the Cafeteria?* New York: Basic Books, 2003.

Telles, Edward, and Vilma Ortiz. *Generations of Exclusion: Mexican Americans, Assimilation, and Race*. New York: Russell Sage Foundation, 2008.

Terry, Don. "Latino Gang Leader Convicted in LA Ethnic Cleansing Campaign." Hate Watch, Southern Poverty Law Center, January 15, 2013.

Thoits, Peggy. "Managing the Emotions of Others." *Symbolic Interaction* 19, no. 2 (1996): 85–109.

Thompkins, Douglas E. "School Violence: Gangs and the Culture of Fear." *Annals of the American Academy of Political and Social Science* 567, no. 1 (2000): 54–71.

Tilly, Charles. *The Politics of Collective Violence*. New York: Cambridge University Press, 2003.

Toch, Hans H. *Violent Men: An Inquiry into the Psychology of Violence*. Chicago: Aldine Press, 1969.

Toft, Monica Duffy. *The Geography of Ethnic Violence*. Princeton, NJ: Princeton University Press, 2003.

Trub, J. David. *Zips, Pipes, and Pens: Arsenal of Improvised Weapons*. Boulder, CO: Paladin Press, 1993.

Turner, John. *Social Influence*. Milton Keynes: Open University Press, 1991.

Turner, Mary Austin, and Felicity Skidmore, eds. *Mortgage Lending Discrimination: Review of Existing Evidence*. Washington, DC: Urban Institute, 1999.

United Nations Human Settlements Programme. *The Challenge of Slums: A Global Report on Human Settlement*. New York: UN-Habitat United Nations, 2003.

Vaisey, Stephen. "Motivation and Justification: A Dual-Processing Model of Culture in Action." *American Journal of Sociology* 114, no. 6 (2009): 1675–1715.

Vollman, William T. *Rising Up and Rising Down: Some Thoughts on Violence, Freedom and Urgent Means,* vols. 2 and 3. San Francisco: McSweeny, 2003.

Wacquant, Loïc. *Body and Soul: Notebooks of an Apprentice Boxer*. New York: Oxford University Press, 2004.

———. *Urban Outcasts: A Comparative Sociology of Advanced Marginality*. Cambridge, England: Polity Press, 2008.

———. *Punishing the Poor: The Neoliberal Government of Social Insecurity*. Durham, NC: Duke University Press, 2009.

Waterman, Alan S. "Developmental Perspectives on Identity Formation: From Adolescence to Adulthood." In *Ego Identity,* edited by J.E. Marcia, A.S. Waterman, D.R. Matteson, S.L. Archer, and J.L. Orlofsky. New York: Springer-Verlag, 1993.

Waters, Mary. *Ethnic Options: Choosing Identities in America*. Berkeley: University of California Press, 1990.

Weber, Max. *Economy and Society*. Berkeley: University of California Press, [1956] 1978.

Western, Bruce. *Punishment and Inequality in America*. New York: Russell Sage Foundation, 2007.

Willis, Paul. *Learning to Labor: How Working Class Kids Get Working Class Jobs.* New York: Columbia University Press, 1981.

Wilson, William Julius. *When Jobs Disappear: The New World of the Urban Poor.* New York: Knopf, 1996.

Wilson, William Julius, and Richard Taub. *There Goes the Neighborhood: Racial, Ethnic, and Class Tensions in Four Chicago Neighborhoods and Their Meaning for America.* New York: Knopf, 2006.

Winant, Howard. *The World Is a Ghetto: Race and Democracy since World War II.* New York: Basic Books, 2001.

Winnick, Louis. *New People in Old Neighborhoods.* New York: Russell Sage Foundation, 1990.

Wranik, Tanja and Klaus R. Scherer. "Why Do I Get Angry? A Componential Appraisal Approach." In *International Handbook of Anger,* edited by Michael Portegal, Gerhard Stemmler, Charles Spielberger. New York: Springer, 2010.

Xie, H., D.J. Swift, B.D. Cairns, and R.B. Cairns. "Aggressive Behaviors in Social Interaction and Developmental Adaptation: A Narrative Analysis of Interpersonal Conflicts during Early Adolescence." *Social Development* 11 (2002): 205–24.

Yablonsky, Lewis. *The Violent Gang.* New York: Macmillan, 1962.

Yogan, Lissa J. "School Tracking and Student Violence." *Annals of the American Academy of Political and Social Science* 567, no. 1 (2000): 108–22.

Zorbaugh, Harvey Warren. *The Slum and the Gold Coast.* Chicago: University of Chicago Press, 1929.

Zunz, Olivier. *The Changing Face of Inequality: Urbanization, Industrial Development, and Immigrants in Detroit, 1880–1920.* Chicago: University of Chicago Press, 1982.

Index

Administrators, 12, 13, 15, 110, 133, 206; ethics of study methodology and, 210; expulsion of students and, 157; in middle-class and lower-class schools, 189; as third party in disputes, 102; tolerance promoted by, 67; wariness during initial period of peace, 172

adolescence, 49, 78; group affiliation and aggression in, 79; identity formation in, 50, 238–39n12

African Americans, 16, 39; cultural apprehensions of, 63, 64; curtailment of violence and, 145–150, 152–163; dashed expectations of, 58–59; demographic change and, 181–82, 183–84; disputes and, 109–10; economic apprehensions of, 57; educational apprehensions of, 58; emotional dynamic of fights and, 115–16; ethnic insults and, 112, 113; female, 108, 129–130; first phase of violence and, 84, 85, 86; gang members, 171; group history viewed by, 39, 41; historical prejudice and, 47, 49, 50; homicide as cause of death, 215–16n5; on infrastructure improvements, 180–81; on lack of residential escape option, 70–71; lag in emotional dispositions and, 166, 167–69; Los Angeles housing market and, 56–57; middle-class culture and, 102–103; in middle-class schools, 51, 52; on police presence in schools,

173; probation status of students, 174; reassertion of dominance by, 93, 94; retaliatory responses as newcomers, 97, 98; riots and, 124, 125, 127–130; school busing in Boston and, 12; self-defense as newcomers, 88; shunning and, 76, 77; social apprehensions of, 60, 61, 234n26; stages of collective violence and, 119–121, 122; stampedes at, 131, 132; stereotyping by, 43, 44; tolerance curriculum criticized by, 68, 69; tracking system and, 65, 66, 67; weapons brought to school, 168–69

aggression, 4, 19, 27, 104; adolescence and, 79; in crowds and riots, 29, 223n31; defensive, 90; defined, 20; frustration-aggression hypothesis, 76, 189; group violence and, 27; humiliation and, 96; passive-aggressiveness, 110, 114; stereotyping and, 43; victim's reaction to, 83

Albanian students, 7, 242n51

Anglos (whites), 39, 41, 61

Armenian students, 7

assimilation, 51

Baldwin, James, 35

Balzac, Honoré de, 165

Boston, 193, 194; busing in, 85, 87, 178, 183; data gathering in, 208, 265n4; demographic change in, 69, 237n61;

www.ingramcontent.com/pod-product-compliance
Lightning Source LLC
Chambersburg PA
CBHW020656270326
41928CB00005B/154